Through My Mother's Tears

THE AUTOBIOGRAPHY OF DAVID FLOYD

with
Frederick Williams

Through My Mother's Tears

The Autobiography of David Floyd

with
Frederick Williams

3 DIMENSIONS PUBLISHING
AUSTIN ✦ TEXAS

This is a 3 Dimensions Publication

Copyright @2010 by David Floyd

Library of Congress Control Number: 2009941663

IBSN: 978-1-61658-237-1

Cover Design by Dr. Melissa Duvall

Printed in the United States of America
at Morgan Printing in Austin, Texas

*This book is dedicated, in loving memory
to my late brother and best friend,
Ronald O'Keith Floyd.*

ACKNOWLEDGEMENTS

First I must acknowledge my Lord and Savior Jesus Christ for always making a way when I thought there was no way. I am a living witness that all things are possible through the power of prayer. This has been a very long and arduous struggle, but all along I had a strong and abiding love from my family. Mother, you, Levi, Ronnie, James, and Nicole have been a major driving force in my life. Each and everyone of you helped instill a sense of humility, love and compassion for others deep within my soul. I owe a debt of gratitude to many individuals who were there for me in my direst times of need. Mrs. Williams, my high school Sociology teacher, instilled in me the power of positive thinking, and not to allow anyone to determine my destination, but me. Mr. Maceo Smedley, the Vice-Principal at Brazosport High School took time to help me fill all the necessary paper work for admission to college. I must acknowledge the 1988 Brazosport High School basketball team. Basketball played a major role in my younger years and I have nothing but fond memories of our team. We laughed together, we cried together, and I can say that we will forever be a family. A special thanks goes out to Ms. Phillips at Huston-Tillotson University for the many hours she spent helping me learn to read. Mrs. Marshall, your tough and no nonsense approach is what many of the students at Huston-Tillotson needed, and I was no exception. I took your college survival class, and you refused to allow me to fail, even when I was failing myself. Without the assistance from Dr. McMillan, who was the President of Huston-Tillotson when I showed up that day in January 1990 with only the application for admission, I would not be a college graduate today. He afforded me an opportunity of a lifetime, the chance to attend that fine university when he could easily have told me no, and been justified in doing so. I must thank Bob Kellogg, a man who took me in and taught me the ropes of working within a controlled environment in the City Auditors Office, Austin, Texas. A wonderful man I will never forget is Dr. Earl Avery at Bentley College in Waltham, Massachusetts. I became a successful graduate student under his direction. Mr. John Simms was another man at Bentley College who helped me make the adjustment from undergraduate to graduate student. My very dear and close friend Glen Morgan at Hanson Aggregate taught me to smile through adversity. And finally, Kim Floyd is the person I am most indebted to. She stuck with me through the hard times. Many nights we sat on the floor of my apartment, one time without lights, and went through reading exercises for hours. Kim and I got married and she gave me two handsome sons, David and Daniel. If there is a mother of the year award she deserves it. I must also acknowledge those individuals who helped make this dream a reality. Frederick Williams, my writer and now friend, worked with me for over a year, interviewing my family and visiting Freeport, and just like a miracle, took all my collective experiences and put them on paper for all posterity to read. Joan Hall, my editor, made sure we got it right. If you want an excellent person to make sure you dot all the I's and cross all the T's, then you need someone like Joan. And of course, my book cover designer, Dr. Melissa Duvall did an excellent job in capturing the real essence of *Through My Mothers Tears*, with the beautiful book cover of Mamma and me together. And that cover tells the entire story. And finally, with a very deep and abiding love, I say thank you to LaTisha Blanchard for the support she has given me in completing this project, for the dedication she has provided to keep me strong, and for the love we share to keep me focused and positive for our future together.

PART I

CHAPTER 1

————— ✦ —————

I will never forget those four words my brother James said to me on Martin Luther King's birthday in January 2008. They will remain with me for the rest of my life. About ten o'clock that morning I pulled out of the driveway at my home in Austin, Texas going to participate in the Annual Martin Luther King parade, when my cell phone rang. I figured it was my buddy from home, Troy, calling to find out what I planned to do after the festivities. Instead it was my baby brother.

He didn't say "hello" or "how you doing," he just calmly said, "David, Ronnie is dead."

Now as I think back on the few seconds it took him to say those dreadful words, darkness engulfed me and I blanked out momentarily. Ronnie couldn't die; it wasn't his turn. After all he was only thirty-six. Ronnie couldn't break that chain we shared with the rest of our siblings.

Those years, when we were still young, Mama had made roll call starting with the oldest. "Levi Douglass," she would shout, then me, "David Alexander," followed by "Ronald O'Keith," then "James Edward," and finally the baby of the family, "Nicole Janelle." Now one of our links was gone and that chain would never be the same.

I regained my composure and pulled over to the side of the road. With both hands squeezing the steering wheel, I shouted,

"Ronnie's dead, it can't be."

I turned the car around and rode back to the house. Knowing just how much I would miss my brother, I felt relieved nevertheless because his suffering had ended. Since childhood, Ronnie had been overweight and his failure to control his weight problem ultimately led to diabetes. Over the past four years, he endured the most extreme pain. Ronnie hid his misery quite well, but those close to him could feel it through his diminished smile and humor.

The previous week I had driven to Freeport to visit Ronnie in the hospital. I hadn't gone home for Christmas that past month and didn't see him on New Years, so I was determined to see my brother before any more time passed by.

As I walked into the intensive care unit at Brazosport Memorial Hospital, he managed to lift his head and signaled for me to move in much closer to him.

"Come on over here so I can bop you upside the head," he said in between deep and laboring breaths.

I strolled up next to the bed and took his hand. I held it tight, something I never did years ago when we were young and always fighting. I don't think there are two brothers who fought more than the two of us while growing up. At that time it seemed the natural thing to do, but now, as he lay dying, holding his hand seemed natural. He was my brother, and I loved him.

"Man, how you feel?" I asked

"Like I want to get out of this place and go home. You know hospitals are for sick folks and dead ones. I don't like either one of those conditions, so next time you talk to me, I'll be back home with Mama."

"I know you will, brother, 'cause you got the power."

I sat and talked with Ronnie for a couple of hours and then left assuming I'd see him again. The thought never occurred to me that the next visit to Freeport would be to bury him. Our chain wasn't supposed to break because we had survived through conditions short of hell. With the exception of Ronnie, we all had escaped and built new lives, with new horizons, lifted up on the shoulders of our collective efforts. Now one of us was gone and that just didn't seem right to me.

I pulled into the driveway back at home. Safely parked, I allowed the tears to blur my sight. My legs felt heavy, my energy drained from me. I hadn't been there for him in his final hour. My consolation was to know he understood why I couldn't be in Freeport. Why, a long time ago I had to get out of that place where hopelessness is contagious instead of contained. I would wait a couple of hours and then head out for home. I sprawled across the couch and crossed my ankles. I remembered Ronnie and my life in Freeport.

Chapter 2

Nothing in life has ever come easy for me, not even birth judging from the facts Mama told me in later life. It all started on Highway 288 as the ambulance screamed up the highway with sirens blaring. Mama was stretched out in the back with an attendant monitoring her blood pressure and heartbeat. My Daddy sat next to her stroking her forehead and offering comfort, telling her to hold on just a little bit longer. Soon they would be in Galveston at the hospital and in the delivery room. It would be the only time that he would be there for her.

Like most shrimpers who arrived in Freeport in the spring, he would be around for only the summer months and then off to Florida to spend the rest of the year. Most of the men dropped by the east end of Freeport, which was the Black section of town, to drink, fight, party, and then take off. And always leave babies behind. There were a lot of shrimpers in Mama's life, and none of them ever lasted. Daddy was only one of many.

"We're losing her," the attendant shouted to the driver through the window. "We still have a ways to go and her pressure is out of control."

"Do something, damit," Daddy screamed at the attendant.

Mama lay there quietly in excruciating labor pains. It was probably one of the only times she remained absolutely still and quiet. My memories of her are of constant screaming, cussing, and beating all of us. Finally, she tried to rise up, but fell back and lost consciousness.

"Come on, do something." Daddy scowled at the attendant.

The attendant glared up at Daddy and said, "We're taking her back." He tapped on the window and signaled for the driver to turn around and head back to Freeport. "We don't have time to make it to Galveston. She'll have to deliver in Freeport." Years later Mama would share with me that she preferred to give birth at John Sealy Hospital in Galveston because it was a much larger and nicer facility than the one in Freeport. She had no choice, they had to get her back or she could lose the baby and possibly her life.

Once back in Freeport, the attendants rushed Mama to the delivery room with Daddy right behind them. He stopped short of going inside the room with them. Mama had made it quite clear that he was not to be in there when she delivered. He knew all hell would break out if she found out he had been in that room. The doctor on duty that night was a young army officer recently discharged and had taken up residence in Lake Jackson, a suburb, just north of Freeport. They paged him to delivery and he practically ran into the room. He examined Mama and decided to induce labor. In the early morning of January 5, 1970, I entered this world having been delivered by Dr. Ronald Paul, a man who would go on to win a seat in the United States Congress, and in 2008 make a serious bid for president of the United States.

My earliest childhood memories are of the time I spent with Mama and Grandma. Over the years, Mama became so accustomed to a shrimper woman's life that she left Levi and me with Grandma and followed the men back to Florida.

Mama and Daddy's relationship was always up and down, and usually down more than up. Right after my birth, we lived in a one-bedroom house, rented to Mama by her godmother Ms. Goode, on Spruce Street. Levi was two when I was born and we both shared a room with Mama and Daddy. I am not sure what kind of relationship they shared, but it was not one that involved loyalty. That's what led to their break up. While she was pregnant, Mama warned

Daddy not to mess around on her. After I was born, she found out that he was seeing some other woman and planned her getaway. She waited until he left one day, packed all our bags and took Levi and me over to Grandma's house. She told Grandma she was going to the store and would be right back. Mama took off for Florida and did not return for six months.

Over the years staying at Grandma's house became my nightmare. She was the pillar of the family, the glue that kept all nine of her children in line. But she suffered from color fatigue and racial self-hatred. Even though she was dark-skinned and her children were dark-skinned, she did not like the darker hued members of the black race. My Grandfather had been a very light-skinned man, who abandoned her with six children in Galveston, Texas. For a while she lived with her children in a shelter and finally made her way to Freeport. Despite that experience she still preferred light-skinned people and would verbalize her preference in front of anyone, to include her grandchildren. At age four she made me aware of the differences in skin color between Levi and me.

Among all of Mama's children, Levi was the only one with light skin and because of that Grandma made it known that she favored him over me. It seems like only yesterday that she looked at both us and told a friend she "preferred Levi because he had pretty skin" and I an ugly complexion. When speaking of men she might date, she would blurt out, "If I'm going to date a man, he's got to be light and pretty like Levi. Ain't nothin' a dark, crusty man David's skin color can do for me."

When I first heard her say that it cut deep within, but I didn't fully comprehend the devastating implications those words would hold for me in future years. Grandma thought something was wrong with me and she favored Levi. I couldn't understand why, since I loved her as much as he did. I stayed angry with her all the time and with Mama who ran off and left me to take that abuse. I didn't understand how she could leave me with such a cruel person and why she didn't come home. After all she was only going to the store. I would lie in bed and cry practically every night until crying lost its purpose.

Mama would make many more trips to Florida leaving Levi and me at Grandma's house and with each trip my feeling of alienation grew deeper and stronger. I often slipped off and went down to the dock. I stood right at the edge of the water, closed my eyes and imagined me being lifted over the water, all the way to Florida and Mama there to meet me. If I had a strong enough determination, I could convince myself that I wouldn't have to return to that horrid place, where I wasn't liked and not wanted. I stayed there until the sun disappeared beyond the water and one of the shore men told me to "get on home." How could I possibly "get on home" when I didn't have one to go to? When I got back to Grandma's house no one bothered to ask where I had been and I offered no explanation. Instead, I went straight to the bedroom, stretched out on my side of the bed and continued to dream.

That next spring when Mama returned, to my disappointment, we lived with Grandma for several months. I didn't want to be there. I wanted us to be in our own home away from the meanness at Grandmother's house. We finally did move to 8th Street, only a few blocks away. While living there, Mama got pregnant, not by anyone we knew. The man never came to our house, and in fact, remained a stranger to all of us. Ronnie was born in the summer while the shrimpers were in town.

Daddy never came around. However, there was a man called Fillmore who stayed with us for a while after Ronnie's birth, but he was not Ronnie's father. I had two brothers and neither one of them knew their father. I was rather fortunate because I did know my Dad and would from time to time see him around town later in life. Mama never went back with Daddy, but he would be in and out of my life until his death. We never had any permanence of a father and son relationship. That's because Mama never established a permanent relationship with him. He seemed to love her, but she never felt that way toward him.

We stayed together as a family until the fall of 1974 and then Mama was off to Florida, leaving Levi and me with our Grandmother once again. She took Baby Ronnie with her, probably because he was so young. That deplorable feeling of depression strangled the life out of me as I cried, watching Mama leave me once again. She told me she would be back real soon, but even at that age, I knew better. Memories of standing at the dock and looking out over the water returned, and I knew once again I would pay a lot of visits to that place. At that young age I lived with the fear of being alone.

Levi and I got excited whenever the mailman delivered letters from Mama, because we knew there would be money for the two of us. Levi always got more than me, but at least Grandma didn't dislike me to the point of not giving me any at all. After a while I became accustomed to Levi's portion being greater than mine. I always received the worst end of the stick, Ronnie went to Florida with Mama while I stayed with a grandmother who made it clear she preferred my brother to me, and Levi was given more of the money Mama would send to us during the winter. At the young age of four, my visits to the dock were often, and my tears were many. Crying, I believed, would always be a part of my life.

In March of 1975 I was five years old when Mama showed up at Grandma's house. It was one of the happiest moments of my young life. I was ready to return to our house on Spruce Street. To my disappointment Mama moved in with us at Grandma's house instead.

We lived there a couple of months and then a man named James Cooler showed up at the house. He was the first man I considered as a father. Mama seemed to like him a whole lot. Levi and I also liked him because he had a lot of money and freely shared it with us. A couple of days after he showed up we left Grandma's and moved into a house a couple blocks away on 7th Street. Big James bought all new furniture, including twin beds for us boys. Ronnie and I shared a bed, and Levi had a bed to himself until Little James was born later that year. Big James and Mama slept in the other bedroom right next to ours. The house on 7th Street was extremely small, and it seemed that we walked all over each other. There was very little privacy, including in the bedrooms. But it was home, and for a while, I found happiness because we were a family.

Soon after Little James was born, the peace we found as a family was shattered. The first time it happened traumatized the three of us. Little James was still a baby and not aware of the nightmare we were about to live. It happened late one night after we went to bed. Big James and Mama had been out at the Blue and White Café, a local bar on 7th and Spruce Street, a block from our house. He had been drinking heavily and did something at the club to anger Mama. As soon as they hit the door, the battle began.

"Don't talk to me, you black bastard," Mama screamed.

Levi shot straight up in the bed. Ronnie and I did the same. Baby James was sound asleep, lying in the bed next to Levi. We looked at each other, shock and fear all over our faces. I thought I had been dreaming, but with my brothers sitting upright in the bed, I knew it wasn't a dream.

"Lower your voice, Shorty, and stop that cursin'. I don't want ta hurt ya." James shouted.

"You drunk motherfuckah, you couldn't hurt one of them roaches on that fuckin' counter," Mama screamed.

"Why ya want ta mess with me this way?" James warned.

"Cause all you want to do is get drunk and act a fool," Mama kept screaming.

"Git out my face Shorty, fore I have ta hurt ya."

"Don't you hit me, you black motherfuckah," Mama's high-pitched voice resonated throughout the house and especially in the bedroom where we sat scared to move. "You drunk bastard, get away from me."

"What ya call me?" James now shouted and then we heard the

blow land directly against Mama's face, and her body slammed to the floor. A cold and fearful chill shot through my body. Ronnie couldn't hold it and peed all over himself. Levi jumped out of the bed and shot out of the bedroom. I followed close behind and Ronnie behind me.

Mama struggled to her feet, but James had her by the hair, dragging her into the living room. She flailed away with arms going in every direction trying desperately to hit him and break loose from his grip. Finally, she landed a blow to his head, but that seemed to only anger him. He brought his balled fist around in a circular motion and caught Mama right above the nose. Blood shot on both them, all over the floor and the furniture.

"Let my Mama go," Levi screamed and jumped on James' free arm. I kicked him on his legs, and Ronnie did what little he could. He tried to pry Mama loose from James' grip. We knew this man could hurt us, but didn't care. All we saw was the pain he'd inflicted on Mama. We were determined to make him let her go. Levi went at him like a mad person, just swinging and kicking. I followed his lead, also swinging and kicking. Ronnie continued to pull on Mama.

Finally James unloosed Mama, tossed us aside, stormed off to the bedroom and slammed the door behind him. When he threw me off him, I landed in the corner. I lay there with my head aching and stared at Mama. She lay on the floor crying and bleeding. That would be the first of many times I would see her in that position all beaten up at the hands of a drunkard who knew only one way to take out his frustrations against a world in which he lived but probably did not like.

Over the years I tried to see Mama through her tears and understand why she would allow this to happen. It had to be the semblance of security these men provided for her children and herself. Mama was willing to take the abuse as long as the man fed her children, kept the lights on and kept clothes and shoes on us. That was the measure of the men in her life. Even though Mama worked all the time, she feared the unknown and the thought of having to make it on her own. The irony of her life was, even with these men, she still was alone. I could always feel her loneliness when she cried, which was often. Mama lived much of her life through her tears and pain that served as a wall around the real person.

There is never a good reason for a man to beat up on a woman. There was, however, a time just before I began kindergarten when Mama refused to leave James alone. She'd badgered him to the point it seemed like she wanted to fight. She pushed him to the breaking point. We watched with the bedroom door cracked open, fearful for Mama's life.

"You sorry son of a bitch," she shouted. "How long you think I'm going to take this bull shit off you?"

"Get away from me, Shorty," James shouted and turned away from her. "I ain't in the mood."

"Fuck your mood, niggah." Mama moved as quick as he did and blocked him from leaving the kitchen. "I don't give a damn about your mood."

I squeezed both fists tightly in anticipation of the pending battle. I knew Mama wouldn't back down. But also that Big James would only take so much of her confrontation.

"Shorty go on 'bout your business 'fore I have ta hurt ya," he slurred his words. As usual, he was drunk. It was an extremely hot night and he obviously wanted to be left alone. But in that small house, where walls seemed to collapse and pen you in almost rubbing next to who might be in the room, there was no escape.

Big James seemed to be seeking that small space of freedom from Mama and her badgering. But she refused to allow him that moment of solace. That was not her style. She had to fight. I wanted to go out there and pull Mama away. I didn't want to see her again lying on the floor with blood gushing from her mouth and nose. But there was little chance that my intervention would make a difference. Whatever I did would lead to me getting beat down. If I ran out there and tried to pull her away, she would beat me, and if

I didn't I would have to again jump on Big James and get knocked around by him. There was no way he would allow my brothers and me to attack him, without making us pay for it.

Ronnie and I slowly made our way out of the bedroom in anticipation of James's next move. Levi came up close behind us.

"Why you actin' so tired anyway?" Mama continued to badger. "Been out fuckin' around and drinkin'. Now you so tired you cain't do nothing but go to sleep."

"You wrong Shorty, now I done tole ya git out my face fore I have to hurt ya."

"You lying black bastard, I smell another woman all over you."

Abruptly, James came to his feet and with a renewed energy he grabbed Mama, lifted her up in the air, and flung her hurling through the sheet rock wall in the kitchen. She crashed to the floor on the other side.

"I tole ya to stop botherin' me," James shouted, turned and stormed off to the bedroom.

Ronnie and I, with Levi right behind, slowly approached the large opening where Mama lay struggling to get up. We stared down at her, afraid to say anything. She managed to get to her feet, climbed back into the kitchen, staggered to the bedroom and slammed the door. I stood there, traumatized by what I just witnessed and fearful over additional fighting that might break out again inside the bedroom. All three of us finally got up enough energy to stagger back into our bedroom and close the door.

Fear can hardly begin to describe my feelings that night as I lay in bed next to Ronnie, who had managed to drift off to sleep and snored in my ear. I could also hear Levi's even breathing. He lay very still next to little James who managed to sleep through the entire ordeal. I didn't know whether Levi was sleeping or just lying there like me, in anticipation of more arguing and blows. Why didn't Big James just go away and leave us alone? At that moment I felt isolation and helplessness, emotions I eventually learned to overcome.

CHAPTER 3

In fall 1975 I entered kindergarten at the O.A. Fleming Elementary School. When school started Mama was again in Florida with Big James. Levi, only seven at the time, escorted me to my class. O.A. Fleming was about one mile from Grandma's house, and we made that walk everyday until Mama returned in the spring.

Grandma prepared breakfast before we left, but once we walked out the door we were on our own. I can never remember Grandma picking me up from the school, or even visiting during parents' day or for Parent Teachers meetings. That's how it would be my entire school life, with Mama also. We had a small group of five who would take the same route along a dirt trail behind an old lumberyard every day going home. A few years earlier my cousin had been hit and killed by one of the trucks carrying lumber out of the yard, so the owner built a trail in the back of the building for kids returning home from school. We did a little bit of everything along that trail. We fought, broke bottles, and sometimes threw rocks at each other. It may have been safer to walk in front of the yard and take your chances with the trucks than to be behind the building where no one could see you and anything possible could happen.

Fortunately, nothing serious happened on what became known as "nigger trail." But I would rather stay on that trail than face Mrs. Davis at the after school day care where I had to go because Grandma was still at work when I got out early in the afternoon. This woman cared for children for the specific reason of tormenting them. She wasn't only mean, but also vicious.

One afternoon a young boy no more than two years old, peed on himself. It irritated Mrs. Davis and she flung the boy across her lap, grabbed a belt and beat him on his legs. The boy screamed, but it did no good, she just kept beating him.

Once again I found myself traumatized as I watched her inflict pain on that boy, just as Big James inflicted pain on Mama. Even at that young age, I knew not to say a thing or do anything to anger Mrs. Davis. That would only have made matters worse.

I'd stay there until Grandma got home from her day job cleaning some rich, white lady's house. Grandma's little house was always crowded. Besides Levi and me, my Uncle Lynn, who was already grown, and Cousin Patrick stayed there. We always battled over control of the television and the kids won out. Levi, my Cousin Patrick, and I loved to watch *Hee Haw* and *Good Times*. But often we lost control when Grandma insisted on watching some program that didn't interest us. She loved her Curtis Mathis television and we would be forced to sit in that small house and watch it with her. Grandma's house was only a two bedroom and Levi, Uncle Lynn and I had to sleep on a pull out couch in the living room. Sometimes we couldn't go to bed until Grandma finished watching television. That was all right with us because we hated going to bed, even though we had to get up and go to school the next morning.

By first grade my insecurity and reading inadequacies were well established. That year for some reason Mama didn't go to Florida. When Big James pulled out with the shrimp boat, Mama stayed behind and it was hard times for us. We lived a life of feast or famine. With Big James around we had plenty of food, spending money, and good times. When he left, the money dried up, and we struggled from day to day. Mama worked at various jobs, but never made enough money to sustain us as a family.

Because of our dire situation, it was tense around the house with Mama always on edge. If we even looked wrong she grabbed a strap and commenced to whip all of us. As far back as I can remember

Mama whipped me more than any of my brothers. Probably because I had the biggest mouth and just didn't know when to shut up.

Home was not the only place I got whipped. Throughout the kindergarten and into the first grade, my teachers physically whipped me. As my reading inadequacies worsened, my behavior became more destructive. And the whippings became more often and intense.

We always had oral reading at 11:00 in the morning, the last subject before lunch. I dreaded 11:00 because Ms. McWilliams, my teacher, would eventually call on me. I tried to figure out what passage from the book I would read when it finally got around to me. While the others read their paragraph, I desperately tried to figure out the words in my part. Sometimes I asked the little girl sitting next to me to tell me the words with the hope of memorizing them and simply speaking instead of reading. That led to a whipping because Ms. McWilliams claimed I badgered the other students. She paddled me and sent me back to my desk.

Sweat broke out on the inside my hands, as they got closer to my turn to read. Certain words I could associate with objects, such as the word dog placed below the picture or next to a dog. Same for cat, cow, house, and tree. I did just fine with those words, but others that had no association with an object baffled me. It made me both angry and frightened at the same time. Finally, when it was my turn I simply froze up. My mouth would not move, my tongue became heavy and my brain went blank.

"Come on David, we don't have all day," Ms. McWilliams scowled. "David these words are easy. A kindergartner could read this. I believe you are just being lazy." Her attack made it much more difficult.

I felt all the other children staring and just waiting for me to mess up so they could laugh. That was the most difficult part, the kids staring and laughing. If I stuttered or failed to pronounce a word correctly, they laughed and it reverberated like an echo chamber over and over. The laughter increased the longer I stood there with that book in my hand. Readings, stories, and words seemed deliberately designed to humiliate me. They gave reason for other kids to look down on me. I no longer cared about reading and I only wanted revenge. I wanted to hit and hurt the ones laughing, tell them it was no fun not knowing how to read and hoping someday the same fate awaited them.

Giving up, Ms. McWilliams said, "If your mother or someone in your family would only come to one of the meetings they'd know you can't read."

If she had taken the time to contact Mama and tell her of my problem then that might have been just enough to let Mama know I needed help. No one did a thing, and with each week, I became more angry and much more violent, because most of all the other students could read, and I couldn't.

During recess I got my revenge on the students who laughed at me. I had no problems blasting them in the face with my fist, knocking them down, and on some occasions, kicking them while they were down. It could be a boy or girl I didn't care. I stormed out of the classroom and onto the playground looking for the most convenient target. Some times I waited until after school and caught one of the culprits walking home down "nigger trail".

When they saw me they knew what was about to go down and I'd walk right into a barrage of swinging arms and fists. Kikki and Tanya were my favorite targets. Those sisters had no problem fighting back. Kikki, at that age, packed quite a punch, but I'd walk right through it and match them blow for blow. Their younger brother, J.B., would eventually become my best friend. For years we shared our lives together, both on and off the basketball court. But in the first grade, a year before he started school, I fought his sister practically every day, up and down "nigger trail."

Whippings by the principal of the school and Ms. McWilliams became practically an everyday occurrence for me throughout the entire year. After a while I don't believe Ms. McWilliams needed a reason, she just assumed I did something wrong and whipped me. I was the target of her wrath. The more she tried to discipline me, the more defiant I became.

By January, ours was a confrontational relationship. I no longer cared about my behavior in the classroom. I talked all the time, laughed at other students, played tricks on Ms. McWilliams, and sometimes threw a punch or two. My dislike for school grew stronger every day while my inability to read also grew worse on those very same days.

Outside the school, my brother Ronnie became the target for my anger and frustration. Few days passed that we didn't fight. Out of respect for the oldest, I never fought with Levi, and James was too young, although one time he did chase me into the bathroom with a kitchen knife and a bottle of Clorox. But that didn't come until years later when James was older.

During these early years, the battles were restricted to Ronnie and me. We loved each other and if anyone outside our family said or did something insulting to either of us, we would take up for the other.

As early as four years old, Ronnie was overweight. His problem stemmed from his inability to stop eating. Ronnie was the victim of a cruel and vicious circle. As he picked up weight, others would increase their level of teasing, his self-esteem would dissipate, and to compensate, he would eat excessively, and his weight continued to go up. All his life he would be overweight to the point that it became a crisis. He lacked the will power to do anything about it.

Mama failed to recognize the dangers. She always bragged that Ronnie was a healthy boy with plenty of meat on his bones. That was a good thing to Mama, so she didn't take his weight problem seriously.

Ronnie's low self-esteem was directly associated with the laughter and teasing from others because he was fat. My low self-esteem was directly associated with the derisive laughter from the same people because I could not read. We took our anger out on each other. With the slightest provocation, we'd start throwing fists at each other. Ronnie always won the skirmish if he could get me in his grip. One time he got me in a bear hug and squeezed all the air out of me. He could always claim victory if our battles were confined to inside the house because there was no room for me to maneuver and get away from him. Outside it was a different story. I was often victorious out in the open with room to move around.

It got to the point I fought everyone. The more I fought, the less importance I put on reading. I also attached a great deal of importance on basketball. That began the summer after I finished first grade and at the time J.B. and I became very close friends. That summer morning, when my Uncle Lynn walked into our house dribbling a basketball, changed my life from that point until I graduated from high school.

Uncle Lynn told Mama he was taking Levi and me down to the local gym to teach us how to play the game. We hurried out the door, following closely behind him. We had no idea what we were in for. Even though he told Mama he would teach us how to play the game, what he proceeded to do was teach us how to take a beating on the basketball court. He showed no mercy on either of us. We tried to shoot the ball over him. He not only smacked the ball away but also knocked us to the ground. All summer long it was one beating after another. No matter how discouraged and angry we became, he didn't care, he'd just keep beating us down.

After a while when he showed up to take us to the court, we cried. Mama finally asked him why we cried when it was time to go? He never answered and she never persisted and we continued our daily beat down.

Levi finally gave up and told me one day on the way to the gym that he wasn't going to play anymore, and I would have to fend for myself. I derided him for quitting, telling him that he couldn't give in, and if he could only get that one ball through the hoop, his entire attitude would change. Defeat was something early in life I refused to accept. One day in the gym, Uncle Lynn tossed the ball to me and told me to make a move.

"Don't be a chicken shit," he taunted. "I want you to figure a way to get around me and score. Don't quit like your brother."

I felt the blood flush in my head when he called me a quitter. I took the ball and dribbled directly at him as he stood between the basket and me. I knew he would knock me firmly on my butt.

Just as he extended his arm to knock me off balance, I took aim and released the ball. As I crashed to the floor I watched the ball sail through the air, and float through the net.

I lay there in amazement. I won, even if it was a temporary victory. It would be the last basket I ever scored on Uncle Lynn, but an important one for my confidence.

I scored a basket on Uncle Lynn and that compensated for my inability to read. At that time in my life it was a sufficient substitute.

From that moment on basketball became my life. Nothing else mattered, not the teasing, the whippings, and especially not the reading. When I finally got my own basketball, I never got caught without it when not in school. Perfecting that game was my only goal so I dribbled all the time. Neighbors began to complain to Mama that they could hear that ball hitting the pavement late into the night.

One night an irate neighbor rushed out of her house cursing me and threatening to take my ball. I took off running and amazingly did not miss a dribble as I hurried away to a safer place to perfect my skills. If she had caught me I would have fought her because no one had a right to deny me this one joy.

CHAPTER 4

"The boats have docked and now it's going to be good times," Mama shouted and smiled. "We going to eat good and y'all going to get new clothes and everybody gets shoes. I'm going to see to that."

Mama's jubilation simply meant that the shrimp boats had arrived in Freeport for the summer. It always happened in May. Men, who made a living on the sea between Florida and Texas catching shrimp, ascended on our city and had only one thing on their minds, to party. It was not far from the boats to the bars, brothels, and plenty of good times, sprinkled with a lot of trouble, right there in our neighborhood. Freeport's east end, the name given to the black and poorest section of the city, was where it all happened and we, as young boys, experienced it first hand and up close.

The Blue and White Café was the hot spot in the east end. My great aunt's husband owned it, and we young people often hung out on the patio, playing our own games. We were not allowed inside, and even trying to look in would guarantee us a whipping from Mama. However, on one occasion, the temptation was too great to pass up. Levi, J.B. and I were in the patio area when the shots rang out. We all froze in place and I wasn't sure if I should run inside to see what happened or turn and run home. We could hear screaming from inside. A couple of the patrons ran out and kept running up the street. Something bad had happened inside. We moved closer to the building and stood right under the window.

"I wanna see what happened," I whispered to the others.

"No, David," Levi scowled at me. "Mama will beat your ass real good if she finds out you looked inside there."

"I don't care," I tried to rise up on the balls of my feet, but still couldn't see inside. I then turned to Levi and J.B. "Come on, give me a boost."

Evidently, curiosity got the best of Levi. He and J.B. each grabbed a leg and hoisted me up so I could see inside. There on the floor lay a man named Don with blood all over him. His body began to flop around like a fish out of water. Gray matter from the bullet wound to his head had splattered against the wall closest to his body. The patrons inside stood with frightened and shocked looks. The women screamed and covered their faces, and the men stared down at him. One of the shrimpers finally tried to restrain his flopping body, holding him still until he drew his final breath. We heard the police sirens screaming toward the café. Levi and J.B. let me down, and we took off running toward Lincoln Park. When we got to the park, Levi asked, "What happened in there? What did you see?"

"Don was flopping around just like a fish," I said. "It was like this." I laid on the ground and started flailing my arms and jerking my body about. We all laughed. As I look back on that dark day in my life, I now know that incident had a profound effect on me. I have tried to blot out the memory and forgive myself for mocking another man's tragedy. I have also rationalized my behavior because I was only seven years old. But I still feel a sense of shame and remorse for being so insensitive to a brutal act of murder. Don's death is nothing a seven year old should witness, but then it was the east end and we had to take the bad with the good.

The only good emanating out of that pathological lifestyle we lived as children was the financial security the shrimpers provided while docked in Freeport. With Mama's lifestyle, it was always an extreme, either feast or famine. When the shrimpers were gone, it was famine times. Even though Mama worked, she never made enough money to cover all our expenses. Four young, growing boys can be expensive. Child support from any of our fathers was unheard of and just wouldn't happen. No one knew Levi's father but Mama, she hardly had anything to do with Ronnie's father, Daddy was too busy making babies all along the Gulf Coast, and Big James only provided when he was in town. The last summer just before Mama put James out, we ate well. However, without any help, we had a steady diet of beef tip stew. I reached the point that I detested beef tips, but if I wanted to eat, I had no choice. It was better than going hungry every night. Before James left we ate good. We'd go to the Barbeque Pit and Raspberry's Restaurant, two of the most popular places to eat in Freeport. Then one night it all ended.

Big James' drinking and chasing women wore thin with Mama. His womanizing finally brought their relationship to an end. I may have played a part in the demise. Again we all were playing outside the Blue and White Café when we watched Big James walk up to the joint with another woman on his arm. He saw me and pointed his finger.

"You'd better keep your big mouth shut," he whispered to me.

No way I would do that. He was disrespecting Mama and I had to let her know. There wasn't much I could do about the beatings he gave her, but there was something I could do about his cheating. As soon as he went inside I started to leave.

Ronnie grabbed me and shouted, "You better not tell. You gonna get Mama beat."

"Yeah, you know she going to say something to him and then they gonna be fighting," Levi added.

"I don't care," I shouted back at them. "Mama got a right to know about this. You know what he's doing with that woman."

"You don't know nothin', and you need to leave it alone," Levi scowled at me. "You gonna get us all in trouble anyway 'cause we ain't suppose to be down here."

"I said I don't care. I'm gonna tell Mama." I broke loose from Ronnie and took off running.

"You stupid ass, David," Levi shouted as I ran off. "And you ain't nothin' but a tattle tale."

I told Mama what I saw, and that evening tension mounted in the house. By ten o'clock Big James wasn't home. Mama had gotten some black trash bags and tossed all his belongings inside. She put them outside on the sidewalk leading up to the house. When I told her about Big James I didn't think this would be her reaction. Levi kept chiding me for what I did.

"Big James going to come up that sidewalk and when he see all his stuff out there, he going to kill us all," he said.

"He ain't gonna do nothin'," I came back at him. "Mama locked all the doors and he ain't got no key."

"Are you stupid?" Levi shouted. "He can break that door down with one little kick."

"He ain't gonna do nothin'," I kept saying. My fear came through in my words. Would he really try to kill all of us or only me for telling on him? After all, he pointed at me when he went in the Blue and White Café.

I kept looking out the bedroom window for any sign of him. This one time I prayed he would stay with that other woman instead of coming home. I could hear Mama pacing back and forth in the living room, waiting for the confrontation. Would he finish the job this time? James had already bloodied her nose and blackened her eyes since he'd been back. And I kept visualizing the time last year when he picked her up and tossed her through the kitchen wall. Maybe this time he would end it once and for all and get away with it. No one in the east end ever went to jail for killing someone black. The police would show up, do an investigation and case closed. That is what happened when Don got shot, and with Moppie who was killed right near Lincoln park. I had run over to the car and saw half Moppie's head was blown off. The front windshield had brain matter and blood across it. By age eight, I had witnessed two brutal murders. Now I stared out the window waiting for the man to show up who just might kill my mother.

Finally James stumbled up the sidewalk toward the porch. He hesitated for a moment and looked down at the trash bags blocking his path. I froze knowing he would open one of them and find all his belongings. Instead, he stumbled around them up to the porch and tried to open the door. He took a step back and stared at it when it didn't open. Again he grabbed the knob and jerked on it. I just knew the entire door would come crashing down, but it held. James balled up his fist and banged on it. It felt like the entire house shook, but the door didn't give.

"Shorty, open this damn door," he shouted. "What the fuck you think you doin'? Open this damn door."

"Hell no," Mama shouted back. "Go to that bitch you been with all day spending money on her ass."

"Open this door. I ain't been with nobody," he continued to shout, his voice rising with each word. "That blabber mouth little bastard David been running his mouth again," James took his fist and again banged on the door. All of a sudden it seemed to hit him. He turned and walked back to the trash bags, opened one, pulled out some of his clothes, then stuffed them back into the bag. James rushed back on the porch and beat on the door. "You bitch, what the fuck you doing? You'd better open this door. I'll kill your black ass."

My body stiffened. The threat was out there. Levi said he could easily break down the door. I backed away from the window and sat on the edge of the bed where Levi, Ronnie, and Little James sat. I knew they were also afraid. Would we all die that night? Levi and I stared at each other and both picked up the fear in the other's eyes.

"Shorty, open this door, damn it."

"Get the fuck away from my house. Go back to that bitch you been fuckin' till ten at night. You going to fuck her and spend money on her ass and think you gonna come in my bed and lay down, you a damn fool."

Suddenly, the pounding and cursing stopped. Could he possibly have given up and decided to leave? Hope spread across my face. Levi and I jumped from the bed and ran over to the window. We watched as Big James backed off the porch, picked up his bag of clothes and headed down Seventh Street away from our house. We found out later that he went down to the docks and slept on the boat. He made that his home until the boats pulled out for Florida.

CHAPTER 5

That fall when Mama put James out I entered the third grade and it turned out to be as frustrating as the other years. I had really come to hate school simply because I could not perform in the classroom the same way I could on the basketball court. The other kids continued to laugh at me in the classroom, but had to respect my basketball skills that continued to improve even at that age. My classmates waited in anticipation for when it was my turn to read. I couldn't figure out why the teachers kept insisting that I read in front of the class. Mrs. Brown, my third grade teacher was relentless in her demands.

"David, take your time and concentrate on each word," she said.

I tightly gripped the reader, stared at the words but nothing registered.

"Don't you want to pass third grade?" she asked.

"Yes, m'am."

"Well, read for me."

"Jjjjohhnn llliked tttto." As I stuttered through my words the others laughed. "Leave me alone," I shouted. "Leave me alone." I threw the book on the floor and ran out of the room with tears flowing down my face.

Mrs. Brown caught me in the hall, grabbed my arm and jerked me all the way to the principal's office.

"Why did you throw your book down and run out of the class?" Mr. Waniack asked, even though he knew why. I did it so many times in the past with the same results it seemed rather ridiculous to ask why. Before I would cry and explain that no matter how hard I tried, the words just wouldn't come out. And when the others laughed, I couldn't stand there and let that happen. But he never heard me. He didn't feel my pain and embarrassment. Mr. Waniack didn't understand that I wanted to read the words in that book more than anything else. I had nothing left inside after each battle but he didn't care. This time was no different; he grabbed his paddle and said his famous two words.

"Bend over."

After a while I became immune to the whippings since they happened practically every day. I must hold the record for the student who received the most whippings at O. A. Flemming Elementary School. Mr. Waniack never considered the possibility that something was wrong with the way they tried to teach me to read. Or possibly they really didn't try to understand. The teachers at the school humiliated me every day for the entire year but still passed me on to the next grade. How could they not understand that I desperately wanted to overcome my handicap? Just like I scored that first basket against my Uncle Lynn, I wanted to conquer this challenge also. Unfortunately, this one I couldn't do alone. I needed their help, but instead got their disdain.

Mama never knew I couldn't read. She assumed that since I was being passed to the next grade, all my learning abilities were developing satisfactorily. I was too ashamed to tell her and the other kids knew they had better not. So Mama was in the dark. I compensated for my failures with an extremely competitive spirit in other subjects. We had a math contest that year. The person who knew their multiplication tables best would win a Baby Ruth candy bar. Mrs. Brown tried to discourage me from participating. With reading, she badgered me to do something I couldn't do. With math, she discouraged me from doing something I could do. I won that contest and it was the proudest moment in all my elementary school years. I really enjoyed that Baby Ruth.

That year I witnessed death once again. This time it was my mother's sister, Aunt Marilyn Ruth. Levi and I both loved her because she seemed to understand the pain we felt living in such a chaotic state all the time. Her life was also very chaotic. She would show up at Grandma's house periodically, hang around for a week and then take off. Listening to Mama and Grandma talk, I knew she was on the run from law enforcement. Somehow she was involved in various crimes, and if she wasn't one step ahead of the police, then it was the criminals she associated with. But she did have a natural ability to relate to children at their level, and that's all we cared about. That was Aunt Marilyn Ruth. One day she took Levi and me out for a soda. She told us that she had to leave and go back to Florida where she had lived for the past five years. She had business to take care of back there.

And then she whispered to both of us that we would never see her again. Her life would end in Florida, and that we must be strong for Grandma, Mama and her son Patrick who had always lived with Grandma. I looked at Levi for some sign of how we should respond. Aunt Marilyn Ruth's words frightened me and I wanted to run away. I wanted to hide from the reality that I would never see my favorite aunt again. Would she die the same way as Don, lying on the floor, covered in blood and flopping around on the floor? Or like Moppie in the car, with half his head blown off, blood and brain matter splattered all over him and the car.

Tears filled my eyes and Aunt Marilyn Ruth pulled me close. Did Levi feel the same as I did? If so, he controlled it much better than I did. I didn't want to lose Aunt Marilyn Ruth, but as we all got up and headed back to Grandma's house, I was determined to live up to her request and be strong.

That night we said our good byes and watched as someone we all loved walked out of our lives forever. The following week word got back to Grandma that Aunt Marilyn Ruth was murdered. Mama went to Florida to retrieve her body and bring it back to Freeport for a proper burial. The authorities never caught her killer. I didn't attend her funeral. Mama knew I was too emotional to sit through that ritual.

Mama decided we needed to move out of the house on Seventh Street. I guess she wanted to get rid of all remnants of James. It had to be tough on her walking into that kitchen every morning with memories of having been thrown through the kitchen wall. In fact, anywhere she went in that small house carried memories of a beating. We moved back on Spruce Street near our old house.

There were now five of us, Mama, all my brothers and me. Our problem was the house we moved into just could not accommodate more than two people comfortably. The entire place was about 700 square feet, so we practically stumbled over each other. Often we would fight for the bathroom. Sometimes if you really had to go, you went outside. Once you got into the bathroom, to get to the toilet was like maneuvering around an obstacle course. When you entered there were two holes in the floor. You had to jump over the first hole to a small surface and then you had to jump over a second hole and land a couple feet from the toilet. So in order to relieve yourself, you had to jump, jump, and sit. Once you sat on the toilet seat, your eyes stayed glued on to those holes for fear something might crawl out of them. Many times I just went outside to avoid the hassle.

Mama did the best she could with the little she had. She wasn't yet thirty years old and faced the prospect of four boys to raise on her own. She worked at the local laundromat as a helper, taking loads of clothes and washing them for the customers. We would often help her, but it was heavy work, didn't pay much, and always left her frustrated.

With the shrimpers gone, Mama had no access to extra money so she made us cut corners on expenses. One of the corner cutters was the amount of food available for each of us. The dinner table became a war zone, especially with Ronnie, who could eat his share and everyone else's share. I seemed to be his favorite target. Even at the age of six, Ronnie was having severe weight problems. The more he gained, the more he ate. Given the small amount we had to share, he had no options but to take from our plates. We developed the habit of eating fast and finishing before he did. One time I didn't make it and he reached over and took a small piece of cake I had been saving throughout the meal. He swiftly took his fork and without looking scooped my cake and tossed it in his mouth. I was furious. I jumped up and punched him right in his jaw. He grabbed a fork and caught me right below my eye. Mama came in the room and we both ended up in the bedroom with a strap firmly administered to our rear ends.

It was not only with food that Mama cut corners, but also with electricity and water. She exploded on any of us who left a light on, and when she determined something could be done without a light she would insist we turn it off. Oftentimes we had to be up early in the morning before the sun rose and get ready for school in the dark. But that was not nearly as bad as the water situation. She insisted that all four of us use the same bath water. Levi being the oldest and James the youngest got to use the bath water first. After they soaked and washed their dirty bodies, then Ronnie and I would climb into that same water. Levi laughed and teased us because we had to use his filth to try and clean off our dirt. I made sure none of that water got in my mouth.

One night Ronnie and I waited outside the bathroom for Levi and James to finish bathing. After about ten minutes they came out and we hurried inside. I made the jump across the hole in the floor and was just about to get in the tub when Ronnie jumped and missed. His body fell to the ground. He got back up and his head protruded right above the opening.

"Hurry up and get out of there," I hollered." Ain't no telling what's down in there.

My words apparently frightened him, 'Shut up David, you making me scared. I can hear the rats down here." He grabbed the edges of the floor and started to pull his overweight body out of the hole. He failed on his first attempt.

"We got to get you out of there before you get bit." I jumped out of the tub and reached for his hand. I wasn't sure I'd be able to help him because of his weight. I pulled and he struggled to use his other hand to help pull himself up. We failed a second time. Ronnie was nervous and began to shake. I thought I would have to call Mama for help, but I wasn't sure what she could do. Mama, a little woman, would probably get pulled down into the hole with Ronnie.

"Something just ran across my foot." Suddenly he panicked, wrapped both hands around the edge and with one great thrust pulled himself out of the hole. Mama showed up just as Ronnie got out. She was angry not at him for falling in, but at situations like this that caused us to live feeling aggravated all the time.

My aggravation led to more fights between Ronnie and me. We had to do so many things together that by evening we just didn't want to be around each other. It seemed that Ronnie was gaining weight daily. He was in the first grade and much bigger than Levi and me. No matter how big he got, I never backed down to him. We would fight anywhere. And at the end of those fights a beating from Mama would be waiting for us. Levi figured that since we were going to fight regardless of the whipping we could expect, that it made sense for us to get up early in the morning, fight, and get it over with before Mama got up. He woke us early one morning, demanded that we get up and fight and get it out of the way. We both looked at him like he was crazy. We weren't just going to jump up and start throwing blows at each other. There had to at least be the semblance of provocation, so we just rolled over and went back to sleep. Later on that day, we did fight, and we did get a whipping, and at that point Levi's advice seemed awfully good.

The only place I found any peace was on the playground shooting hoops with my best friend, J.B. We played one on one until late into the night. Mama didn't mind as long as she knew I was at

Lincoln Park. She always kept close tabs on all of us. If we had to be home at a specific time, you had better be there, or she would come looking for you with a switch in hand. But for some reason she always gave me a lot of leeway when I was out playing basketball because she knew exactly where she could find me.

At eight years old I manipulated my way through the third grade while living in a very small house with holes in the bathroom floor, bathing in dirty water, feeling the sting of mama's many whippings as well as those from the principal at O. A. Fleming, losing my favorite aunt to a murder, and playing basketball all my spare time. But I still could not read.

CHAPTER 6

In the spring the shrimpers docked in Freeport, but Mama did not show her usual exuberance. She had just taken up with Jerry who was different from the other men she dated. He was not a shrimper, he did not drink, he did not beat Mama, and he took a genuine interest in us. We all liked him a great deal. His biggest problem, which was major, he did not work or bring money into the house. But at least there was a peaceful atmosphere for the few months he managed to stay around.

Even though Mama was dating Jerry, she took all of us down to the dock to see Big James. She especially wanted Little James to see his father. We really didn't want to go. Our memories of him were of the beatings inflicted on Mama. On the way to the dock I thought back on that night when he showed up and all his things sat in front of him in trash bags. That night I knew he would kill us all, but instead just turned and walked away. Now we were going to meet him. That made no sense to me. What if he became violent? What if Mama said something to trigger that temper? But she insisted we all go, and there we were, waiting on the dock for him to get off the boat.

James was not the first man we saw that we knew. It was my Dad. When he spotted us he hurried over to where we stood.

"Hey, Shorty, how you doing girl?" he asked Mama completely ignoring me.

"I'm fine, but don't you see your baby," she said and pointed directly at me.

"Hey boy, how you gettin' along?" he asked, but did not hug or even touch me. He showed no emotion at all.

"I'm playing a lot of basketball and getting real good," I replied.

"Okay, but don't be a big mouth and brag on yourself." He then turned back to Mama. "Maybe I'll see you at the club later on."

"Maybe you will," Mama said looking over the top of him at Big James who had strolled off his boat and headed in our direction. "When you see me, make sure you got some money." She put one arm around my shoulder and pulled me in close to her. "This boy needs a lot of things and ain't nobody going to give it to him for nothing."

She then pushed me away. "I'll see you when I see some money."

"Yeah, yeah," Daddy scowled. "Hey man, how you doing?" he said as he walked away and Big James walked toward us. I held my breath for a moment hoping Big James wouldn't attack Daddy for talking to Mama. Daddy was a little man, standing 5 foot 3 and James much bigger. Even though word on the street was that Daddy whipped men bigger than him, I had experienced Big James' fury and couldn't see Daddy matching up well in a battle with him. But the two shrimpers shook hands, did a slight hug and Daddy walked away.

My fears now shifted to Big James. After the rather turbulent departure last fall I didn't know how he would act. Would he pick up Mama and throw her in the water, would he hit her right in the face as he had done in the past, or would he be congenial?

"Shorty, how you and these boys doing?" he asked. I sighed in relief knowing he would be congenial.

"We fine, but we need money and your boy needs all new clothes. He's growing an inch every month it seems like."

James pulled out a wad of bills rolled up together. Without counting, he peeled off a number of twenties and put them in Mama's hand. "Ain't nothin' Shorty," he remarked. "Ain't nothin' at all."

Mama placed Little James out in front of her. "Say something to your boy," she said.

"How you boys doing?" he asked.

"We fine," Levi answered taking the lead to respond for all of us.

I wondered why he didn't speak solely to his son. Why he didn't pick him up, hug him and even kiss him? He hadn't seen his son in six months and some kind of emotional attention seemed appropriate. But my father hadn't done those things with me, why should I expect James to do them. These men, who spent so much time at sea, where love is not portioned out, could not give affection, but could dish out pain. At least Big James gave Mama some money. That's more than what my Daddy did. I guess that made him the better of the two men. But did James believe that would earn him an invitation to move back in with us. I dreaded the thought. I would rather Mama give him the money back than wake up to the sound of blows against her flesh.

My fears were quickly dispelled when a week later Mama brought Jerry home to be our new dad. That night in bed, Levi and I exchanged views on this new male addition to our house. We didn't think he would last long because he was not a shrimper and since he didn't have a job, he couldn't help provide for the family.

Mama had finally decided to leave the shrimpers alone. I didn't know what Jerry did for a living, but I knew he would not be pulling out returning to Florida in the fall. Even if he didn't make it with Mama, I knew he would be somewhere around Freeport. Because he was such a nice man, he'd never make it with Mama, even though I was pulling for him.

He spent a lot of time with my brothers and me; something we were not used to. Big James always gave us money, but never spent time with us, not even his own son. In fact Little James and I were not his favorites. He showed favoritism toward Levi and Ronnie because they knew how to keep their mouths shut.

Mama was no saint. In fact, her behavior was quite hypocritical during the years Big James lived with us. When he left the house in the morning to go down to the café or the docks, Mama would grab all of us boys and leave out the back door. There was a trail in the back that led to the house where Ronnie's father lived. She would take us inside, sit us down on the floor and then disappear in the back room with him.

We never felt compelled to tell Big James. If Mama did it, we accepted it, but it was not acceptable for Big James to cheat. I accepted nothing from anyone I felt would hurt Mama. And that is why I liked Jerry. He didn't seem to be that way.

That summer Jerry decided to enroll Levi and me in Little League baseball. Freeport did not have organized basketball for the youth, but it did have baseball. I don't know where Jerry got two baseball gloves, but Levi and I had our own. I played shortstop and pitched. I was awful as a pitcher and the other team scored on me with relative ease. I got to the point I didn't like the sport. One game Jerry wasn't there, and the coach didn't allow me to play at all, not pitcher or shortstop. I confronted him and asked why. He told me I didn't know how to shut up and that I was always running my mouth. It was annoying to him and all the other players, coaches and umpires. I needed to learn to keep my big mouth shut and just play the game. Until that day came, he was not going to play me.

I imploded within, but I didn't say anything. I knew I wasn't going to sit there while the other players had the opportunity to play and all I could do was watch. I turned and stomped off. Gary Park, where we played our games, was close to Grandma' house, so I headed over there and that was a grave error. When I walked up to the porch, Daddy stood there, talking and drinking with some friends of Grandma. He didn't make the Florida trip that year, instead hung around Freeport. Even though he was no longer in Mama's life, he regularly visited Grandma.

I stomped up on the porch and tossed the glove away from me. I was about to go in the house when Daddy grabbed me and swung me around.

"Hey boy, what you doing?" he asked.

"I ain't playing that game no more," I answered and tried to pull away.

He jerked me back to him. "Why, what happened?"

"The coach won't let me pitch and he won't let me play shortstop either. I know I'm better than that boy playing shortstop." Again I tried to break loose and go in the house, but his grip tightened on my shoulder.

"You telling me that you quit?" he shouted with spittle hitting my face. I realized I had made a mistake, and it probably would be costly. "I'll be damn if a kid of mine is going to be a quitter." He snatched me off the porch and found a rope, dipped it in a bucket of water, and commenced to beat me. In unison with each blow, he would shout, "I ain't going to have no quitter. You'll learn that a Floyd never quits."

That was one time I wished a Floyd would quit; quit beating on me because my butt and legs ached and welts exploded all over me. I also wished I had stayed at the baseball game or gone straight home. The beating was almost as painful as the ones I would get years later at the hands of Bobby, another of Mama's lovers and our tormentor.

Next day I returned to the baseball team but knew my chances of playing were negligible. I also knew I'd rather sit there on that bench angry because I was not playing, than to face the wrath of my father. He was the only man I ever feared. Daddy was known as a brawler and even though most of his opponents towered over his 5 foot 3 frame, he battled much larger men and would often win. I experienced the fierce power behind his swing, and was determined to steer clear of it in the future.

Levi and I were right about Jerry. By the end of summer he was gone. Even though he seemed to be nice to Mama and took time with us, he did not pay the piper so he had to go. With Mama you had to pay to play and since he didn't work, he was out. Mama always criticized the local men of Freeport, complaining they weren't willing to spend money on a lady. The shrimpers were the gentlemen and knew how to treat a lady real nice. Evidently Mama measured being nice by the amount of money a man would give her.

It couldn't be by any other standards since getting thrown through a sheet rock wall didn't disqualify Big James. We figured she was still seeing him because we were still eating real good. And we knew she was still seeing Ronnie's father because of those afternoon treks on the back trail to his house.

CHAPTER 7

———◆•◆•◆———

"Hey David, you sure are dumb. You can't read nothing," Hayward Barnes taunted me on the way out of the classroom to recess. "You all see him holding that book and just staring at it," he continued his taunting in front of the other students. "Boy you dumb."

Reading was our last subject before we went outside for recess and it all seemed like a repeat performance from last year when the same students would tease me. I stood before the class and stuttered my words, Mr. McDonald, our teacher, lost patience with me, and the other students laughed. This time Hayward took it outside the classroom, which would be his mistake.

We were in the middle of dodge ball and I had the ball. I watched Hayward as he made it safely to a base free of attack from whoever had the ball, which in this instance happened to be me. After he came to a stop I reared back and threw it right at his head with all the power I could muster. Smack…it caught him right in the face. He grabbed his head and held it between his hands. He then charged toward me and I readied myself for the battle. Mr. McDonald stepped between us and directed his wrath at me.

"David Floyd, over to the sidelines. What's wrong with you? You can't go around throwing balls at the heads of other children!" he exclaimed. "Get over there against the wall and don't move." He pointed toward a corner of the school building. "Your other teachers warned me about you, nothing but a trouble maker. If you put as much time into trying to read as you do into making trouble, maybe you'd make some progress."

I stomped over to the building and leaned against it. I didn't bother to tell Mr. McDonald what Hayward said. It wouldn't do any good because he had made up his mind about me. In fact, all the teachers at O.A. Fleming had decided I was a lost cause and would simply float from grade to grade until I dropped out of school. I disliked them as much as they did me and couldn't wait for my sixteenth birthday so I could get out of what to me was prison. While standing there I kept my eyes trained on Hayward. I'd make him pay after school.

A large group of students stood in a circle down "nigger trail" in anticipation of the fight soon to commence between Hayward and me. Word had spread like wild fire what happened during recess and they all knew I was going to even the score. I believe I had more fights than any one else along "nigger trail." It seemed like every day I fought someone and when I couldn't find another person to go to blows with, I would chose Ronnie. On this particular day it was Hayward.

Ronnie walked next to me as we headed down the trail. We saw a group of kids surrounding someone. We knew that someone was Hayward. I rushed right into the middle of the circle and positioned myself face to face with him.

"Why you want to go and hit me with that ball?' he asked with clenched fist ready for action.

"You know why, boy," I replied with as much base in my voice as I could muster. "I ain't going to let you make fun of me."

"I won't only make fun of you, I'll kick your ass," he said and lifted his arm to strike me.

Before he could land a blow Ronnie came crashing through the circle of on-lookers. He had a piece of steel and managed to wrap it around his fist. He landed a blow right above Hayward's eye. Hayward fell to the side and blood from the blow shot everywhere. The on-lookers scattered in all directions. Hayward burst out in a screeching yelp, covered his eye and took off running. Ronnie and I were the only two left standing there.

"Come on, let's get out of here," I shouted. We took off running and didn't look back. We hit the front door of our house still running.

We ran straight to the bedroom, slammed the door shut, and sat on the side of the bed. We had to figure out what to do next. Fortunately, Mama was still at work. Little James was at the baby sitter's and Levi hadn't made it home. I finally noticed all the blood on Ronnie's hand, got up and grabbed him by the arm.

"Come on, we got to wash that blood off you," I said.

We headed through the living room and kitchen into the bathroom. He scrubbed thoroughly and then we looked for any blood on his clothes. If Mama suspected we had just busted another kid in the head with a piece of steel, she would wear us out. There was no evidence of the fight and we could only hope no one would tell her. It would be a very long night.

Ronnie and I made it through the night without the wrath of Mama crashing down on us. She didn't say anything the entire evening but had to know something was wrong because we were so quiet and subdued. Ronnie stayed in the bedroom but I hung out in the living room while Mama helped Levi with his homework. Every once in a while, she would glance at me. I knew a question about my behavior was coming. It didn't and I felt relieved when we finally went to bed.

After the incident on the playground, I thought Mr. McDonald might be sensitive to my feelings and stop embarrassing me in front of the rest of the students. That wasn't going to happen; he still called on me. One day I came up with a scheme I thought might work. Each student was required to read one paragraph from the reader. I counted the number of students before me and figured out what I would have to read. Instead of listening to the others, I practiced what I was expected to read. In my mind I could read it like poetry. I knew once they got to me I would have conquered my problem. Finally, it was my turn and it all went blank. I tried to read the first word, "Wwwhen," I stuttered.

I could feel all eyes on me and finally heard the snickering from the other students. "Shut up," I shouted. "Why you got to laugh." Out of the side of my eyes I saw Hayward laughing again. "Shut up," I shouted a second time.

"David Floyd stop that shouting in my classroom," Mr. McDonald said. "In fact get out of here and go to the principal's office. I'll be right behind you."

I threw the book on the floor and rushed out of the room. Mr. McDonald caught up with me before I made it to the principal's office. When we walked into the office, his staff knew why we were there. They let us go right into Mr. Waniack's office. He looked up from his desk and over the top of his glasses.

"Not again," he said.

"Yes," Mr. McDonald answered. "I can't allow this boy to continue to disrupt my class." He firmly placed his hand on my shoulder. "This has to stop. He doesn't want to cooperate and I'm convinced he doesn't care about learning."

"Thank you Mr. McDonald," the principal said. "You can go back to your class. I'll take care of him."

Mr. McDonald turned and stormed out of the room. Mr. Waniack got up and came around from his desk. He grabbed my arm and pulled me over to the corner. "So you want to continue your disruptive behavior do you?" he said. "Well I can paddle as long as you can act up." Again those words "bend over."

He not only whipped me but lectured me also.

"You are nothing and you'll never amount to anything, David," he said and then whapped me with the paddle. "You're nothing but a trouble maker." Whap. "If there was some way I could get you out of this school, I would do it." Whap. "Now get back to your class and see if you can do something right for a change."

I returned to class angrier and more defiant than ever before. Not because of the paddling. I was used to that, but because this man told me that I would never accomplish anything in life.

Mr. Waniack's combination of physical and mental abuse brought me to the realization that I could never be broken through physical pain, but only through the mental. This understanding would serve me well for the next three years when Mama brought Bobby into our lives.

"Hey, young David, dance for us," Bobby Robeson shouted from his bar stool inside the Blue and White Café. As usual Levi, J.B. and I hung out in the patio area. After a half-hour of playing games we decided to go inside and buy chips and cokes with money we hustled doing small chores for customers going inside. When we walked in, the jukebox was blasting away with a James Brown tune. I admired James Brown because of his smooth and graceful routines. I practiced them many times at home in the middle of the living room.

"Here, this is for you." Bobby threw two quarters at me. I grabbed them right out of the air and went to work.

As James Brown's "Please, please, please don't go," resonated throughout the room, I moved to the center of the floor and performed his moves, sliding my feet across the room and then bending my knees and moving my body to the rhythm of the song. I then fell to the floor, and Levi moved in to help me up and simulate putting a coat around my shoulders, which had always been a part of James Brown's act. He then helped me across the floor and suddenly I broke from his grip and danced my way back to the middle of the floor, continuing my James Brown routine. Bobby, along with all the other patrons inside broke out in a loud cheer, encouraging me along. It was through this performance, which I did many times, that I first met Bobby. He was a fixture in the place and always paid me to dance. That was the beginning of what became a very turbulent relationship.

Bobby was not one of the shrimpers. Word spread he was a college graduate from some school in Alabama. He majored in electrical engineering and was a pretty smart man. But just like most men in

Freeport he loved to drink. A few weeks after I met him in the Blue and White, he began to date Mama. Less than a month before, she had broken up with Jerry and now she had someone new. Mama didn't let any grass grow under her feet.

Shortly after they started dating, the police arrested Bobby and charged him with the murder of my close friend's mother, Shirley Anderson. Rumors had it that he mistakenly killed her with a shotgun. The round was meant for someone else. The district attorney indicted Bobby even though the police never found the weapon and had no witnesses.

Mama was irate over his arrest and insisted that we write him letters of encouragement while he was locked up. We wanted to see him beat the charge because we were all convinced it was a trumped up bad rap against him. In rallying to the defense of Bobby, we forgot that a young Black woman was brutally murdered. Levi, Ronnie, and I used to rush to the Blue and White Café to find out what happened at trial. Then we would hurry home to find out what Mama knew since she dated the man and had more contact with him and his lawyer than anyone else.

The excitement behind Bobby's trial was short lived. After two weeks he was acquitted and set free. We probably would have forgotten about Bobby but for the fact he moved in with Mama and became the new man of the house. For about two months things were good among all of us. Initially he spent some time playing different games and wrestling with me quite a bit. He didn't mess with Ronnie because of his size. It was during one of these tussles on the couch that two shotgun shells fell out of his pants pocket. He quickly snatched them and stuffed them back into his pocket. During his trial he had vehemently denied owning or having access to a shotgun. Why would he be carrying shells if he didn't have access to the weapon? Prior to actually seeing those shells I assumed he was innocent. Now my doubts began to grow. If he had actually killed Shirley, then we all had to be careful around him. We had heard many old timers say, "Once you killed the first time, the next is much easier."

Not long after Bobby settled in, we moved to the west side of town. I found it much different over there. I was no longer real close to J.B. and Lincoln Park. It became more difficult to hang out in the patio at the Blue and White Café. It was a new life style with the exception of the drinking, cussing, and whippings now being inflicted on us instead of Mama. Bobby drank a lot, did not work and we couldn't figure out why she kept him around, since she had gotten rid of Jerry because he failed to bring money into the house. Our greatest nightmares occurred on the afternoons Mama would be at the Goodwill working, and we were left alone with that maniac.

CHAPTER 8

"He passed me and I'm going on to the fifth grade," I shouted to Ronnie as we headed home on the last day of school. How could that be? I couldn't read a thing and Mr. McDonald knew that as did all the other kids in the class. It made no sense, but I didn't complain. I sure didn't want to spend another year with him, and he definitely did not want me in his class again. More than any other reason, that's why he moved me on to the next level with the rest of the students.

Levi was now in his second year at Freeport Intermediate and would be moving onto the seventh grade. He was the smart one in the family; an excellent student in math, could read, and had an outstanding skill for writing. Levi definitely was college material. I wasn't, even though I needed college as a stepping-stone to the National Basketball Association. There was still no organized basketball for elementary school students in Freeport. I developed my skills on the playground at Lincoln Park. We had moved further away, but I still found my way over there. J.B. and I spent all our spare time throwing up hoops, with the exception of the time Ronnie and I spent at the docks trying to earn summer money.

We decided to work cleaning the hatches and the engines of the shrimp boats docked at the pier. We'd get up early, grab something to eat and head out running. Less than five minutes after we started toward the docks, Ronnie would stop running and shout out to me.

"Come on David, wait up. I'm out of breath and I got to walk."

"Oh, man, you got to start losing some weight," I taunted him. "We going to be late getting down there and ain't nobody going to hire us."

Ronnie walked at a slow pace a few feet behind me. "You always say that, but we always get work," he retorted. "They hire us cause they all like your Daddy."

"They hire us cause I'm good. Now hurry up before we lose out." I started to jog forcing him to walk faster in order to stay close behind.

There were at least thirty shrimp boats lined up next to each other. As I jogged along the dock, I looked for the boats with the owners on board. After a while, you know the owner from a deck hand. When the situation was right, I walked right up to the owner and asked him,

"Want your hole and engine cleaned?"

"How much?"

"We can do the entire job for twenty dollars."

"Ain't you Runt's boy?"

"Yessir, I am."

"Okay," the owner reluctantly agreed. "But you boys better do a damn good job." He waved us on board.

Ronnie headed for the hatch and I went to the engine and started the rigorous job of cleaning in over one hundred degrees heat. As we worked I heard the owner grumbling, "Twenty damn dollars, too much for that little work. Boys ain't nothing but young hustlers. Better be glad they're Runt's boys or I wouldn't give them no more than ten dollars for the entire job."

"And I wouldn't do this hot work in this hot hole for no ten dollars," I whispered in retort to his complaint.

Ronnie and I finished cleaning the boat in about three hours. We did only one boat a day because the work tired my brother out. If I started looking for more work after we finished a job, he complained,

"I ain't doing no more, David. I'm too tired."

I always conceded and we would start toward home. But I insisted on getting the last word, "Man, Ronnie, you'd better lose some weight or you ain't ever going to be able to do nothing and you sure ain't going to live long."

Life with Bobby had become unbearable, especially during the summer when we were out of school and he did not work. The first few months he lived with us all he did was curse and shout. But he soon took it to another level.

Levi, Ronnie and I were playfully wrestling all over the living room when he came bursting through the front door like he wanted to kill someone.

"Get the fuck off that furniture you little motherfuckers!" he hollered.

The glare in his eyes frightened me, and I came to an abrupt stop.

We jumped to our feet and started toward the bedroom. He grabbed Levi before he could make it inside, placed his body in front of the entrance and blocked Ronnie and me.

"You all been acting up in this house since we moved over here. Looks like Shorty can't control your asses." He dragged Levi over to the end table, took the extension cord from its sockets. Bobby drew back to strike Levi when I shouted, "You ain't got no right to whip us. We ain't done nothing to you and you ain't our daddy."

"Oh, you the big mouth bastard, ain't you," he screeched. He let Levi go and instead grabbed me by the arm. "Bend your ass over boy, or I'm going to hit you wherever I can."

"You'd better start hitting because I ain't bending over." I didn't want this man beating on my brother because I didn't know if he could handle it. Levi hadn't endured the kind of beatings I had at school or at home. Mama would whip him but never as often as me, and I don't believe he ever got whipped at school, so I was better prepared to handle Bobby's violent attack. Chances were he could break my brother, but no way could he do that to me.

Bobby beat me for a good five minutes, hitting and cussing as he went along. When he finished, he grabbed Ronnie and then Levi. No doubt he was enjoying this exercise of power over us. The same kind of enjoyment he must have felt when he pulled that trigger and killed another human being. This was a new experience for us. We got whippings by Mama, and I got plenty of whippings at school, but no man that Mama brought in the house to live had ever laid his hands on us. Would she allow this to happen if she knew? We weren't about to tell her because he had already killed once and that old man had warned us that the second time was much easier.

Just like it was easier to kill after the first time, it seemed easier for Bobby to whip us after the first time. It became a habit, and he loved to do it. It didn't really matter what we were doing to earn a thrashing, he would grab anything, a belt, strap, or cord and begin to wail away. His greatest thrill came when he whipped me because I showed no emotion. I refused to cry no matter how hard or how long he thrashed at me. That infuriated him and it soon became a mental game between the two of us. I was determined that he would never break me down, no matter how many times or how many licks. He was powerless if he couldn't conquer my determination not to cry. That was the beginning of a strong will that never let me down, no matter what the situation.

Levi finally reached a point he could not take the beatings any longer. After one particular intense beating from this maniac, one that drew blood from all of us, Levi decided we had to tell someone what was going on. The only person we knew was our Grandmother. The three victims of the beatings, Levi, Ronnie, and I, all took off one afternoon to her house. She looked somewhat surprised when we came running through the front door and right up to where she sat watching her favorite television programs. Levi took the lead.

"Grandma, you got to help us," he shouted.

She knew something was seriously wrong because she cut off the television to listen to us. "What in the world is wrong with you children?" she asked. "You look and act like you saw a ghost."

"Grandma, you got to stop him from beating on us," Levi continued. "He just beats us so bad that we start bleeding."

"What? Who beats you?" she shrieked.

"Bobby, Grandma," I now got into the conversation. "He thinks he's our daddy or something and he can beat us whenever he gets ready."

"What?" Grandma again exclaimed. "Does your mother know about this?"

"I don't like him and wish something would happen to him," Ronnie added.

"Hush boy, let your brother tell me what's happening," Grandma instructed Ronnie.

"Bobby is mean, and he killed that woman," I shouted.

"Let Levi explain what's happening, and you other two hush."

"He been beating us all the time for the past six months," Levi said. "We don't really have to do anything wrong, but he comes in drunk, while Mama is at work, and just attacks us. He don't care what he beats us with. It can be a belt, strap, anything he can find."

"I asked you all does your mother know about this?" Grandma again questioned us.

"No, 'cause we scared to tell her," I said. "We don't want him to do nothing to hurt Mama. You know he killed that other woman."

"Stop saying that boy," she said to me. "You don't know for sure what happened."

"That man is mean and I just know he did it," I continued.

"Boy, I told you to stop that talk. I'm going to tell your Mama what's going on," she said. "She got to get that man out her house if he's abusing you children."

"Don't get Mama hurt," I shouted.

"That man ain't crazy," Grandma shot back. "If he do anything to hurt Shorty, her brothers will tear him apart. Now you all can stay here if you want to until we get this straightened out."

"I'm going to move back here with you, Grandma," Levi said. "I don't want to be in that house no more with that man."

"You can't do that," I shouted. "You can't leave Mama and Little James in that house alone with him."

"That's right," Ronnie said. "We got to go home and help Mama."

"You all can go back, but I ain't ever going there as long as that man lives there," Levi said.

"Levi, how you just going to leave Mama there?" I directed my anger at my brother. He was being a coward running away from our collective problem. We all needed to stick together in order to protect each other. I was not about to leave my brothers and Mama alone in that house. I didn't know exactly what I could do, but I would try anything to help them out.

He stayed there with Grandma while Ronnie and I returned home. Levi didn't even come back with us and get his clothes.

That night Mama acted funny. She gathered Levi's clothes and took them down to Grandma's house. Mama's attitude towards Bobby seemed different. She was real quiet and kept staring at him with a look I saw many times just before she tore into me. I wondered would she fight him as she had done with Big James, would she put him out, something she also had done with a number of men in the past or would she just let it continue? It would be quite a while before I got the answer to that question.

CHAPTER 9

In the fall I entered the fifth grade with a stronger will than ever before to succeed. It was not based on reading, but achieving without knowing how to read. Despite my major handicap, I seemed to be progressing in life. The strength derived from my constantly improving basketball skills. I was, hands down, the best ball player in my age bracket at Lincoln Park. But that was no longer enough to feed my competitive nature. I wanted to show off my skills throughout the city and along the Gulf Coast. I craved more competition and couldn't wait until I moved on to the sixth grade and intermediate school. But first, I had to fool another teacher in order to pass on to the next grade. It would be a long nine months, especially having to face Bobby every night and his need to inflict pain on me. I was battle tested and now ready for all the challenges I would confront that year.

Mrs. Silva, the fifth grade teacher, showed a genuine interest in my welfare and wanted to help me overcome my reading problem. Unlike previous teachers, she didn't taunt or threaten me. Instead, she went out of her way to help me through each reading. She worked with me privately using a kindergarten reader, *Buttermilk Bill and the Train*, as the reading material. I failed miserably.

That Christmas, Mrs. Silva cast me in the school Christmas play as a toy soldier. She knew how well I danced and gave me that role as an opportunity to demonstrate my talent in front of the other students and parents. It was one of the highlights of my elementary school years. I displayed my moves and rhythm before the entire audience and was deemed the star of the play. Mama never showed up for the play and that was a disappointment. I would soon get used to Mama being a no-show. She failed to attend any of my basketball games throughout intermediate and high school. For a while after Christmas, no one laughed at me, but only gave compliments for my outstanding performance.

At the end of the year, Mrs. Silva did as all the other instructors had done before her, promoted me to the sixth grade, and I prepared to finally leave O.A. Fleming Elementary School onto Freeport Intermediate. Unlike the others, however, Mrs. Sylva passed me not for the same reason as my previous instructors. She did it because she understood how badly I wanted to read. For the first time in my short education I felt that someone really did care. A student's skin color didn't matter to her. She showed much compassion for all students and definitely gave me a heavy dose, sometimes in the form of "tough love" but it was love.

Mrs. Sylva was a no nonsense person and definitely wielded a heavy paddle. I learned not to mess around in her classroom. But ultimately, she did the same as all the others, and that is to send me on to the next level of learning when I had totally failed to master the first level.

My situation with Bobby had gotten much worse. The whippings were coming more often and severe. Ronnie and I were at the point we really did hate him. We were convinced that he had murdered Shirley, and we had regrets for the time we spent pulling for him to beat the charges. I wanted to tell Mama about the shotgun shells that fell out of his pockets the time we wrestled. But I did fear the man, and so I decided against telling her. Little did I know at that time Grandma had pretty much convinced Mama to be careful around him, and that she was convinced he had committed the murder. Mama, also, walked in fear of him. That is why it took her so long to finally confront and put him out of our lives.

That spring when the boats returned from Florida, Bobby decided to become a shrimper. I don't know if that was forced on him because he knew Mama liked shrimpers or because he couldn't find any other work. One fact he understood well, he could not live there with Mama without working. He knew many of the captains on the boats because of his association with Mama, and when he found out there was an opening on the boat, *Retirement Plan*, he jumped at the opportunity to get aboard. Those twenty days he was out at sea were golden for us. Ronnie and I played and moved around the house without worrying about him. The only whippings we got came from Mama and that was like a cakewalk compared to the ones inflicted on us by that crazy man.

Mama even relaxed some. That angry look no longer dominated her facial expressions. She laughed with Ronnie and me. We all took bets as to how long Bobby would last at sea. We also bet that when he returned he would not go back for another twenty days. Later in the evening when alone in our bedroom, we laughed at him. If he crossed one of the shrimpers like Big James, he would end up in the bottom of the Gulf. To us that wasn't such a bad idea at all. He thought he was some kind of pretty boy, but those kinds of men just didn't make it out at sea. It took more than looks to survive out there. It took toughness. That night we fell asleep confident that Bobby would return in twenty days a defeated man.

We counted the days in anticipation of his return to Freeport. When that day finally arrived, Mama made us all go down to the dock to meet him. Ronnie and I didn't want to go. We dreaded the day when we would see him again, and Mama actually made it worse forcing us to greet him. None of our predictions came true. He rushed off the boat, spotted us and headed our way. He looked to be in perfect shape. His right arm, the one he wielded his weapon of punishment with, was intact, and Ronnie and I could look forward to the end of our tranquility.

It only took until a little past noon the next day for him to spring into action. Mama was at work and Baby James at the baby sitter, when he came busting through the front door. We were playing in the living room throwing a miniature football to each other.

"Take that shit out of here," he scowled and then dropped down in the middle of the couch right in the direct line of the ball's back and forth flight.

Ignoring his warnings, Ronnie shot a pass to me. I grabbed and shot it back to him. This time I threw it just a little lower and right over Bobby's head. He flung his arms in the air and tried to catch it. He missed and Ronnie threw it back to me.

"You fucking kids hear what I said," he shouted. "Quit throwing that ball in the house. Take that shit outside."

"You ain't my Daddy, so you can't tell me what to do," I shouted right back at him. Ronnie held on to the ball. Probably in anticipation of what was coming.

"Your Daddy." Bobby sat up on the couch. "That no good piece of shit got babies all over the place and don't take care of none of them. And he sure don't take care of you."

If I'd had the ball I would have fired it right at his head as I did on the playground with Hayward. But Ronnie held it and that was probably a good thing. "My Daddy's a better man than you'll ever be," I screamed at him.

"You think so, huh?" He jumped off the couch and looked around as if searching for a weapon for a beating. I broke for the bedroom, but he grabbed my arm. Bobby dragged me into the kitchen, still searching for the proper weapon. I kept trying to break his grip, but he was too strong. Ronnie rushed him and tried to break his hold. He smacked him with his loose hand and tossed him into the kitchen table. Ronnie crashed to the floor. "You keep your fat ass right there. I'll get you soon as I finish with big mouth."

Bobby finally spotted a thick rubber hose attached to the faucet and the washing machine. He loosened it from both connections and whaled away. He hit every conceivable spot he could find.

"I bet this shit will make you cry now," he shouted as the hose hit my legs, butt, and part of my lower back.

Of all the whippings I'd gotten over the years, this one hurt the most. With each blow the pain worsened, but I continued my struggle to break loose from his grip, and I did not cry. I recalled my resolve to never let another person break my will, exactly what he wanted to do. The more I fought, the more intense the blows. I wanted to beg him to stop because of the excruciating pain, but I couldn't do that. He couldn't win. If I lost this first time I would be losing the rest of my life. He kept hitting, and I kept hurting until he finally tired. He threw me to the floor and stormed out of the room. Ronnie was spared the rod that day. Evidently Bobby wore himself out trying to wear me out. I ran to my room in deep pain, flopped down on the bed and threw the covers over my head. I didn't want my brother see me break down and cry.

That night I realized Mama was afraid of Bobby. Before, she had no idea just how severe the beatings had become. But when she came into the bedroom, after he left the house, and saw my condition she had to know. In order to compensate for her inability to stop him she blamed me.

"Why you keep doing things to Bobby to make him so angry?" she asked standing at the door. She never thought to come over and sit next to me on the bed. She never thought to soothe both my physical and mental wounds. She gave none of it a second thought. Instead she stood there and chastised me.

"You always running your mouth, David. You got to learn when it's time to shut up. Grown men ain't going to tolerate no back talk from a kid."

"Mama, he came after me and Ronnie," I said in a weakened voice.

"What you mean he came after you? What were you all doing?"

"We was just tossing the football," I pleaded our case.

"In the house?" she shot back at me. "He should've whipped your ass. In fact, I should give both of you another ass whipping," she said, but not with the usual vigor. Mama knew I was hurting real bad, and should have done something other than threaten me. She should have put him out on the street.

The pain Mama inflicted on me that night was not physical but mental. She was about to break me down, something I swore would never happen. I didn't let Mr. Waniack do it or Bobby, and no way I would let her do it. My only defense was to turn away from her, and for that brief time in the bedroom, I hated Mama.

After that night I stayed away from the house as much as I could. J.B. and I practically lived on the playground at Lincoln Park shooting hoops. Mama didn't complain. I believe she was giving me space to recover from that ordeal. Ronnie would hang out with us, but he was not much of a basketball player. He just wanted to be away from Bobby's madness. He would usually take off for home about the same time Mama would get there. Ronnie hadn't reached that same point of alienation from her because she never talked to him in the same disdainful manner she did me. Mama was much more sensitive to his weight problem and therefore careful how she talked to him. He felt secure at home if she was there. I didn't feel secure at all and because of that I wanted to stay away as much as possible. Levi had Grandma, Ronnie had Mama, and I had basketball. I was perfectly happy with that arrangement.

CHAPTER 10

Two weeks later, Ronnie and I had the opportunity to get away from home for twenty days, but not from Bobby. One of my schoolmate's fathers was captain of the shrimp boat, the same one Bobby had joined onto. We would be going out with him. Ronnie and I were so happy we didn't care that he'd also be aboard. And how much damage could he do on a boat with other men around? I would find out.

On a blistering hot summer morning we climbed aboard the boat with the rest of the crew. Ronnie and I ran to the back of the boat and fell out on the deck. Many times he and I boarded these boats to clean the engine and hatch areas. I always wished we could sail out into the ocean. Now it was happening and we felt like real men, rough and tough kind of men who frequented the Blue and White Café, drank heavily, fought viciously, and then disappeared back out to sea. We were a part of that group and I knew I would enjoy every day we were out and would never want to return home. At least that is how I felt that first morning. It wouldn't take very long for all that to change.

The first day both Ronnie and I were sick from the constant motion of the boat. Ronnie was really miserable to the point that he could only get up to throw up. My seasickness lasted one day, his five. I worried about him making it through the twenty days. This was not a situation we could just turn around and go home. This wasn't Lincoln Park or the patio area at the Blue and White Cafe, but a small shrimp boat so far out into the ocean that we saw only water everywhere we looked.

To make matters worse, our schedule called for us to sleep during the day and work all night. We reversed our timetable for those twenty days and adjusted to the habits of the shrimp. Ronnie, Tim and I had a specific job. Once the shrimp were caught in a large net and pulled up to the deck, we had to pop off their heads. When we first started out after dark, Bobby and the other two men on board lowered the net into the water. The captain started the engine and the boat moved forward at approximately thirty-five miles per hour. We rode for about four hours with the net dragging along behind us and catching anything in its path, eight feet below the surface.

The captain had the most tedious task while the boat moved along in the water. He had to be alert for any jagged mountain tops extended up from the ocean floor. Our boat descended about eight feet under water, deep enough to hit one of those jagged ends and tear the boat apart. Sensory equipment, located next to the steering wheel, alerted him when he neared the mountaintops in sufficient time for him to move around them. If we didn't veer around it, the boat would be torn apart much like what happened to the Titanic. I was scared all the time thinking that the Captain wouldn't hear the warning or the equipment would fail. Suddenly being at sea as a man wasn't so much fun.

At that age I didn't appreciate how magnificent the sky looked on a clear night. Millions of stars twinkled above me with their brightness uninterrupted by city lights. But I was much too frightened by the vast amount of water all around us to appreciate the beauty of the night. I feared that we might hit a jagged edge and disappear under tons of water. Then when Bobby and the other men pulled the net out of the water and dumped its contents, I had no time to concentrate on my fears. Not only did the net capture shrimp, but a little bit of everything else. All sorts of ocean life slithered around the deck searching for an escape back into the water. Most of what we caught was shrimp and our job was to behead them expeditiously so the men could throw the net back into the water.

Time was crucial to the Captain and he wanted to maximize every minute we spent at sea. He rode us hard and Bobby stayed on Ronnie and me. For the first couple days he didn't attack us, but by the end of that first week, he verbally did his damage. Physical attacks were coming soon.

By sunup all I wanted to do was sleep. As soon as the Captain called it quits for the night, I'd run to our cabin and fall out on the mat spread on the floor for us. Ronnie always wanted to eat, no matter how tired he felt. We both wanted to get away from each other. He was bugging me to no end with his incessant whining and crying that he wanted to go home. I wanted to go home also, but all I had to do was look out at all that water and know we weren't going anywhere for a while.

One early evening before our work for the night begun, I messed around on deck and decided to go fishing without the use of a pole. I tied one end of a fishing line around my index finger tightly, placed a hook at the other end and tossed it into the water. I didn't know that a school of fish followed our boat because of the scraps of shrimp heads that we tossed back into the water. These fish would eat anything. When I tossed the hook into the water, they attacked it. I could feel that something had attached to the hook and was trying to break free. I panicked and didn't know what to do. The line tightened around my finger and I couldn't get it off. The tightness hurt, and I believe it cut off my circulation. I shouted for help. First Ronnie ran over there, but he didn't know what to do. He grabbed my hand and pulled in the opposite direction of the tug from the fish. I held on to him tightly. I could see me going overboard and disappearing under all that water. Ronnie pulled so hard he slipped and fell down on the deck. I went down with him because I refused to let go of his grip. The fish seemed to get stronger as it struggled to get loose from the hook. Finally, one of the men shouted out to Bobby.

"Hey, you'd better give your boy a hand."

Bobby dropped the net he had prepared to throw out and sauntered over to where I struggled for my life. He pulled out a long knife and cut the line close to the end tied to my finger. For a second I thought he would cut my finger. At that point I didn't care. I would rather lose part of my finger than end up in the ocean. As soon as he cut the line I grabbed my finger with my free hand and started to rub the pain away. I was busy nursing my wound and didn't see Bobby snatch a long rope lying on the deck and double it over into one piece. Suddenly, I felt a strong grip on my arm and my whole body swung toward Bobby.

"You dumb little motherfucker, you can't do nothing right," he shouted.

I tried to break loose from his grip, but he was too strong. I couldn't believe he would actually whip me right in front of the entire crew. But he did. He brought the rope back as far as he could and then whipped it forward hitting me right below my butt. Again, I tried to break away. I even turned and took a wild swing at him. That only infuriated him. His blows came at a much higher intensity. When he finished, he threw me down next to Ronnie who watched it all from the deck floor. I got up and took off toward my cabin, went inside and fell down on the mat.

For the remainder of the trip I said very little, performed my chores, and then retired to the cabin. I wanted to be off that boat so badly I was tempted to try swimming to shore even though I couldn't swim. Mama had to get rid of this demon. I didn't know how, I only knew she must.

My despondency and anger waned when we arrived back in Freeport and the Captain handed me a three hundred dollar check for my work. Ronnie got the same amount, even though he had spent the first week on his back. Even after he got over his seasickness and began working, he always did much less than I did. When I put my feet back on solid ground with three hundred dollars and no more rocking boat or crazy Bobby, I didn't care how much Ronnie made. We both headed right to the store and cashed our checks. The remainder of my summer vacation would be great because I had more money than ever before, and it was all mine.

Mama quickly put an end to the idea that all the money was mine. She took half of it for bills that had accumulated and then I bought Levi and Little James all new clothes for school. With the remainder, I bought new clothes for me. I was about to begin a new adventure in my life; I now entered Freeport Intermediate School and a whole new group of students with whom to relate.

Freeport Intermediate served three different elementary schools. Jane Long Elementary from the west end delivered students from predominantly white upper middle class families. Valasco Elementary students came from across the river and were middle class. My school, O.A. Fleming, held predominantly lower income students with a good mixture of races. They all came together in this one intermediate school, pretty much unfamiliar with each other. No doubt the teachers favored those students from Jane Long because their parents were the most influential in the city and took a great deal of interest in school affairs. They considered east-end students the troublemakers and rabble-rousers. I was designated as the worst of the group.

The very first week of school I lived up to my reputation. Mr. Westbrook, the principal, had a bulldog face and all the students laughed at him when he was not around. I took it a step further. One morning he caught me running in the hall because I was late to class.

" Stop that running," he shouted at me.

I came to a stop and walked by him. Once I passed him I said, "Whatever, bulldog."

He replied in a stern tone, "David Floyd, I am not going to put up with your mess. To my office."

I followed close behind as we marched down the hall and into his office.

He said, "You are not going to bring your disruptive behavior to my school, bend over, three licks."

I bent over and received my initiation at Freeport Intermediate with three whacks to the rear end. That marked my first, but it would not be the last.

CHAPTER 11

One day after school Ronnie and I walked through the door at Grandma's house and were greeted by Levi with, "Mama's pregnant!"

"No she ain't," I shouted. "Ain't no way Mama going to have that fool's baby."

"Unless she been messing around on Bobby, she going to have his baby," Levi said. "I heard her tell Grandma. And I don't believe Mama going to mess around on that fool. He already done killed one woman."

The three of us plopped down on the couch, and Levi turned on the television. My favorite program, *Good Times*, had just come on, and Thelma was into one of her arguments with J.J. I was in love with Thelma as were half the young black men in America. To me she was the prettiest girl in the entire world next to Marcia, another young beauty who attended First Emmanuel Baptist Church. It was because of her that I started attending Sunday school and sang in the youth choir. I met her during the summer Bible school retreat. I started going to church to be close to Marcia, but after a while I found myself feeling close to Reverend C. E. Richardson, the pastor. But I did like Marcia a whole lot and was determined that someday she would be my girlfriend. At that moment, however, I was content to stare and gloat at Thelma.

"I sure am glad I ain't living with you all no more," Levi said bringing me out of my daydreaming. "There ain't going to be no room at all in that little house."

At that moment I wanted to holler out how I felt about him

running off and leaving the rest of us to deal with Bobby. I had to protect Mama, Ronnie, and Little James from Bobby, but there was no one to protect me. He should have been there to help me out when Bobby attacked me with that rubber hose, or when he beat me on the boat.

Thelma was now holding hands with her fiancé, talking and standing very close to him. I could feel my pressure rising. He was tall, handsome, and of course, light skinned. His kind always seemed to get the prettiest girls.

"I hope it's a girl," Ronnie said. "We got enough boys."

"Yeah, then maybe you won't try to take her food like you do us," I said taking my attention off Thelma long enough to respond.

"That means Mama ain't never going to leave that man," Levi said.

"I don't know about that," I said. "She didn't have no problems getting rid of my Daddy, and Big James, and Jerry."

"Mama done had a whole lot of different men," Levi said.

"And she done got rid of a whole lot of them, too," I said.

"Let's hope there's at least one more," Levi scowled.

Thelma had just started another fight with J.J. so we all turned our attention back to *Good Times*.

After school, I always stopped by the gym and watched the seventh grade team practice. I wanted to practice with them so bad, I could taste it. I was ready for seventh grade ball even though I was only in the sixth. It didn't matter because none of those guys could have handled me. My confidence was solid and I could play way beyond my age.

During the summer, at Lincoln Park, I would get picked by the men to play with them. One man told the others that, "David Floyd is quite a baller and he's going to go a long ways." After that I knew I could make it against any opposition. But since I was only in the sixth grade they wouldn't even let me practice with the team. I had to spend one more year playing sandlot ball with J.B., my best friend, at the park. We both were getting good and looked for the day when in high school we could play together.

In the classroom, nothing had changed. The only difference now I changed classes every period and wasn't with the same students all day. Once my reading class ended, I didn't have to worry about feeling embarrassed because those same students wouldn't be in my next class. The fact that I could not read no longer bothered me. The intermediate school teachers would do the same as they did in elementary school, and that is pass me on to the next grade. But during class the students taunted me when I failed to read. I threw the book at them and the teacher sent me to Mr. Westbrook's office, where he punished me.

Since I knew I would get whipped, I developed a new game plan. Before it was my turn to read, I did something foolish in order to get kicked out of class. My teacher sent me to the principal's office and he gave me five licks. My obstreperous behavior to authority was getting worse. I no longer feared Mr. Westbrook's paddling me. In fact I challenged him. One time he had just finished laying the wood to me, and I turned to walk out. As I passed by him I said, "That don't even hurt, bulldog." He snatched me back into the room and added another five. That became my pattern of behavior throughout the entire year.

In March 1981 Mama gave birth to a little girl. They named her Nicole. She broke the cycle of boys in our family. How do you treat a little girl? We didn't know. We had to be more delicate with her, something that was not part of our behavior. I was angry because there was no room in that small house for another body, and there was hardly enough food for those of us already living there. But Mama seemed happy to have a little girl even if Bobby was the father.

I began to notice a change in Mama. She seemed to be distant from Bobby, always hollering at him. We had witnessed that behavior in her before and knew exactly what it possibly could mean—another locked door with trash bags full of clothes on the walkway.

I crossed my fingers and wanted that to happen real soon. Even with the new baby, we could make it better without him around and no more violent whippings, which still came on a regular basis. Mama had tired of him beating on us all the time, and no longer feared him the way she did in the past. It was only a matter of time before Mama finally broke off that relationship. It happened one night when she had gone out and left all of us, including baby Nicole, at Grandma's house.

"Ms. Sylvia, Bobby got a knife to Shorty's throat," my friend Daniel rushed through Grandma's front door and shouted. "They down at the Super Port Disco and he said, she ain't leaving him."

We had been sitting in the living room watching a late night television program. Grandma held Nicole, but still jumped up first, followed by Uncle Lynn.

"Where you say they at?" Grandma screamed.

"Down at the Super Port Disco."

Uncle Lynn slipped on his football cleats, grabbed his gun, and ran out the door. Levi, Ronnie, and I ran right behind him. In the past the three of us did battle with Big James when he beat up on Mama. Now we had help. We were elated that our Uncle Lynn took the lead. He had the reputation for being a real brawler. Finally, the big bad Bobby, who beat up on kids, was about to meet his match. Bobby fought dirty and I just hoped Uncle Lynn was ready to match his tricks. I also hoped we would get there before Bobby cut Mama's throat.

When we finally reached the spot where Daniel said Bobby held Mama hostage, no one was there. We could hear the neighbor's dogs barking back behind the club. I feared we would find Mama lying there in a pool of blood with her throat cut. Instead, Bobby stepped from behind the building where he was hiding.

"Where's Shorty," Uncle Lynn shouted.

"She's gone home, man."

"Why you put a knife to Shorty's throat? " Uncle Lynn asked.

"I ain't put no knife to her throat. You think I'd hurt my baby's mama."

"Yes," I whispered.

"You shut up," Bobby scowled at me. He glared at all of us. "Get out of here. Get your little black ass home. It's after one o'clock and you ain't got no business out here this late."

"I don't want you hitting on my sister, you understand?" Uncle Lynn's tone was harsh and strong.

Suddenly, Bobby pulled a sportsman's knife from inside his jacket and pointed it at Uncle Lynn. "I don't want you trying to tell me what to do."

"Oh, you going to pull a knife on me?" Uncle Lynn shouted.

"We going to fight gangster style and I'm going to cut you up."

I froze momentarily. I wanted to help Uncle Lynn, but I couldn't get to Bobby without also getting cut. The three of us backed up a little, fearful of what Bobby would do.

He moved toward Uncle Lynn who stood his ground and coolly pulled his pistol out of his pants pocket.

"Boy, I'll blow your fucking brains out," Uncle Lynn warned. "We can fight gangster style, but I just don't think you going to last too long." Uncle Lynn pointed the gun in Bobby's face.

Bobby straightened up and stared at the gun. He threw his knife on the ground. "No, we going to fight fair."

Uncle Lynn pushed the gun back in his pocket. With balled fists he moved in close to Bobby. They both took a couple swings at each other, but missed. Uncle Lynn caught Bobby on the side of the face with a glancing blow. It shook him up a little, but didn't hurt him. Bobby charged at Uncle Lynn, swinging wildly. Uncle Lynn stepped aside and connected again on the side of Bobby's face. The blow slowed him down, but he kept moving around. Bobby had yet to land a blow. Out of frustration he charged Uncle Lynn and that was his mistake. Uncle Lynn moved slightly to his left, and connected with a solid right to his face. It sounded like he had crushed all the bones. He sailed backward from the blow and landed on the ground. Uncle Lynn then moved in and kicked him in the side, the face, the groin, and anywhere he could find an opening. Bobby curled up in a fetal position to protect himself from the many blows coming at a rapid speed.

I smiled with satisfaction as I watched him lying in that position and taking a beating. Taking one just like he had given to my brothers and me. For us, this was the "chickens coming home to roost." I wanted Uncle Lynn to just keep beating him for every beating he'd ever given us. Finally, Bobby did not move. He lay there like a dead man. I began to worry because I didn't want Uncle Lynn to go to jail for killing this man. He wasn't worth it. Uncle Lynn gave him one final swift kick to the ribs, turned and walked away. We followed closely behind satisfied that Bobby Robeson had finally gotten what he deserved and satisfied that he would not return to our house.

CHAPTER 12

Mama began to worry a lot about Ronnie's weight. He could do very little but lie around the house and eat. He couldn't walk more than a block without having to stop to catch his breath. He gave off all the signs of being a juvenile diabetic. Our fighting days were just about over. I felt sorry for my brother, and wanted to help him and not fight him, even though he would push me to my breaking point. Food was still our major problem. He had a voracious appetite. He couldn't help himself. When he saw my food he had to reach over and take it off the plate. I don't think I would have cared if we had a lot to eat, but it was always very little. Mama bought all our groceries with the food stamps she got through the state of Texas program. In fact, she gave us an allowance in food stamps. When we got those stamps Ronnie and I would take off for Krogers Grocery Store and load up on candy. That didn't help Ronnie's condition at all.

During school I didn't see Ronnie because he was still down at O.A. Fleming and wouldn't come to Freeport Intermediate for another year. He did poorly in his classes because of the burden of his weight, and the school officials wanted to send him to Special Education. Mama wouldn't hear of it. She told them Ronnie was not physically handicapped, but only over weight. She took him to the doctor and they told her to put him on a strict diet but she wasn't able to do that to him. Ronnie would complain and cry about being hungry all the time and Mama would give in. She wasn't helping him, but she didn't know how to turn him down she felt so sorry for him.

Ronnie and I still shared one of the twin beds and that was a real burden. He took up all the room. I always found myself sleeping right at the very edge. Ronnie and I slept together throughout my teenage years. We were like two peas in one pod and I didn't want anything to happen to him. At that age you never tell your brother or any other male that you love them. It made you appear weak. We lived in an environment that frowned on any kind of affection. So that word was not a part of our vocabulary, but I know I loved my brother and worried all the time that something terrible would happen to him.

For the first time in my life, calmness existed in our home. Bobby was history. The night Uncle Lynn beat him badly he did show up at the house. Mama had locked all the doors and windows and ignored his pleas to get in. He actually broke out a window, but didn't dare come in. He had Uncle Lynn in mind and didn't want to get beat down anymore. He stood there at Mama's bedroom window begging her to let him, but she refused. Ronnie, and I laughed at him and it was therapeutic. I listened from the bedroom at this weak, beat up man I had feared for three years. With Uncle Lynn's beating, all fear was gone. I can't say I hated him because he was my sister's father and that would come into play when I saw him six years later in Austin, Texas, a broke, beggar on the streets.

I moved to the seventh grade without a lot of confusion at home. Mama seemed more relaxed and content with life. She didn't have a man and seemed to be all right with that. We were still poor because Mama didn't make a lot of money on her job and none of the five fathers paid child support. Adding to my calmness was the fact I knew I would now be able to play organized basketball against other teams throughout the area. I was good and I had prepared myself for this next step for years. I could show off my skills in front of the entire student body.

I felt exhilarated playing basketball in an inside gymnasium instead of the playground. Tryouts were held in October, two months after school started. I was one of the first seventh graders to show up. Walter Pipkin, who should have been in the ninth grade, but was held back twice also tried out. It seemed a little unfair that he could participate with the seventh graders since he was two years older than most of us and much bigger. Troy, a lanky tall kid who lived down the street from us when we lived on the east side also tried out. He had played with J.B. and me at Lincoln Park. Troy was nothing like J.B. and me. He came from a stable two-parent family, and they tried to make sure he had as little contact as possible with us. He was a good basketball player, with his height and lanky arms. The fourth spoke in our wheel was Donald Wilson. I didn't get to know Donald until seventh grade when he transferred to our school from Bay City. Donald had the potential to be a great basketball player, but after two years, he lost interest and gave it up. The four of us knew we would make the A team. We were too good to be put on the B or C team. They were for those boys who wanted to play basketball but did not have the necessary skills to compete at the highest level.

After a week of tryouts Donald, Walter, Troy and I started on the A team. I loved my coach because he was the first black man or woman I ever had as a teacher or coach. He taught gym and coached the A team. Coach Ronald Wallace nicknamed me "Sleepy" after Sleepy Floyd who played for Georgetown University at that time. Finally, I felt I had a male figure in my life that wanted to teach me instead of beat me. Coach Wallace became more than just a coach to me. He became the father figure I needed in my life at that time. I give him a lot of the credit for my ability to stay on a positive course in life when it would have been real easy for me to go down that road of self-destruction so many of my classmates took.

Mr. Westbrook also recognized Coach Wallace's influence over me. The paddling didn't work so he found another way to reach me. The times I ended up in his office, which were still many, he called Coach to come and talk with me. That way definitely worked. Coach always took me to his office and talked so that I understood.

I can hear him now, "Sleepy what do you want to do with your life? Do you think you can fight your way through life and win? I've seen so many of you young black boys come through this school thinking you the baddest dude to ever walk these halls. But you know where a lot of those boys are now? They are in prison with their lives completely ruined. Is that what you want to happen to you? Don't you expect more than that, and don't you deserve more?" His words penetrated like never before and I began to respond to his lectures. I had a couple fights at the beginning of the seventh grade, but abruptly stopped. I changed my attitude in the classroom and did away with my obstreperous behavior. He was the first man in my life that I respected and wanted to prove to him that I could succeed. On the basketball court, I had my first opportunity to show him how good I really could be.

Ten players made the A team under Coach Wallace. On the first day of practice we assembled in the bleachers in the gym. Excitement exuded throughout my body and I couldn't wait to get out on the court and prove I should be a starter. I suffered my first setback that day as I noticed all the other players had new tennis shoes and I didn't. When the school first announced tryouts for the team, they told those of us who couldn't afford new leather tennis shoes there was a box full of used Chuck Taylor canvas shoes. We could pick through the pile and find a pair that fit us. They were old and used. However, I had no choice but to dig through the pile and find a pair I could wear. As I sat there listening to Coach explain the rules we must follow as players on his team, my mind wandered. I had to find a way to get a pair of Nike leather shoes or I really believed I would be at a disadvantage. My only problem was how to ask Mama for the money to buy a new pair. My thoughts went back to last year when I made all that money working on the shrimp boat and now I had none of it. If I had known then about the different shoes, I would have saved some for this occasion. But now I had no choice. I had to ask Mama and didn't know how that would be received. It didn't take long to find out.

That evening I approached her.

"Mama, I made the basketball team at school," I said.

"That's good," she replied.

Her lack of enthusiasm gave me second thoughts about asking. But I had to. My teammates had the best and I wanted the same.

"Mama, I need a better pair of tennis shoes. I had to get an old pair someone else wore before me. I need my own."

"What's wrong with the ones you got from the school, they got holes in them or something?"

"No Mama, but they ain't the best, and everybody else got new ones, they're called Nikes."

"David, all I got is light money right now, and I sure ain't going to have my lights turned off so you can get some damn tennis shoes. If you want new ones, ask your Daddy. He's in town."

"Where is he?" I asked

"You know where, the only place he spends any time other than in some woman's bed."

I had never asked Daddy for anything. That wasn't the kind of relationship we had. He never volunteered to give me any money, and I never asked. My reluctance to ask him was strong, but my determination to get those shoes stronger. I took off and headed for the Blue and White Café.

The place was crowded when I got there. The music blared and folks moved around the room engaging in various discussions. Daddy sat at the bar with a couple of women on each side. He was laughing and appeared to be in a good mood. Maybe my timing was just right, and he would be amenable to my request. I had no way of gauging him since we never discussed money. My last encounter with him had been years ago when he beat me with the wet rope for quitting baseball. No need to hesitate, I headed straight for him.

"Daddy, I need something from you," I said getting right to the point. I didn't know how to engage in small talk with him. We didn't have that kind of relationship.

"What you want boy, and why you coming up in this here place?" he replied.

The sternness of his voice and his question made me nervous. Would he beat me again for asking? It didn't matter; a beating was something I could live with. Not getting the new tennis shoes I couldn't live with. I took in a deep breath and slowly let it out. I was ready.

"I made the A basketball team at school," I started out.

"So what, I'd expect nothing less than that," he said. "And you better not quit like you did with baseball when things don't go your way. You hear me?"

"Yes sir," I answered. I stood staring at him trying to work up enough nerve to ask for the tennis shoes.

"Well, go on now," he ordered. "This ain't no place for kids anyway. I don't know what your Mama's thinking about letting you come down here to tell me some shit like that."

Intimidation turned to anger. How could he possibly refer to my good news with that kind of language? I didn't care, so I blurted it out.

"Daddy, I need money to buy me some new tennis shoes. All I got are the old used ones that the school gives us. The other players got Nikes and Reeboks and I want a pair.

Daddy glared down at the shoes I had on and said.

"Seem to me like you already got some shoes, now get on out of here."

I wanted to stand up to him and tell him just what I felt. Why couldn't he do something nice for me? Why couldn't he do something once in his life that would make me feel good about him? Why couldn't he be like Coach Wallace? Instead I turned and rushed out of the Blue and White. Just as I reached the door I heard him tell the bartender. "Free round of drinks for everybody. It's on me."

I cried all the way home and couldn't hide the tears from Mama when I walked into the house.

"I guess he told you no," she said.

I didn't say anything. I ran to my room and fell out on the bed, still crying. I was getting to the age when I questioned everything. I lay there tears streaming down my cheeks thinking, "Why me?" Grandma favored Levi and would do anything for him, Mama favored Ronnie, Little James and now Nicole. But I was no one's favorite. Mama must have picked up my hurt. She came into the room and sat down on the side of the bed.

"That no good bastard, he ain't no father." I don't know why she said that to me, but I agreed. "Come on David, you going to get those new shoes, even if we have to sit up in this house in the dark."

Mama took me to the store that night and bought a pair of Nike tennis shoes. I was on top of the world, and most important I couldn't wait for the next practice so I could show off my new Nikes.

Our lights did not get turned off. Mama, as she would usually do, figured out a way to get the money. She also figured out a way to get even with my Daddy in the only way she knew how. Mama caught him heading back to the boat one night, and busted a coca cola bottle over his head. He had to get stitches, but I didn't care. Later on in life, when he really needed me, I would treat him better than he had treated me the time I needed him.

CHAPTER 13

Mama cried a lot, and when she did, I cried with her. I felt her pain and it always made me sad. From early on, I had a mixed relationship with Mama. I guess it could be considered love/ hate, though I don't really believe I ever did hate her. But I could get awfully angry when she beat me for no reason at all. That happened one time right after she had surgery on her foot. Levi had moved back home after Bobby left, and we were all playing in the kitchen. Because of the surgery, Mama's right foot was all bandaged up and she could hardly walk. For some reason, she decided to whip just me. Somehow Mama managed to grab me, took her belt and began to swing. I turned my body away from her so she couldn't hit me directly on the butt.

"Keep your ass still," she hollered.

"I ain't going to let you whip me Mama,' cause I ain't done nothing wrong." I tried to break from her grip but failed.

"David, damn it, hold still." She swung and caught me on my legs.

My anger took control. I began stomping, trying to get her on the bandaged foot.

"Boy what you think you doing?" she shouted.

"Let me go Mama," I screamed. "I ain't going to let you beat me. I ain't done nothing wrong."

"I'll decide when you done something wrong. I'm your Mama, damn it, and I'll whip your ass whenever I want to."

Finally, I came down hard and just missed hitting her on top of her bandaged foot. I ran into the bedroom. I felt terrible about what I tried to do, but she had no right to beat me. I never complained about a whipping if I did something wrong. But I refused to be whipped this time, and not in front of everyone. Mama had it hard and I should never have fought her, but right was right and what she tried to do that day was wrong.

I guess she needed some kind of release from all the stress in her life. Mama struggled with four boys and a girl to raise alone and with no financial help. She had the additional burden of Ronnie's physical problems, which seemed to grow worse by the month. She knew other kids would tease him, but when adults did it, she went ballistic. She always told Ronnie that he could lose weight, but they could not lose their ugliness.

Mama became an enabler to Ronnie's problems. Instead of forcing him to stick to a diet, she gave in and allowed Ronnie to continue stuffing himself. Because there was always so little to eat at our house, he really didn't have that many opportunities to indulge.

Bill collectors dunned Mama, and often she made me answer the phone and tell them she wasn't available. The burdens of her excessive responsibilities took a toll on Mama and made her angry all the time. But nothing angered her more than the perception that Grandma favored her other grandchildren over us, with of course the exception of Levi. It always exploded over at Grandma's house on Sundays.

It was understood by the entire family that we would have Sunday dinner at Grandma's house. After I started going to Sunday school, Mama decided to attend church. That was a major breakthrough and Grandma just knew it was Jesus' intervention in her life that finally got her back in church. No more Sunday partying on our porch. Church should, however, be a place that you go to bring the family closer together. That didn't happen in our family. After service the entire family, which included, my aunt Clevella, Rosalie, Henrietta, my Uncle Lynn and Ronnie, along with Uncle Ronnie's wife, my aunt Sharon, and at least sixteen kids assembled in Grandma's little house.

While the grownups were inside preparing dinner, we kids disappeared outside and played some kind of game. Grandma's house was packed deep with people. It is a wonder they didn't argue more than what they did, which was quite a bit. Most of the time the argument would be over Mama's kids, and especially Ronnie and me. We could do nothing to satisfy Grandma and our aunts. Our Uncle Lynn and Uncle Ronnie never complained, but those women just waited for us to make the wrong move and then they attacked. That set Mama off, and I don't care if we hadn't yet eaten, were eating, or had finished, she'd load all of us up and march home. If we hadn't eaten, we'd complain that we were hungry. We could smell the fried chicken, and knew Grandma would have greens, corn bread, potato salad, and always the best coconut cake ever. When we got home, there was very little to eat and never anything to match what we had left at Grandma's. Mama had to practically fight Ronnie to get him out of there. He would cry all the way home and complain about being hungry. Before Mama left she had some appropriate words for whoever was the villain in her eyes. Often times it would be Grandma. For some reason Grandma loved to go after Ronnie and me. I guess it was because Ronnie was too fat and I too black. Mama would go a few days and not talk to her family, but by the next Sunday we all were back over there and the war would be on again.

Through all this confusion at home, my only light at the end of the tunnel was looking forward to our basketball games at school. I put all my effort into being the best because I had to and because I wanted to impress Coach Wallace. The first game I scored 18 points to include the winning basket right at the end of the game. My teammates depended on my ability to get the ball across half court and distribute it to the open player. If I couldn't find anyone to pass to, I would pull up and take my patented jump shot.

Word spread throughout the school that I was one good basketball player. Word also spread that I still couldn't read. Because I couldn't read I was slow in all the other subjects. In fact, that was true of all five starters on the team. We were all assigned to the developmental classes, designed to assist slow learners. We could play basketball, but couldn't master the subject matter for seventh graders.

The development classes were a joke. The teachers didn't expect us to learn. In fact they gave points to the student who erased the blackboard or did other chores. Grades didn't depend on our grasping the subject matter, but doing mundane jobs in the classroom. None of us seemed to care because our energy was geared toward the basketball court and winning games. Apparently that was all the school cared about, also.

We did pretty well that year. We won five games and lost three. Bay City McCallister Junior High School was the powerhouse and I was determined to beat them before I graduated. The player opposite me in the Bay City game played me hard and I him. We came out even in our individual game against each other. Little did we know, as we went after each other in a very competitive way, that his sister was also my sister. He had a different father than her, but my Daddy was also hers. It would not be the last time I would meet someone related to me through Daddy on the basketball floor. I guess Bobby had been right the time he told me that all my Daddy could do was make babies.

After basketball season ended I lost interest in school. Coach Wallace kept me on the right path. I never gave into the temptations that surrounded me every day I attended school. One time an older boy approached me with a deal.

"Hey David, you want to make some fast money," the boy who hung around the school asked.

"What I got to do?" I asked him.

"I got a couple of packages I need for you to deliver," he said.

I knew exactly what that meant and did not like or trust this boy.

"No I think I'll pass," I said and kept walking.

Chapter 14

J.B. and I had become like brothers. That summer we spent all our time together. If he wasn't over to my house I was at his. He was always welcome at my place, but his mother did not like me and didn't like me always hanging around. She told him I was a loud mouth and loved to brag all the time. That was true and an accurate representation of me. I told everyone I would be a National Basketball Association star someday. I was going to make millions of dollars and buy Mama a house in Lake Jackson, where most of the rich white people lived. After high school I would go on to Baylor University, play four years of college ball and then be drafted in the first round by the Houston Rockets. Despite J.B. 's mother's dislike for me I still hung out with him, and most of the time it would be at Lincoln Park.

I now had one year of organized basketball under my belt, and J.B. would begin his career of organized ball in the fall. As the older more experienced player, I told him what to expect. Told him about Coach Wallace for whom he would be playing. When there were no other people at the park we played one on one and I showed him some of the moves I learned my first year.

Ronnie often followed us to the park, but was much too big to play basketball. I know it frustrated him, because he often became irritable and wanted to fight. In my earlier years I would accommodate him, but now I had my mind firmly planted on playing ball. I had no time to fight. When we first arrived at the park, he played for about five minutes, and then quit from exhaustion.

We also played football at the park. I was good because I was quick, but it was not my favorite sport. I had planned to play both sports my eighth grade year. I figured I would be the quarterback for the team. A deliberate blow to my face during a game of "Kill the Man With the Football" put an end to those dreams. We were on the grassy area at the park. Most of the boys were at least three to four years older than me, but that didn't bother me at all. I loved to compete against older boys. I always had to compete against Levi. But the rules of this game should have been enough to scare me off. They didn't. The danger involved and the size of my big mouth turned out to be a disastrous combination for me that day in the park.

The game started with the football tossed high in the air just like the tip off in basketball. The person who caught the ball would then have to run from one end of the field to the other, dodging the other boys who would be out to tackle him. The person with the ball had no help. He had no blockers and couldn't lateral the ball to a teammate because you had no teammates. The game really had no purpose other than to tackle and often hurt the person with the ball. If you made it through the hordes to the other end of the field you had bragging rights. And bragging was right up my alley.

Fifteen boys gathered at one end of the field. Previn Phillips, my cousin, two years older than me, tossed the ball in the air. No one but me wanted to catch it because they all wanted to be tacklers and not runners, but me. I grabbed the ball out of the air and took off, dodging, juking, and moving real fast. My quickness and slick moves helped me scoot through all the tacklers, leaving them on the ground, until I was across the goal line.

I had to rub it in.

"You bunch of slow punks can't catch me," I said laughing at all of them. "Come on, throw the ball up again, and I'll run through all you slow fools like I just did."

If looks could kill, I'd be one dead sucker. But looks didn't do anything but reveal the frustration they all felt because the youngest person on the field beat them down.

"Shut up, David," Levi scowled. "You talk too much. Just play the game before you make somebody mad."

"I don't care about none of y'all getting mad. In fact I'll go through you all a second time. Come on Pervin, toss it up." I was too arrogant to take heed of my brother's warning.

Pervin tossed the ball in the air and no one went for it but me. I grabbed it and set out again running and dodging everyone in my way to the other end of the field. For a second time I made it without getting tackled. Now the level of my bragging increased.

"You some of the slowest suckers I ever seen," I said all the time laughing in between words. "Maybe y'all should go play with the girls. They probably could beat y'all."

Energized by two fantastic victories I was ready for a third go at these guys. "Come on let's go," I said moving into the middle of the circle. "Throw that sucker up and let me beat y'all again."

The looks had hardened and I knew it was time to be quiet, but that was not my nature. "You up for getting whipped again."

Previn threw the ball up, I grabbed it and took off. I don't know how I was able to do it, but I eluded all of them for a third time. Once I crossed the goal line at the other end, I fell on the ground, stretched my arms and legs out and laughed. I kept laughing until it hurt. I enjoyed this and didn't want to stop. They couldn't catch me even if I slowed up.

"David, you'd better shut the fuck up," one of the boys said. "You going to get your little ass whipped."

"By who? Not you cause you can't even catch me how you going to whip my ass."

"David, shut up," Levi said again. "Boy you going to get hurt, and I ain't going to help you cause you talk too much."

I glared at my brother, but didn't want to get into an argument with him, I trotted back to the middle of the circle. One more time," I said to Previn.

"Okay, you little motherfucker, but we going to get your ass," Previn shouted and threw the ball in the air.

I grabbed it and started to make my break toward the other end. But this time, they all locked arms around me and I couldn't get out. I spotted a small opening between my cousin and another boy, who had broke loose, and shot for it. Before I could make it, Previn used his forearm and blasted me in the face. He didn't try to tackle me because I could have out maneuvered him. Instead he gave a jarring blow that tore into my lip and split it wide open. Blood shot into my mouth and down my front.

I jumped to my feet and started to wipe the blood. Then I realized he did it on purpose. He didn't try to tackle me. He just went for my face. He was angry because I taunted them, and this was his way to get even. I grabbed a palm branch with spikes that had fallen from a tree and started for him. He took off running. I was right behind him cussing and running. But the blood poured out of the wound to my mouth so I finally had to stop. He got away, but I vowed I'd get even with him once my lip healed.

Levi finally caught up with me and grabbed my arm.

"Come on David, you got to get to Grandma's so she can take care of you."

We ran the few blocks to Grandma's house, all the time I wiped blood from my mouth. I went right into the bathroom and tried to wash the wound clean, but it kept bleeding. Grandma came to the bathroom door and glared at me.

"What on God's earth happened to you?" she asked

I couldn't talk because of the swelling around my mouth. Instead Levi talked for me.

"He got hit playing football at the park."

"I told you kids about playing that football," Grandma said. "I knew eventually one of you was going to get hurt. Now just look at you."

Again I tried to plead my case but the words just wouldn't come out.

"Come on, I got to get you to the hospital and get that stitched up before you bleed to death."

Fear shot through my body when Grandma said, "bleed to death." I had no idea that a wound to the mouth could cause a person to die. Why did I run my mouth so much, and why did Pervin have to hit me in the mouth? Was I going to die? We climbed in my cousin Patrick's car and they drove to the hospital.

They closed the gash in my mouth with twenty stitches, but nothing could be done for the swelling. I looked just like a boxer who had his butt whipped real good. The doctor finally gave me some medication that relieved the pain. I went home and waited for Mama to get there when my second ordeal would begin.

"Them motherfucking bastards, who did this to you David?" Mama asked when she got home and saw the condition of my mouth. "I'll kill them bastards about my boy."

I felt relieved. This time Mama wasn't angry with me, and it didn't look like I would get a whipping. She actually took up for me and would have hurt Pervin if she knew he was the one who had inflicted this wound on me. She would have hurt any of the boys involved in this. Levi had been involved and didn't try to stop them, but I didn't dare tell Mama for fear what she might do to him.

———◆———

CHAPTER 15

Teachers in the Freeport school system maintained an active grapevine of student information. What a student did in the first grade stayed with him throughout high school. I found that out when I entered Mr. Graves' math class the first day of school. I took my usual seat in the back of the room feeling good that I was starting my last year at intermediate school and confident I would have an excellent year as the starting point guard on the basketball team. I also knew all my teachers would pass me just as they did every year since kindergarten. Even with my lip busted and still swollen, my spirits were high. That is until Mr. Graves called out my name.

"David Floyd, come to the front."

I slowly lifted my body up and strolled to the front where he sat at his desk.

"David Floyd, I am giving you fair warning that I will not tolerate any of your nonsense in my class."

Suddenly my mood changed. All my insecurities re-surfaced and instead of holding my head high, I looked down at the floor. How dare he spoil my good feeling even before he knew anything about me. At least that's what I thought.

"I ain't done nothing in your class," I protested.

"I know you haven't and I plan to keep it that way. Mr. Westbrook informed all your teachers for this year about the problems others have had with you all the way back to kindergarten. I want you to know the minute you cause trouble in here, you will find yourself in Mr. Westbrook's office, and I know you're aware of what that means. Do you understand?"

"Yes," I said sharply.

He gave me a hard stare and said, "Get back to your desk and don't start trouble."

I felt all eyes on me as I returned to my desk, and I hurriedly sat down. I couldn't wait to get out of there and go to football practice where I was viewed as a star and not the school dunce.

I had busted my lip one week after football practice started. For that week I played quarterback and would have started at that position for the entire season. But my mouth was so badly swollen I couldn't call signals or tell the players what play we'd run. I was disappointed when coach switched me to tight end. I was no longer the leader, the one in control. Instead I was just another player on the field following someone else's orders. That, I did not like. As point guard on the basketball team, I controlled the ball and the other four players on the court with me. I wanted to do the same on the football field. Because I couldn't, I lost interest in the game and wanted only for basketball season to hurry up and start.

Despite my setback on the football team, I was still a star athlete at Freeport Intermediate. No one teased me any longer because I couldn't read and was still stuck in developmental classes. I was part of that elite group of athletes every school has. We ate lunch together, hung out during school breaks and walked the halls together. And there was always a group of girls following close behind us, especially from the sixth and seventh grade classes. It was from that group that we found our girlfriends. Kim Peeples, a sixth grader, was my choice.

Kim was a pretty girl with long black hair, olive skin, and brown eyes. She had attended Valasco Elementary School. Valasco was a suburb of Freeport where the middle class and upper middle class workers and managers at Dow Chemical lived. Kim's family was the direct opposite of mine. She came from a two-parent home, with a father who was a manager at Dow. She had a stay-home mother who took interest in her education. Given my background and home life compared to hers, there was no way Kim's parents would approve of me. My inadequacies took over whenever I tried talking to her.

I walked Kim to class and carried her books but never tried to hold her hand or even touch her. I lacked the nerve to even kiss her on the cheek. Kim, as my girlfriend, consisted of me walking her to class, always carrying her books. We did that until the end or my eighth grade year when I moved on to high school.

The first day of basketball practice, I couldn't wait to get out of class. I paid no attention to any of my teachers or the material we covered. My mind was on the basketball court and how I would show everyone up and prove to be the best player on the team. I couldn't let anyone beat me at basketball. The game was my salvation for all my other inadequacies. It made me somebody. Others could laugh at my lack of performance in the classroom, but not my performance on the court. By eighth grade, I had come to accept that I probably would never read from a book. David Floyd was a failure as a student who teachers just passed on from year to year in order to get rid of me. But David Floyd would be the very best at basketball and that would be my future. The only thing that could stop me from achieving on the court was my big mouth. That is exactly what happened temporarily when we started practice.

I figured we would have the same starting lineup we had on the seventh grade team, with me as the point guard and running the offense. The first practice I performed extremely well. I beat my opponent off the dribble, distributed passes to my teammates, and scored easily. However, every time I would do something that showed my superior skill, I would brag. I talked all the time and after a week of this, my teammates and Coach Kerr tired of me. I didn't care because I was standing out like a bright shiny star in a pitch-black night.

My star stopped shining when Coach devised a drill every player had to perform in order to make the A team. Anyone who failed would be sent down to B team. The drill called for each player to jump up and touch the bottom of the backboard. It seemed like a simple enough drill, but only if you could jump and you weren't 5 feet 3. I couldn't jump, and I was that height. Coach knew that and that's why he devised the drill. Panic set in as I stood in line watching Troy, Walter, and Donald easily touch the backboard. The same frightening feelings passed through me that I experienced in elementary school when I waited my turn to read lines from a book. Why would Coach do this to me? If I couldn't make A team then my failures would be complete and there was no longer anything I could believe in. Finally, it was my turn. I jumped and failed miserably.

"Do it again," Coach said.

"Come on David, you can do it," I heard Walter say.

I tried again and failed again.

"Try it one more time," Troy said. "You gotta do it. You gotta make A team.

I heard Troy, but it didn't register. I turned and walked away. My feelings of rejection overwhelmed me. My anger dictated my behavior. I stormed down to the locker room and slammed my fist against the locker. The tears filled my eyes, but I managed to hold them back. Coach had embarrassed me out there on the court and in front of my teammates. He wouldn't do it twice. I refused to cry and instead swore that I would get even. If it took me all season, I pledged that I would make him regret placing me on the B team simply because I could not jump.

Next day Coach demoted me to the B team.

It didn't take all season for me to prove him wrong. It only took a scrimmage between the A and B teams a week later. In four days, A team would play its first league game and Coach wanted to use the B team to sharpen their game. I started as the point guard for the B team and paired up against the boy who took my place at that position on A team. My buddies, Troy, Walter, and Donald felt bad for me. They knew I should be playing with them. But they had to play me the same way they played any opponent and that was to win. That was fine with me because I planned to play them the same way.

When the scrimmage began I smothered the boy playing across from me. I was all over him so tight you would've thought we were one. Because of my tenacious play A team couldn't get the ball out of the back court. I stole the ball from my opponent with ease. I could tell from their gestures Walter, Troy, and Donald were angry. We ended up beating them and Coach knew he'd backed himself into a corner. If he didn't move me back up to the A team, they would get slaughtered the entire season. If he brought me back up, he would have to admit his mistake. Next day he decided it made more sense to eat a "little crow" and bring me back up. "Eating crow" would only last a few days; refusal to put me back at my rightful position would cause problems for the team the entire year.

We had an excellent season and I performed to my own high expectations. I led the team in scoring, assists, and steals. My confidence was back to where it was before the incident with the Coach. I was the star of the team and walked the halls of the school with my chest stuck out and with a bounce in my step. I still couldn't read but knew the teachers would pass me on because I was David Floyd, superstar. I was ready for high school and would play varsity basketball my freshman year at Brazosport High School.

CHAPTER 16

At the ages of thirteen and fourteen J.B. and I were ready to venture out. J.B.'s grandfather bought him a car, and his mother allowed him to drive it without a driver's license and no insurance. And Mama allowed me to ride with him. One Friday in July, we decided to go to a concert featuring Lisa Lisa, Curtis Blow, Force M.D., and Slick Rick. It was in Houston at the AstroWorld and J.B. was going to drive.

That Friday we left Freeport about six in the evening all dressed to kill. If someone told us we weren't the sharpest dressers at that concert they would have to fight. I dressed in dark green parachute pants with big pockets, a lighter green Izod LaCosta shirt, with the long tail in the back hanging over the pants. I wore white K-Swiss shoes with light green laces. I had it going on.

When we parked the car, J.B. stuffed the keys in his pants pocket and we made it to our seats inside the park. During the Lisa Lisa performance we both jumped up excited and full of energy. Neither of us noticed that J.B.'s keys dropped out of his pants pocket. During the intermission we strolled along the pavilion and every once in a while tried to talk to the girls who looked awfully good.

After the concert we made it back to the car, J.B. reached in his pocket for the keys and then desperately searched all his pockets.

"Man I don't have my keys," he said.

"What? You don't have the keys," I shrilled. "What did you do with them? Did you have them when you went inside?"

"I don't know, I guess I did." J.B. sounded irritated with my badgering.

"What do you mean, you guess you did?" I was full of questions, but had no answers as to what we could possibly do. In fact, my next question was, "What are we going to do?"

With the concert over, no one left. People had taken the party outside in the parking lot. I had never seen that many people in one place in all my life. It was rather intimidating. These were Houston's thugs, and I wanted no part of them.

"I got to call Granddaddy," J.B. said. He pointed to the Astro Hall Hotel near the park. "Lets walk over there and see if I can catch him at the club?"

We made it through all the partying and loud music to the Astro Hall, called his Grandfather and hurried back to the car. I sat on the hood and glared at the action all around me. That was a big city Houston crowd, and I wasn't ready for them. I could go for bad in Freeport, but I wasn't about to get tough in Houston. After about an hour, Uncle J.B., that's what I had come to call him over the years, showed up. We were relieved when his car turned into the parking lot and headed toward us.

We spent a couple weeks with Uncle J.B. in Houston. It was two of the best weeks I'd ever spent with anyone. He owned a night-club in the Third Ward. His house was connected to the club. It reminded me of the Blue and White Café absent all the drama. Uncle J.B. always carried a big wad of money in his jacket pocket. He closed the club at three in the morning and woke us up about four. We went with him to an all night diner called Dot's; they had the most delicious and biggest pancakes I'd ever eaten.

After two weeks of fun we headed back to Freeport and prepared for school. J.B. moved on to the eighth grade at Freeport Interme-diate and I the ninth at Brazosport High School. That year was especially important to me because I now attended high school, that much closer to college and the National Basketball League.

My first year of high school began in the middle of the infamous 1980's, the decade that marked the growth of gangs, crack cocaine, and a constant string of black youth my age killing each other. East end housed much of that same kind of activity, but my closest friends, J.B., Darrell, Troy, and Thomas stayed clear of the drugs, gangs, and killings. We were from the hood, but we were not of the hood, and east end was definitely the hood with all its accompanying negative attributes. There were fewer killings, less drugs, and smaller gangs in Freeport, but it was just as intense as any large city, and we as young men witnessed it all. Many of our childhood friends who attended O.A. Fleming and Freeport Intermediate with us had fallen by the wayside. They dropped out of school, got involved in drugs, and we watched as they laid out their personal road map to one of the many prisons cropping up in Texas faster than high schools or decent housing. Unlike these young men, we had dreams of our future. J.B., Darrell and I dreamt of some day playing in the National Basketball Association. Troy and Thomas were determined to pursue college degrees through any means necessary. The two of them lived very structured lives, with two parent families and strong men as role models. That was missing for J.B., Darrell, and me.

Despite the difference in our home lives, we were as close as five young boys could be. At the end of the summer before I started high school and after J.B. and I returned from Houston, we hung out practically everyday shooting hoops and then at night standing under the street light at Sixth and Poplar. We'd talk about our dreams and mostly we would talk of getting out of Freeport after graduation from high school.

The best part of our friendship was that we served as watchdogs for each other. If it appeared that one of us might be heading in the wrong direction we would jack him up, and sometimes all of us would get involved. Even though it was the worst of times for us, especially J.B., Darrell, and me, standing on that corner below the light helped us make it through simply by leaning on each other. They gave me the strength to keep fighting my reading disability and when I entered high school I was confident they would all be with me as another episode began in my life.

CHAPTER 17

David Floyd, the boy who could not comprehend a kindergarten reader was now in high school. I knew my status
would be much different from what it had been at Freeport Intermediate. It was like the end of an era for me being a big man on
campus to a small fish in a very large pond. I anticipated the same
problems I'd encountered in the classroom all my life would be
waiting for me in high school.

They assigned me to developmental classes to include developmental English. I would be called on in that class to read orally from
different books, but I no longer feared my failure because all the
other students in the classroom had been with me since Freeport
Intermediate, and they certainly didn't have a right to laugh. They
lacked the requisite skills to be in regular classes. The school system
categorized us for the entire student body to recognize as slow learners or non-learners.

I had no illusions of learning over the next four years. But somehow I would make it just as I did in the past. It became clear that
the school officials didn't care if a black child couldn't read, do math,
or any of the subjects you were asked to pass in order to graduate.
Many young blacks in my condition had graduated with no chance
of success, and many of them were stuck in prison with no future.
That's how I felt at that time in my life. Eventually I would come
to realize that attitude was self-destructive and sometimes used as
an excuse not to learn.

What irritated me most was that my past followed me from one
school to the next. The first day of class I was summoned to the

principal's office. I had just settled in when my teacher called out, "David Floyd you're wanted in the principal's office."

The first period of the first day and I had to report to the principal. I didn't even know the location of his office, and it had already started. I spotted a boy who lived in the east end.

"Hey where's the principal's office?

"End of the hall and make a right. You can't miss it." He chuckled. "Damn man, this is the first day and you already in trouble?"

"No, I ain't got in no trouble," I rejoined in a belligerent tone.

"Oh, that means the principal got your permanent file," he said and walked away.

"What's a permanent file?" I asked but he had already turned the corner.

As I hustled down the hall, I wondered about the permanent file. Was it like a police record, and did they only have it for students who had gotten in trouble in the past? I figured I'd find out soon enough. I walked into the office and looked at a number of students my age sitting in chairs along the wall. I strolled up to the counter and waited until one of the clerks finally approached me.

"I was told to come to the principal's office," I said.

"What's your name?" the clerk asked.

"David Floyd."

"David Floyd, yes, have a seat along the wall, and I'll call you when it's time for you to see Mr. Cervenka." Mr. Cervenka, the vice-principal, handled disciplinary problems at the school I learned.

I found a chair and sat down next to a boy who had gotten into trouble at Freeport Intermediate School. I knew then what this was all about even though I had no knowledge of the permanent file.

While I sat there waiting, my eyes wandered from one girl to another as they made their way into the office. Brazosport High had some of the prettiest girls in the entire world. Everywhere I looked there was either a black, white, tall and short one. As a star athlete, I figured it wouldn't be long before I'd have my pick.

"David Floyd, Mr. Cervenka is ready for you now," the clerk called out.

Reluctantly I made my way into Mr. Cervenka's office. He stood by the door and stared at me like I was a prize calf, then closed the door.

"David Floyd, am I going to have any trouble out of you?" he asked making his way back to his desk.

"No, am I going to have any trouble out of you?" I said. He had no right to ask me that since I'd just arrived at the school. It was that permanent file the boy in the hall told me about, and I didn't want to be a part of anyone's file.

"I can see already that mouth of yours is going to earn you a lot of trips down here. I'd suggest you put a muzzle on that mouth." He glared across his desk at me.

I sat there and said nothing. Instead, I stared out the window at the trees outside his office. This time I wouldn't say a word. Maybe he'd leave me alone and let me go back to class. I could detect that I was probably very close to my first paddling.

"Your other teachers and principals have put up with your nonsense, but I won't," he growled and his brows furrowed.

I wanted to ask him how he knew about my previous teachers and me. Did they have a secret file on all the students at Brazosport or just the black ones?

"Do we understand each other young man?" He stood up, walked to the door and opened it. He again glared back at me waiting for an answer.

I accommodated him. No need to get paddled the first day of class because I knew over the next four years I would get plenty.

"Yes Mr. Cervenka, I understand." I sat waiting for him to order me up and out of his office. I didn't have to wait long.

"Good, then you're excused. Go to your class."

My accommodating spirit only lasted a week before it came to an end in American History class. I had just sat down and we all were waiting for our teacher to arrive. Brad Kottle, a very large white kid, stood in front of the class clowning around. Brad was a true red neck all the way. His family probably flew the Confederate flag at his house. He was a young white man who had absolutely nothing going for him and so he had to create his own worth through putting down Blacks. While we waited for class to begin, he got racial. He held his history book high in the air and opened it right to the center page.

With a big grin, Brad shouted, "If you want to hide a hundred dollar bill from a black person, just put it in the middle of a book and close it." He busted out laughing.

No one laughed as all the other students turned and looked at me. The room grew tense and I hesitated only for a moment. Then I sprang into action. Harvey stood 6 feet 2 and weighed at least 240 pounds. I stood all of 5 feet 6 and weighed a mere 130 pounds. I didn't care; he had dissed my race and me. He had to pay. I jumped on him, and he pushed me against the blackboard bloodying my nose. I wiped the blood away and quickly turned on him, hitting him with a right to the face.

Just as I struck him our teacher walked into the room. He stood there long enough to comprehend what was going on then turned and hurried out of the room. The two of us rumbled all over that classroom, and even though I was much smaller than him, I held my own until two hall monitors rushed in and broke us up.

"At it already aren't you David," one of the monitors said. He held my arms. For some reason they did not hold Brad but allowed him to go back and sit down. The teacher finally came back into the room.

"Get him out of here," he said to the monitors.

"Alright Floyd, let's go," the monitor instructed me. "To the office."

They dragged me down to Mr. Cervenka's office. He shook his head and didn't ask any questions. He grabbed his paddle and told the men, "bend him over."

That was the first of many visits I would make to Mr. Cervenka's office. And none of them were friendly.

I encountered Brad again after school on the football field. We both were playing freshman ball, he on the line and I as a running back. That day of practice coach called both of us over to the sidelines and warned us to put any lingering differences aside for the good of the team. I couldn't dismiss what Harvey said that easily, but I did put it in check and resolved that I would cooperate with him for the good of the team and for no other reason.

Since I had reached the conclusion I would never learn to read, I concocted an elaborate scheme to cheat my way through the courses where testing depended on my ability to read. It called for cooperation from my friends, especially Troy and Darrell. They were in my English class, and all tests were based on comprehension of material we had to read. The plan worked in other classes with other friends. During a test Troy would do something to divert Mrs. Shaw's attention. While she dealt with Troy, Darrell slid the answers to all the questions over to me. I would copy them and then pass them back to him. It worked perfectly, and we never got caught. I did that in every class for four years with the exception of math. Those classes I could handle without help. I was good with numbers, and as long as it didn't involve reading, I could work out all the math problems. Throughout my four years I only failed one class and that was geometry. I couldn't read or comprehend the theorems and could not solve the problems.

I didn't think anything was wrong with cheating. It was survival for me, and without the cheating, I wouldn't graduate. Ultimately it served me well. If I had failed to graduate from high school, my will power to achieve may have been broken and I never would have learned to read.

CHAPTER 18

A t fifteen and now in high school, I was ready to declare my independence from Mama's control over me. For years my curfew had been ten o'clock and Mama was usually home by that time to make sure I met that deadline. It didn't matter if she'd been out at the club, she always made it home to make sure I was there. As long as I was at the park playing basketball she didn't mind if I stayed out a little later. But I had better be at Lincoln Park, or all hell would break loose. That is exactly what happened one night Walter, Curtis and I hung out near the Super Port Disco, the same place where Uncle Lynn had beaten Bobby.

"David, look at the bunch of white boys over there," Walter said and pointed to at least ten whites about our age standing in a circle near the Super Port Disco.

"What's going on over there?" I looked in the direction Walter was pointing. "What they doing this close to the east end?" Super Port Disco was located right on the border of the west and east ends. Since it was primarily a black club we considered it east end property.

This was one of the few times I wasn't with the usual gang. I never made it a habit to hang out with Walter because he smoked marijuana. I wanted no part of that action. But sometimes it felt good hanging out with him because he was two years older than me and used to beat me up when we were younger. Curtis was also with us. It was unusual for J.B. not to be with us. Troy and Thomas could never hang out after ten.

The three of us stood there trying to figure out what those white boys were doing in that circle. Whatever it was, they seemed to be having lots of fun. I couldn't take it any longer. We didn't invade their neighborhoods after ten o'clock because if we did it would end up in a trip to jail.

"This ain't going to happen on our watch," I shouted to Walter and Curtis then ran in the direction of the boys.

They turned and glared at us just as we reached the circle. I stared into the middle and lost control. Daddy was lying on the ground, barely conscious. He had thrown up all over himself and his pants were soaked from his urine. Daddy was stone cold drunk. The white boys circled around and taunted him. They weren't beating up on him, just mostly laughing and calling him names.

I broke through the circle and hurried over to Daddy. I tried moving him away from his tormentors but he was too heavy. One of the boys from school recognized me and turned his taunting on me.

"David Floyd, is that your Daddy?" he asked.

"None of your damn business," I scowled. "You'd better get your asses from around here."

"Yeah, and you'd better get your drunk ass Daddy out of here before he pisses his pants again."

When he said that, the battle began. And it wasn't me this time. Walter turned the boy around and smacked him right in the mouth. Curtis followed his lead and snatched another one of the boys and wailed away on him. I didn't join the battle. Instead I lifted Daddy by grabbing him under his arms. I dragged him out of the circle and back over by the club. He mumbled some incoherent words as I forced him over to the building.

"You motherfuckers better leave me the fuck alone," I understood some of his incoherence. "You heard me, motherfucker."

He was all dead weight, and I had to stop. I looked back to see how Curtis and Walter were making out. I felt bad because I couldn't be there to help inflict a whipping on a bunch of white boys. That was like every young black boy's dream, to catch a bunch of vulnerable whites on our side of town. It was payback for that young black who lived over 40 years before us, but had been lynched in Mississippi. It was for the ancestors we never knew, but through stories passed down about the humiliation they suffered at the hands of these white boys' ancestors. It was for slavery, lynching and any other reason we conjured up in our heads. It was therapeutic. The anger and adrenaline were working overtime in Walter and Curtis because the two of them were wailing away at the ten enemies. They actually had them on the run. After sufficient payback for centuries of oppression, the other boys high-tailed it out of there. Walter and Curtis came over to where I was trying to get Daddy on his feet.

"You ain't going to be able to pick him up," Walter complained.

"I can't leave him here," I shot back. "I got to get him back to his boat."

"Is that where he's living?" Curtis asked.

"Yeah, I guess so. You guys got to help me."

"Damn David, by the time we get him down to the docks it's going to be after midnight." Walter said.

"I don't care, I can't leave him here. Somebody might kill him."

"Yeah, but you know Shorty going to tear into you," Walter continued.

"I know but I ain't got no choice."

Walter and Curtis looked at each other, shrugged their shoulders and helped lift Daddy to his feet. Fortunately for us, he wasn't a big man. It took us an hour to get him to his boat. After we dropped him off, I ran all the way home.

"Where the hell you been boy?" Mama asked as soon as I entered the house. "And don't tell me you been playing basketball 'cause I went down there looking for you."

I was lost for words, something unusual for me. If I told her I'd been way over at the Super Port Disco, and found Daddy drunk the whipping would be that more intense. Mama dished out whippings according to the intensity of her anger. If she knew I was beyond my designated area, but had also carried a drunk David to the boats, the whipping was bound to be very intense. Instead I kept my mouth shut. She whipped me, and this time I did not fight back. I was wrong and I accepted the punishment

My Daddy was a serious alcoholic. He drank as much as Big James and Bobby. It seemed rather strange to me that Mama, who didn't drink at all, had such a strong affinity for alcoholics. One other time during that summer after my freshman year Daddy got so drunk it almost cost his life.

On this particular night Mama had picked us up from Grandma's after working late at the Goodwill store. We were pulling into our driveway when I spotted Daddy stumbling toward our house. When the car stopped I jumped out and ran back toward him. I caught him just before he fell to the ground.

"Daddy, what happened?" I shouted. Blood oozed from a deep wound on his forehead. He was disheveled and disoriented.

"Get the fuck away from me," he slurred his words. He took a swing at me and missed.

Daddy was in bad shape and I needed someone to help me get him to our house. "Mama, it's Daddy and he's all beat up," I shouted. By that time they were all out of the car, standing and looking at me. "I can't carry him."

"Levi, go get Wolf," Mama shouted and then hurried toward me. Wolf was married to our Aunt Rosalie and lived right across the street from us. His real name was Willford, but just like most people in the east end, he had a nickname.

"Daddy, you all right?" I asked him simply because I didn't know what else to say. Obviously he was not all right. The gash and blood freely flowing down his face frightened me. I thought he might die right in my arms.

"I told you to get the fuck away from me," he slurred. "I'm going to kill your fucking ass."

"Daddy, it's me, your son David. Don't you know who I am?" I pleaded with him.

"He's damn drunk, David," Mama scowled. "He probably was at the Tropical, got drunk and was running his big mouth. Made somebody mad up in there."

Wolf ran up to us followed by Levi, Ronnie, and James.

"Damn what happened to him?" Wolf asked.

"You know this damn fool been fighting," Mama answered. "Big James wasn't there to protect his dumb ass this time."

"Shorty, this gash is pretty bad," Wolf said. "Whoever did this was damn mad at him." He grabbed Daddy under his arms and picked him up.

"Get the car Shorty, we'd better get him to the hospital before he bleeds to death."

"I'm going with you," I said.

"No you ain't. You're going home," Mama snapped. She brought the car up to the corner, Wolf got Daddy inside and they took off to the hospital.

As I watched them drive off I thought that Daddy was trying to make it to our house. He knew Mama would take care of him, clean his wounds and let him stay there until he healed and then send him on his way. He tried to make it to the person he loved. Men like my Daddy never show emotion, never let love enter through conscious behavior because it would suggest weakness. But just like a wounded puppy will find its way to the person who will care for him, my Daddy was trying to do the same with Mama. Years later he would display the same behavior as he lay in a hospital bed near death.

Next morning, we found out that Knox, one of the regular customers at the Super Port Disco, followed Daddy out of the club and started beating on him in the park. I knew him, and that afternoon, Ronnie and I were determined to get revenge for what he did to Daddy.

"Anybody seen that bastard Knox," I shrieked as we burst into the club.

"Why you looking for Knox?" a man sitting at the bar asked.

"Last night he beat my Daddy half to death, and we going to beat him." I shouted. "So if you know where that motherfucker is you'd better tell me."

"Wait one damn minute little man," the bartender said. He put down a glass he'd just washed and glared at me from behind the counter. "Don't come up in here all loud like you going to do something."

"When we find him we will do something," I shot back at him. "The same something he did to my Daddy." We walked further into the club and stood by the counter.

"You'd better carry your little ass home," another man, a friend of Mama's said. "Your Daddy deserved an ass whipping the way he talked about that man's dead father. Somebody talk about one of my folks like that, they going to get their ass kicked too."

Ronnie and I didn't move from our position at the counter. "I don't care about nobody's dead mamma or daddy, let him know we looking for him and we going to kick his ass when we find him." Ronnie and I backed out of the bar and started toward home. I didn't really know if we could whip Knox, but we were going to try, that is until Mama intervened.

"What you doing down at the club threatening to fight some-body," she shouted at me after getting off the phone. I was sitting in the living room, and again watching *Good Times* when she came after me. She had that intensity in her voice, so I knew a whipping was coming at the end of this talk.

"Mama, Knox beat Daddy real bad and we needed to get even," I said.

"Even my ass, those men will beat you like you ain't never been beat before. You keep your little black ass away from around there." Her voice had increased a few decibel levels. "Knox is crazy. He'll be done cut both y'all. You worry about your own battles and don't try fighting your Daddy's fights."

This time she didn't get the strap, so I got off easy, with just a good fussing. I believe Mama really was proud of what Ronnie and I planned to do. She liked the fact that we stood up for someone we loved regardless of how misguided our intentions. Mama liked that we were not afraid. When I was young she used to march me back out to the park to fight if I had run home to escape a battle. She knew she had taught me well. You never back down if someone comes after you and always stand up and help the people you love. That's exactly what Ronnie and I did, even though we would have gotten obliterated in the process.

Chapter 19

I walked the halls of Brazosport High School with a swagger. I was now in the tenth grade and had one year of high school behind me. My swagger told everyone that I had it together. I could "ball" on the basketball court, and this year I planned to make varsity even though I was only in the tenth grade and the best I should expect is playing time on the junior varsity team. I had such an outstanding freshman year I just knew I would dominate on junior varsity and probably get called up to varsity. I still played football, but my heart wasn't in it the same it was for basketball. In fact, I had considered not playing that year so I could just concentrate on basketball, but I did play running back on the junior varsity team. My problem however was the number of in-school suspensions I received during the football season.

A student received in-school suspension if he was sent to the office for disciplinary reasons three times in the same week. That was a regular occurrence for me, and I spent many Fridays isolated in the room reserved for students serving a one-day in-school suspension. If you received a disciplinary suspension you weren't able to play in any organized sports for that week. I missed a number of football games because of my suspensions. I had been receiving this kind of punishment since sixth grade when I entered Freeport Intermediate

It worked a little different at the intermediate level. There we would not serve the suspension at our own school, but they would bus us to Clute Intermediate six miles from our school. We were housed in a separate room away from all the other students, and marched like prisoners to the cafeteria, where we ate at separate tables. We stayed there for the entire day and then were bused back to our school. Students stared at us like we were prisoners when we got back to our school. They might as well have put a big X across our forehead. Our schoolmates viewed us as being different. Just as students scorned me because I couldn't read, here was a second time I faced the same kind of embarrassment.

Brazosport imposed the same punishment, but instead of being bused to another location, the school had a very large empty room, with no windows, where they housed all students on suspension. All grades were in the same room, with a teacher from each grade assigned to watch over us. I did not get in-school suspensions during basketball season. I didn't want to miss any games so I watched my behavior in the classroom. Once basketball season was over, I was in that one room at least once a week. It was an embarrassing way to be treated. During lunch we would be marched single file to the cafeteria after the other students had already gone through the lunch line. We had to sit at separate tables alone while eating. We could only look straight ahead while eating lunch and after lunch were placed back in a single file line and marched to the isolation room. Students standing in the halls waiting for their next class would call out, "Hey David when you getting out?" just as prisoners ask each other inside prisons. Most of the students in developmental courses did some time in isolation, but I led my class in the number of suspensions during my four years at Brazosport.

The students that spent most time in suspension status were those in developmental classes. It happened most often in Mr. Philpot's class. He taught developmental language and arts, which is a fancy way of saying he tried to improve our reading and writing skills. Walter and Troy were in that class with me, and they did fine because they at least could read. Another student, Liberty Bryant, and I were the hell raisers. We spent the most time in suspension. One episode that really sticks with me happened when Mr. Philpot refused Liberty permission to go to the bathroom.

"Mr. Philpot, I got to go use the bathroom," Liberty said, then got up and walked to the front of the room, placing his body right in front of Mr. Philpot's desk.

"Go back to your seat Liberty and wait until the bell rings. You can use the restroom in between classes."

"No joke, Mr. Philpot, I can't wait that long. I got to go right now."

"I'm not going to tell you again, return to your seat and finish your assignment.

"But Mr. Philpot…"

"Don't try me, Liberty, get back to your seat. I already told you no."

"Okay, if I piss on myself, it's your fault," Liberty said and headed to the back of the room.

"Damn man, how he going to tell you something like that," I chimed in. "If I had to go, I'd go right in here."

Liberty looked around the room and spotted a large plant in a deep container filled with dirt. He whispered to Troy, Walter and me. "Hey you all block his view of me. I'm going to piss right in that plant. I can't hold it."

The three of us got up and slowly made our way over to the plant. We stood close together and Liberty slid between us so that our backs were facing Mr. Philpot and he couldn't see what Liberty was doing. Liberty proceeded to urinate on the plant with sprinkles of it bouncing all around us. He didn't hit us but the floor was hit pretty good. He was in the middle of relieving when Mr. Philpot shouted, "You'd better not be peeing on my plant." He got up and headed to the back of the room. We scattered back to our seats, leaving Liberty holding his penis and still relieving himself right in view of everyone.

"You idiot," Mr. Philpot scowled. "Cover yourself up, there are girls in this room. Get yourself out of here and down to the office."

"I can't, I'm still pissing," Liberty said. When he turned his head to look at Mr. Philpot, he missed the plant and urine covered the floor.

"All right, watch what you're doing," Mr. Philpot now shouted. He stood watching Liberty finish then told him, "Get out of here. I'll meet you in the principal's office." He looked at Troy, Walter, and me. "You three out of here also."

As I got up and headed out of the room I glanced at some of the girls and they were laughing. Evidently they were not offended by Liberty's actions. Troy, Walter, and I received licks, but they placed Liberty on an in-school suspension for a week.

Mr. Philpot was not a bad teacher, and he did the best he could with us. I imagine he considered it punishment having to teach the developmental class which contained the most boisterous and obstreperous students in the entire school. A few in his class really wanted to learn, but many of us didn't think we were capable of learning and achieving in the classroom so all we did was act up. We clowned and we fought because that is what non-learners do when they have lost hope. I had lost hope so I clowned, in Mr. Philpot's class and in all my classes.

My Uncle Ronnie was the junior varsity basketball coach and taught gym at Brazosport. I embarrassed him to the point that I don't really think he wanted to recognize me as a relative. He loved Levi, who was a senior and preparing to graduate. Levi was an exemplary student in the classroom, but a hell raiser outside of class. Uncle Ronnie would constantly ask me why I wasn't more like my older brother. In fact, a lot of my teachers asked me that same question. And the more they asked, the more I cut up in school.

When basketball practice started I knew I would be starting as the point guard on the team. After all I had an outstanding year playing in the ninth grade, and my Uncle Ronnie was the head coach. That day I noticed a young white boy named Andy Ward got more playing time than I did. When the same thing happened the next four days I began to wonder exactly what my uncle was doing. Surely, he wouldn't put a white boy, not nearly as good as me, ahead of me in the lineup. That's what I'd expect a white coach to do, not one who was black and happened to be my uncle.

Then I began to think of the many times he'd walk by the principal's office and see me sitting there and just shake his head. One day he stepped in and scowled at me telling me that I needed to straighten out and change my attitude. Maybe the fact that I wasn't in the starting rotation had something to do with me getting kicked out of class all the time. This was my punishment and when the season started he'd put me back in at my rightful position.

The day of the first game he did no such thing. I sat the bench for three-fourths of the game. I boiled over watching this inferior player get all the playing time. If this was punishment for my terrible behavior, I needed to explain to him what was really happening. I was in the principal's office so often because I couldn't read and didn't want to get embarrassed in the classroom. He would understand because he was my uncle. I never had that opportunity. After the game I approached him.

"Why you got me on the bench, Uncle Ronnie?" I asked. "You know I'm a better point guard than Andy."

"I don't know no such thing, and why you approaching me about my starting lineup." He shot back at me.

Why was my uncle doing this to me? He had to know how important basketball was and without it my life might fall apart.

"You know I'm a better point guard," I insisted on this line of reasoning. Everyone on the team knew I was better than Andy.

"David, I don't mean to hurt your feelings, but at this point you are not better than Andy. He is a junior, and you're a sophomore, and he has more experience. So right now I'm going to leave him in the starting lineup."

Devastated best describes how I felt. My entire world came crashing down on me. If Andy Ward was a better basketball player than me, how could I ever expect to make it to the National Basketball Association? Professional basketball was my dream, and my own uncle was destroying it.

CHAPTER 20

I finished the basketball season riding the bench and finished the school year in the windowless room that was the school equivalent of a prison. I received in- school suspensions practically every week. At that point I didn't care and I even considered dropping out of school until I thought how it would affect Mama. I couldn't do that to her. Regardless of the problems we had growing up, she always insisted her children would finish school. Levi had just graduated and now it was my turn. Mama never finished high school and that is why she was adamant about her children getting their diploma. No way I could let her down and cause more tears than what she'd already shed in her life. Our relationship was always rough around the edges, but I loved her very much.

Dr. Roberts, the only Black PhD at our high school, ran a summer program designed to give work to teenagers whose family income was below the poverty line. We qualified and he put me to work picking up dead fish that had washed ashore as the result of an oil spill from a tanker out in the Gulf. About twenty of us were strapped with that job. I hated it and went into my usual performance when something bothered me, I clowned.

I picked up the dead oily fish and threw them at other workers.

"David Floyd, stop that nonsense and do your work," a supervisor over the workers shouted from a distance.

I paid no attention to her and kept pelting the others with the dead fish. I ran up on one of the female workers and swatted her on the butt.

"That's it, you're out of here Floyd," another supervisor said as he walked next to me. "You're off the job."

I laughed at the girl I'd hit with the fish and walked away. When I got home Mama was there.

"What the hell you doing home so early?" she asked. "And you'd better tell me you got sick and not fired."

"I got fired," I said and headed for my room.

"Get your black ass back out here," Mama hollered. "You taking your ass back down there and ask Dr. Roberts to give you another chance."

"Mama, I can't do that. He ain't going to let me work on that job."

"He'll just have to find another one for you. You ain't sitting around here all day and do nothing. And I need the help. I need that money you make."

Mama found Dr. Roberts' number at the school, grabbed the phone and dialed it. They talked for about ten minutes with Mama practically begging him to give me another chance. When she hung up she turned to me and said.

"He's going to put you on another detail and you better not mess up again. You got to be there in the morning Now get in there and clean that kitchen since you going to be around here all day." She started to walk away.

"Mama why I got to clean up the kitchen? Why can't Ronnie and James do it?"

"I told you to do it, that's why."

I sat in a chair at the kitchen table while Mama went back into her bedroom. My thoughts kept returning to that day when Uncle Ronnie told me I was not as good a player as Andy Ward. I never recovered from the shock. Despite the hurt, I wasn't going to let him destroy my will to succeed just like I never let Bobby break me down, or any of my teachers over the past ten years. I'd go back next year more determined than ever. I'd work on every aspect of my game, and by basketball season, be ready not for junior varsity, but varsity. Mama came out of her bedroom and peeked in the kitchen.

"Boy you'd better stop all that day dreaming and get on those dishes and then mop the floor," she said. "This whole damn place better be clean when I get home."

"Mama, I don't think…" She didn't let me finish, instead abruptly turned and headed out the door.

I got up and cleaned the table, piling the morning dishes into the sink. These were Ronnie and James' dirty dishes so why should I be cleaning them. They were back in the bedroom playing some kind of game. I placed the last plate in the sink and hurried over to the room.

"I need you all in the kitchen," I ordered them.

"For what?" Ronnie asked

"Come in here and find out." I walked back to the kitchen and they reluctantly followed me. "James you don't ever do shit around here. You can wash the dishes."

"Mama ain't told me to do no dishes," James said. He stood there with defiance all over his face.

"I don't care. I'm in charge when Mama ain't here," I shot back at him.

"You ain't in charge of shit," Ronnie chimed in.

"Yeah, you ain't in charge of shit," James echoed his brother.

"You'd better stop that cussing and get over here and do these dishes," I said to James.

"Aint' nothing you can do to make me," he said and moved in closer to me.

I instinctively jump kicked him in the chest. He fell back against the sink. James was big and very athletic. He sprang back to his feet, grabbed a knife and a bottle of Clorox off the counter and came after me. He was so angry he probably would have stabbed me and thrown the Clorox into the wound. I'd made a mistake kicking him and needed to get out of there. He stood between me and the opening to the living room. The back door was too far away so I swiftly made it over to the bathroom, went inside and locked the door. Instantly he banged on the bathroom door,

"You'd better come on out of there," he shouted.

"James, you put that knife and Clorox down and get away from the door."

"You wish I'd get away from this door. But you wrong, I'm going to stay right here until you got to come out."

James banged on the door for a good ten minutes. Finally I heard Ronnie tell him to give it up, and he did. I waited another five minutes before I came out to an empty kitchen. I made sure the Clorox was back on the counter and the knife back in the drawer. I then did the dishes, mopped the kitchen floor and even vacuumed the living room. With the chores out of the way, I went in the bedroom where James was playing some game and Ronnie had dozed off to sleep. James gave me a very hard stare. I grabbed my basketball and took off to the park. That was the last time the two of us would have any kind of altercation until years later when he completed his football scholarship at New Mexico State and was trying to decide what to do with his life.

Next day I started a new job with JTPA but the outcome was the same. Within a week I was fired. In fact, Dr. Roberts fired me a total of seven times within a two-month period. Every time he fired me, Mama would beg to get my job back. I believe Dr. Roberts felt sorry for us. He had known Mama for a very long time and knew her struggle, trying to raise four boys and a daughter with no help from the fathers. We never viewed our family as being different, but the city did. Our family stuck out like a sore thumb, with a bunch of children and no fathers. We were what no one wanted to be; poor and black. It had to be pity, why else would someone fire and hire the same person seven times.

Dr. Roberts finally gave up trying to find the right spot for me on one of the working crews. Instead, during the morning I took a course in typing, and in the afternoon, I worked alone picking up papers and trash around the school. I was elated with my morning assignment. It meant I would spend each morning with Mrs.

Woods. She taught typing at Brazosport and was by far the prettiest teacher in the entire school. I never believed my luck could be so good. She instantly became the love of my life, and I dreamed that someday we would be a couple. That feeeling overwhelmed me and controlled my behavior every day in her class. I had no problem expressing to her just how I felt. I did it in a flirtatious manner.

"Mrs. Woods how are you today?" I asked when I walked in the classroom and sat at the typewriter.

"Fine David, and how are you?"

"Feeling great now that I'm in your classroom and your company."

"Let's just leave it that you are in my classroom and not necessarily my company."

"But Mrs. Woods I want to be in your company more than just in your classroom."

"Don't get started David, or I'll have to report you to Dr. Roberts," she warned. "Or better than that, I'll call Shorty and tell her you're acting up. I know you don't want that?" Mrs. Woods, at one time, had been a friend with Mama. They attended high school together until Mama dropped out.

"Would you do that, Mrs. Woods, and spoil the good thing we got going on?" I asked

"David Floyd, do your work," she snapped at me.

Her next move would be to send me to Dr. Roberts' office and I didn't want that. Not because I feared him, but I didn't want to be away from her. I turned and banged away at that day's assignment. I spent the remainder of the summer learning to type and admiring Mrs. Wood's beauty.

On weekends J.B. and I would drive up to Houston and spend time with Uncle J.B. We always made sure to get over to Dot's for some of her delicious pancakes. J.B. still drove without a license and often our gas gauge sat on empty. The first time I glanced over at the gauge, and the light was lit up, I panicked. J.B. moved behind a truck and assured me that when a car gets behind a large truck it can run off the its fumes. Like a fool I believed him. Fortunately we never ran out of gas. And what is more fortunate for us is that we never were stopped by the police or highway patrol.

We also spent a lot of nights at Lincoln Park perfecting our game. We played one on one and horse when it was only the two of us. We both were convinced that we could make varsity that coming year. I would be a junior and he a sophomore, but we knew the seniors that year were not that good. Even though Andy Ward had started in front of me on junior varsity last year, I knew I could beat him out for the starting position. I was convinced that if I had a coach the previous year other than my Uncle Ronnie, I would have started at point guard. Kenny Casper was the varsity coach, and I built my hopes that he would be impartial in his evaluation of me. He would recognize my superior talent over Andy and elevate me to starter on the varsity team, and I knew J.B. would be right there with me.

Chapter 21

"It's your attitude, David," my ex-coach and mentor Wallace told me. "You got a bad attitude, you're too cocky and you stay in trouble all the time."

I sat on the bleacher seats in the Freeport Intermediate gymnasium. As soon as I received word that I would not be playing varsity basketball I went to see him. To make matters worse, a sophomore, Cooley Darthard, who had very little ability, was elevated to varsity surpassing the junior varsity team. That crushed me and if I hadn't found someone to talk with I believe I'd have imploded. The only person I could share my disappointment with was my former coach. He'd understand and be on my side. As I sat and listened I found that not to be the case. He was telling me what I needed to hear but I wasn't listening.

"I know you don't want to hear this, but you must. You run off at the mouth all the time. That's hurt you in the past and it's going to hurt you now and in the future." Coach reached over and placed his hand on my shoulder. "Get rid of those demons and with your determination to succeed, there isn't anything you can't accomplish."

When I headed home, his words resonated with me. Maybe I was my own worst enemy. The temper and the need to show off kept me in trouble. But it was also compensation for my inability to succeed in the classroom, and there didn't seem to be any way to change that. At sixteen I felt trapped in a vicious circle and couldn't figure a way out. All these years I believed basketball was my escape and now because of my behavior, that way out was escaping me. I was moving in the wrong direction and wasn't sure I could control or change it. The fear of absolute failure momentarily took over, and I felt an overwhelming feeling of anxiety. I had to work my way through this setback or I might not make it to the twelfth grade.

We had a very good junior varsity team. Finally J.B. and I were able to play organized basketball together. Since we had played years and years at Lincoln Park and knew each other's strengths and weaknesses we had an advantage over our opponents. Troy, who should have been on varsity, but just did not have the heart for intense competition played with us. Our team was better than the varsity and would often beat them in scrimmages. I was over my initial disappointment and now determined to outplay Andy.

Just before scrimmage, I would tell J.B. "I've got a contract out on Andy. He ain't going to do nothin' I'm going to be so locked on him." I guarded him so close in those scrimmages he had a difficult time getting the ball across half court. We broke their timing and rhythm and I easily stole the ball from him. Together, the three friends from Lincoln Park, J.B., Troy , and me, none of us seniors, were beating up on the varsity team. I was undoubtedly the most aggressive and determined. It paid off when we played other teams. We played our games right before the varsity, and afterwards we sat in the stands watching them get beat. We were very good, and they were not good at all. After a while the student body gave up on them and closely followed our season.

I made it through basketball season with no in-school suspensions, but as soon as it ended I reverted back to my old ways. There always seemed to be one particular teacher with whom I battled. In the eleventh grade it was Mr. Horad. He taught geometry. I was good at mathematics because it dealt with numbers and not words. That changed in geometry class. I couldn't read or understand the meaning of theorems and hypothesis, so I was unable to solve the problems. When Mr. Horad called on me to solve a problem my defense mechanisms kicked in.

"David did you work out the problems assigned as your home-work last night?" Mr. Horad asked with a frown because he already knew the answer and anticipated trouble.

"No, I didn't," I answered.

"You didn't do any of your homework assignment?"

"No, he didn't do it cause he can't read," a student sitting behind me said. His comment brought chuckles from the other students.

"No, I didn't," I answered trying to ignore the students laughing at me.

"See, I told you," that same student said sounding like a parrot. The laughter continued.

Mr. Horad ignored the jeering and laughing and instead saved his badgering for me. "David Floyd, there is no way you can pass this class without doing your homework. It is part of your grade."

"Whatever, Mr. Hypothenuse head," I scowled at him.

"What did you call me?" he snapped.

"You are a hypothenuse head aren't you, since that's all you seem to know anything about."

The students broke out in laughter and I felt secure again. Instead of them laughing at me, they laughed with me. I diverted their derision from me and onto Mr. Horad. I had been using this particular tactic for years. And it still worked. But as in the past, I paid the price. Mr. Hoad's lips tightened and his brows furrowed. He stood up straight.

"David Floyd, don't you ever call me out of my name. I am Mr. Horad to you, now get out of my class."

"Where do you want me to go?" I asked as if I didn't know.

"To the principal's office, where else?"

"Whatever, Mr. Hypothenuse head," I said and walked out of the class. This time I didn't get in-school suspension. Instead, Mr. Cervenka gave me five licks in his office.

The rest of the semester turned out to be a disaster. I spent as much time in Mr. Cervenka's office and in-school suspensions as

I spent in the classroom. To make matters worse, Ronnie was in his freshman year at Brazosport. Between the two of us, Mr. Cervenka stayed busy. Ronnie's big thing was gambling in the boys' rest room. He would pitch pennies against the wall with other boys. The penny, or sometimes nickel, dime and quarter that landed closest to the wall would be the winner.

One day during the spring semester I came bouncing down the hall and saw a line of boys standing outside the bathroom. Some of them held on to the crotch of their pants, a sure indication they had to really use the bathroom.

"What the hell's going on?" I asked walking up next to the boy at the front of the line. I tried the door but it wouldn't open.

"What you think's going on," he said. "Your damn brother in there against the door and can't nobody get in with his fat ass blocking the door."

My first inclination was to hit that boy right in his mouth. He called my brother fat and I didn't tolerate that disrespect. But Ronnie was wrong because the boy had to urinate real bad, and he did what any person would do in those circumstances. He attacked the boy blocking him from some relief. There was nothing worse than having to go to the bathroom and having to hold it. I recalled that day in Philpot's class when Liberty couldn't hold it and went in the flower pot. Instead of going off on the boy, I beat on the bathroom door.

"Ronnie, open this damn door," I shouted.

I lowered my shoulder and launched my body against the door. It swung open.

"What you all out here hollering about?" Ronnie asked.

"Man, all these boys got to pee," I scowled.

"Okay, okay, go to it." Ronnie walked out of the bathroom and down the hall.

The boys waiting outside made a beeline inside just as the bell rang for the next class. I hurried down the hall to my class satisfied

I had saved the school from a hall way filled with urine and Ronnie a trip to in-school suspension.

That one deed, saving the school from smelling like urine and Ronnie a trip to Mr. Cervrenka's office, could not even start to match all the trouble I caused the rest of the year. I cared less about an in-school suspension now that basketball season had ended. For the remainder of the year I struggled with geometry. There was no way for me to cheat in that class and no way for me to comprehend the material. At the end of my junior year I failed geometry. It would be the only course I failed in all four years at Brazosport, which was an incredible feat for a person who then read at the second grade level.

CHAPTER 22

In the summer of 1987 Dr. Roberts assigned me the job of picking up trash around the school. I promised him that I would work the entire summer without getting into trouble. I made that promise because Mama asked me to. It happened a week after school ended. Mama's demeanor caught me by surprise. She had Ronnie and me at the supper table right after the two of us had fought over food.

Mama had fixed a pot of red beans with neck bones and cornbread. I came in about seven that evening and headed right to the kitchen, grabbed a plate and took the top off the pot. I jerked my head back and frowned when I looked inside. It was empty. He had done it again; he'd eaten the entire supper leaving none for the rest of us. Angry is a mild description of how I felt. I rushed over to the bedroom, opened the door and glared in at Ronnie stretched out on the bed looking at a comic book.

I stood in the doorway and screamed, "Why you eat all the food?"

"I didn't eat it all," he shot back.

"It's all gone and I know damn well James and Nicole didn't eat that much."

"How you know how much they ate?" Ronnie raised straight up in the bed and glared back at me.

"We'll see about this." I slammed the door and hurried outside where Mama stood at the curb talking to Aunt Clavella.

"Mama, you got to do something about Ronnie," I shrieked.

"Boy, what the hell is wrong with you walking up on me like that," Mama said.

"Mama, it's Ronnie," I snapped.

"What's wrong with Ronnie?" A concerned look spread across her face.

I thought for a brief moment that Mama worried over Ronnie's condition. She just knew I was bringing bad news. But quickly my anger took over.

"He ate all the food for dinner. What are the rest of us going to do?"

"Damit, boy that ain't my worry. I fix it for you all and I ain't going to sit there to see who eats what. You need to get home in time to make sure he don't eat it all." Mama turned away from me and continued talking with Aunt Clavella.

I marched back into the house and to the bedroom. Ronnie wasn't going to get away with doing this again. It happened all the time, and it had to stop. When I busted back in the room he jumped up and started toward me. We met half way between the twin beds.

"More than just you got to eat fat boy," I shouted.

"Who you calling fat," he shot back.

"I'm calling you fat and out of shape, and that's why you can't play no sports. If you eat less you might be able to lose some of them 400 pounds you carrying."

"Fuck you, David." He scowled and took a swing at me.

I ducked and hit him right in the mouth. We went at it for a couple minutes, both of us swinging and missing. He came at me and I ran in the living room. He tried running behind me, but was winded after taking only a few steps. From across the room I could hear his wheezing. Suddenly he plopped down on the couch and began coughing. He had trouble breathing.

"You all right?" I asked him.

"Hell, yeah, I'm all right." Ronnie's voice was very low and his words slurred.

For the first time I recognized the reality of my brother's condition. A second reality hit me that I should not be fighting Ronnie.

I should be helping him. I walked over and stood staring down at a fifteen year old who acted and looked much older.

"I don't want to fight you," I said. "We got to stop this fighting each other."

"That'll work for me," Ronnie said between deep breaths.

"I'm going over to J.B.'s," I said. "They always got something to eat."

"But his mama don't like you."

"What's that got to do with me getting something to eat? She ain't home and I'm hungry." I finished, got up and dashed out the house.

That was too close for comfort. I thought Ronnie might die that day. He struggled to get his breath but pulled through. Later that day, Mama sat with both of us at the table and poured out her concerns. Our constant problems in school, our fighting all the time, and the fact that she spent as much time at the school about our behavior as she did on the job was wearing thin on her nerves. She needed our commitment not to fight with each other, and that we would try to stay out of trouble. Mama cried because she wasn't sure the two of us would be able to make it in life if we didn't change our attitudes. How would we survive if something happened to her? I didn't like to see Mama cry and swore if I could do anything to prevent that I would. Memories of her lying sprawled on the kitchen floor, blood all over her from a busted mouth were still burned deep in my memory bank. It was my senior year coming up, I needed to stay out of trouble and do the right thing so Mama wouldn't have to cry. Working the summer job was a great start.

The day finally arrived when J.B., Troy, Rich McGuire, and I would attend a basketball camp at Baylor University. We planned to leave the next morning. That evening I spent over Grandma's house. I don't know why I did, but that night would be one I would never forget. Looking back it must have been fate. I was supposed to be there with my favorite cousin, Patrick, Aunt Marilyn Ruth's only son. He had lived with Grandma all his life.

I believe I was meant to be the last person Patrick spoke to on earth. He was gay and that didn't bother us because he was family, but I believe it bothered him. To be gay in a town like Freeport was not an easy life, and I knew he wasn't happy. I figured at some point Patrick would learn how to deal with it or take steps to end his misery. He did the latter.

That day, just out of nowhere, he expressed that he was happy I was there with him. He knew how much I loved Aunt Marilyn and how much I really did miss her. Maybe he was reaching out to me, and without speaking the words, asking me to share the same strong emotions for him. For whatever reason, he strolled out of the bedroom right after he swallowed a whole bottle of pills, chased them down with vodka, and stood next to me for a short minute. He seemed to wobble while standing there. He threw his head back and his body swerved from side to side.

"You okay, Patrick?" I asked.

"What you think? I don't look all right?" He answered and then stumbled back into the bedroom and fell out on the bed.

"Yeah, I guess so," I answered as I watched him fall down on the bed. Grandma and Levi were outside on the porch. It was an extremely hot day, but I preferred to sit in the hot house than join them on the porch. My insecurities warned me that Grandma just might start making comparisons between Levi and me. She hadn't done anything like that in a very long time, but I still chose to be cautious.

However, watching Patrick's head slump forward and his eyes close tightly, I got up and started for the front door. At the same time Patrick's body was curled up in a fetal position on the bed and he went into convulsions. A foam like material drooled out of his mouth. I flung the screen door open and hollered.

"Grandma, something's wrong with Patrick. He's fell out on the bed and he's shaking and puss is coming out of his mouth.

"What in the world is wrong now?" She got up and went into

the house with Levi right behind her. I stayed outside but looked back in through the screen door.

"Oh Lord, Heaven help us," Grandma screamed. She snatched the phone and dialed 911.

"He's unconscious," Levi shouted. He began pumping Patrick's chest trying to revive him, but it wasn't working. I heard the sirens in the background screaming toward Grandma's house.

It took the emergency medical personnel five minutes to get to the house. One of the young men on the rescue squad had graduated high school with Patrick.

"I know him," the man said. They hurried in with the stretcher, placed Patrick on it and as fast as they got there they were gone. Patrick died in the ambulance on the way to the hospital.

The next day I left with Troy, J.B., and Rich for basketball camp at Baylor University. As we left Freeport I had mixed emotions. I felt bad for feeling good. Patrick, my cousin died right in front of me less than twelve hours ago, and that was an occasion for mourning. But looking out at the Gulf of Mexico through the back window of Troy's father's car, I felt a burst of joy, and most of all I felt good about myself. I could feel Patrick all around me and he was talking to me, telling me it was all right and that he was all right. I would not feel that sense of peace and tranquility again until my Daddy's death.

I had never been further than Houston without Mama, except the few times we were forced to vacate Freeport due to hurricane warnings. Then we would go to shelters in Waco. This time I was going on my own, using the money I had raised last semester by intimidating students going into the cafeteria. For the next few days I would concentrate all my energy into being the best point guard at the camp.

When we arrived at Baylor I could hardly control my emotions. It was my favorite Texas University since my Uncle Ronnie played football there in the 1970s. Often we had the opportunity to watch both their football and basketball games on television, and I planned to play there before moving on to the NBA. This was only a prelude to my future years there.

We slept in dorms, ate in the cafeteria, and played ball in the main arena. Brazosport High School shined during the practice sessions. Troy performed magnificently in the low post, I shined playing against the other point guards there, and J.B. blocked shots and stole the ball from other players with ease. Players and coaches questioned Rich's status. They just knew he had to be either a junior or senior. He appeared too polished and mature for an incoming sophomore.

J.B. and I played against each other for the one on one championship. I defeated him because of my aggressiveness and determination. My overwhelming need to always win worked well for me, except when I challenged Michael Williams, Baylor's 6 feet 4 inch junior guard who made first team All Big-Twelve. I had just defeated J.B., and knew I could take on Michael Jordan, let alone a Michael Williams. I bounced the ball to him and said.

"I beat all these chumps, let me have a shot at you."

"What do you want to play?" Michael asked as he dribbled the ball while standing in place.

"One on one, seven baskets to win," I said. "And don't go easy on me."

He bounced the ball over to me with a firm snap of his wrists. "I won't."

I dribbled the ball from one hand to the next, figuring which way to go. His defensive stance looked perfect, body leaned low, legs spread, and arms lifted. I did a crossover and then broke to my right. I shot right by him and a smile spread across my face because I knew I had him beat. I went for the lay-up and then out of nowhere he came flying through the air and slapped my shot up into the bleachers. He easily skunked me the first game, the second, and the third, as well as the fourth. Memories of Uncle Lynn beating Levi and me years ago and the grown men beating us flashed through my mind. Those times and now, I had to concede the superior skill of my opponent. But I refused to give up until I scored at least one basket. Michael either got tired or just gave in and let me score in the fifth game. I felt content making that one basket against a superior competitor. It was like a victory for me. We finished the camp on a high note but my joy waned as we headed back to Freeport. We still had to bury Patrick.

I refused to attend the funeral. I didn't go to Aunt Marilyn Ruth's, and it seemed appropriate that I not attend Patrick's. I was too emotional then and too emotional at the time of his funeral.

A couple weeks after Patrick's death, Levi joined the navy. After graduating high school, he had spent one year at DeVrie University on financial aid. His major was computer science, a field in which he was quite good. But after one year he didn't receive any additional financial aid, and Mama was too poor to help him.

When Levi returned to Freeport he cried for a long time. I couldn't figure out why someone would cry because they couldn't go to school. I wanted to cry because I had to go. Levi stayed home the entire summer then shipped out for basic training at Newport News, Virginia. I admired my brother and was proud to see him make a decision that would ultimately provide him an escape out of Freeport.

I knew I'd be leaving in another year with a scholarship to play college basketball. It was my next step to fulfilling my ultimate goal, which, despite my disappointment last year at Brazosport, I still planned to achieve.

CHAPTER 23

"You boys are the team I've been waiting for all my life," Coach Casper said to us with much excitement in his voice. "Many of you have played together for years and that means a lot. Now lets get to work and from this day until the end of the season we have one goal in mind and that is to win the state championship.

We jumped out of the bleachers, gathered in a circle and shouted in unison, "Win." We then began our first day of drills in what would turn out to be the most exciting year of my short life. Without a doubt I was the leader of this team. I was designated to start at point guard and control what happens on the court. I just knew I would be playing back up to Cooley but he didn't even bother to try out. Evidently he knew better than the coaches that he was not good enough to start and shouldn't have made varsity over me the past year. But that was all behind me, I had the position and was determined to lead my team to the district championship if not state.

I was the leader because Troy, Darrell, J.B. and the others on the team looked to me to give the team direction and I loved the responsibility. We started the season beating up on everyone. I was easily beating other teams' full court press that produced many easy layups for my teammates. I led the team in steals, and I had a smooth, deadly jump shot. Things were going well, and then suddenly the coach went to a platoon system. Under the new system I shared playing time with a sophomore, Ondrea Wiley, who really wasn't ready for varsity. He had a great jump shot but got rattled when pressed. He couldn't break the full court press and the opponent was able to steal the ball from him at will.

I started the games and we always built a lead, but he would replace me in the second quarter and we lost or almost lost leads. Coach Casper's system frustrated the fans, the players, and especially me. When he finally inserted me back in the game we would again build up another lead. This went on the entire semester, and then the day came when we had to play our arch rival, Bay City, on their home court. Later in the season they would play us on our court, but first we had to beat them in their back yard. That was no small feat, since Brazosport hadn't beaten them at home in over twenty years.

In the locker room prior to the game we were all fired up, but when we took the court for drills, the air came out of us like a deflating balloon. The stands were packed with their fans. It had to be standing room only on their side of the court. As soon as we took the court, their band started playing *"Ain't no stopping us now,"* and all four thousand shouting fans stood up and started rocking from left to right and clapping their hands. To a player on the court, sounds come at you from all directions and merge right in the center, magnifying the intensity. It sounded good because it let us know we were playing in front of a very large crowd, but it made us feel intimidated because none of those fans were pulling for us. To make matters worse, their players were slam-dunking during lay up drills. Our coach never let us slam-dunk during warm ups. He wanted to save them for the game. He strolled among us and shouted, "Pay attention, none of that matters. What matters is what happens when the whistle blows." Finally a large contingent of our fans showed up, and we felt their support.

Coach's advice was so true. We managed to dominate them through the first quarter and then coach made that crazy substitution. Wylie wasn't able to break their press, and Bay City dominated the second quarter, evening the score at halftime. I played an outstanding third quarter, easily breaking their press and setting up my teammates for easy lay ups and short jump shots.

I was playing the kind of game in which the coach shouldn't take you out. But he did at the beginning of the fourth quarter, and it was downhill for us again. Bay City was only four points behind and I approached coach.

"You got to put me back in," I pleaded. "They going kill us, Wylie can't handle getting the ball across court. They got him rattled."

He ignored me and refused to make the change. The fans joined in shouting, "Put David Floyd in." He ignored them. Bay City took a two point lead before he finally got the message. We were going to lose unless he made the switch. He called, "Number nine, back in." He refused to call my name, but instead called my number.

I didn't care just as long as I was back in the game. We were down one point as J.B. hit a foul shot. They brought the ball back down court and scored. The press was on as J.B. tossed the ball into me, and I easily maneuvered through them. We were down by one point and the clock had only five seconds remaining.

Coach Casper jumped off the bench and waved his arm indicating I should take the ball all the way through their defense for a lay up.

I turned on the burners and shot through two of their defenders and just as I started to release the ball I was hammered on the arm. The shot fell off to the right of the basket, but the referee called the foul.

I was in the very situation I always dreamed of, and that is taking foul shots for the win. Bay City called a time out in order to freeze me out. I needed to make the first one to tie the game and second one for the victory.

I slowly strolled into our huddle. I heard the radio commentator say.

"Now it's up to David Floyd. He can win the game for Brazosport and beat Bay City on their home court for the first time in over twenty years."

Hearing my name called gave me an adrenaline rush. Our home games were never on the radio and just knowing thousands of Bay City folks were listening made me a little nervous, but I loved it. I didn't worry about sinking those foul shots. I knew I would.

Before going back on the court Coach warned us, "If you make these two foul shots, all of you get the hell out of here and to the bus." J.B. and I glared at each other. My look told him that didn't scare me. I had been through hell and this was a piece of cake.

I strolled to the foul line, looked at J.B. and Darrell one more time, took aim and dropped the ball through the net twice and we had a one-point lead.

They had no opportunity to score and when the clock went off, we all broke for the exit as a barrage of fans started down from the stands and onto the floor. We got out of there just in time to escape the vengeance. They hadn't lost to us in that gym in a very long time, and they were not happy.

The local police held the crowd back long enough for us to make it outside to the parking lot. We could hear the shouts and jeers from the crowd as they finally broke through the police barricade. By that time, our driver had pulled the bus right up close to the exit and we all shot into the bus, he closed the door just as the crowd reached the bus, and he pulled off, forcing the crowd to clear a way for us. We smiled and waved at the crowd and once they were out of sight, all of us shouted as loud as we could "we won"!!!!!

Our team was one of the best in Brazosport history. We won District for the first time in over twenty years and made it to the second round of the state playoffs before losing to West Orange Stark High School out of Orange, Texas.

With the season over I was convinced of my ability to play college basketball, the last step before the pros. None of the major universities in Texas recruited me, and the coach didn't help out, so I did it all on my own. My determination was unrelenting. I refused to deal with anyone at the universities I contacted other than the head coach. Sometimes I would wait on the phone for an hour and on a number of occasions the person on the other end hung up on me when I insisted on talking only to the head person in charge. After a number of rejections I finally talked to the head coach at San Angelo State University. He invited me to come up to his school for a tryout.

I was elated when I boarded the bus in Freeport heading for San Angelo, with a transfer in Houston. This was the second time I would be a long way from home without Mama. I had no hesitation because I knew the tryout would be an overwhelming success. I made it to Houston but found out I had missed my connector bus. It would be twenty-four hours before there would be another one. That was the longest twenty-four hours of my life. I sat there afraid to go to sleep because of the winos and street sleepers in the depot. I slept all the way to San Angelo.

The coach and two assistants gave me a vigorous workout, testing my skills against those of a couple of other boys already on the team. I held my own, and at the end of the tryout, the coach told me that he would give me a scholarship to play ball there. He also told me it was contingent on my high school grades and test score on the ACT. My first obstacle would be graduating from high school. One class stood in my way to graduation.

Every year since elementary school I had one teacher with whom I was bound to have a confrontation. My senior year it happened the second day of school, much faster than in the past. Usually it would be at least a week before I entered into battle with some teacher. And also this time the battle came to me, I didn't initiate it. The day of senior registration I signed up for accounting simply because so many pretty girls also enrolled in the class. I knew nothing about the subject matter, didn't know what to expect, but loved the idea of being surrounded by some of the prettiest young ladies in the school.

The second day I strolled proudly into the classroom and was met at the door by Mrs. Artiss Hassenback.

"David Floyd, what are you doing in this class?" she asked.

"Taking accounting," I said. "What are you doing in here?"

She frowned and snapped back at me. "Don't come in here thinking you're going to start trouble."

"Why you think I'm going to make trouble?" I asked but did not wait for an answer. "I don't go around starting trouble."

Mrs. Hassenback didn't answer but continued here badgering. "You have a terrible reputation at this school and other schools you've attended. I will not put up with your nonsense."

"Whatever," I said and walked toward a desk at the back of the room.

"And what makes you think you can pass accounting?" she asked.

I hesitated momentarily, turned and stared at her. I thought no need to get kicked out of class the first day and continued toward the desk I'd chosen right between two of the prettiest girls in the class.

Brazosport allowed the students to chose their own classes without the aid of a counselor. I chose every advance class that was available just to be defiant, with the exception of Mrs. Williams' class. Even though she taught advanced sociology, I needed to be in her class because she was my anchor in a sea of storm with all my other teachers. I enrolled in the other classes as a statement that I was as good as any other student in the school even though I could not read. Amazingly I got along with all the teachers and did quite well in advanced algebra.

That was not the case with Mrs. Hasenback. Our relationship was so turbulent that eventually Mama intervened in order for me to graduate. The catalyst for our major confrontation was Stacy Boone, the daughter of the head football and track coach at the school. Her perceived status as Boone's daughter gave her a feeling of superiority over others. She quickly found out that would not work with me, but I ended up paying the price for challenging her.

I stood in the aisle of the classroom talking with another student when she took her seat in the back. Mrs. Hassenback came into the room and said, "All right, everyone sit down and stop the chatter."

I ignored her and continued talking.

Stacy stood up and shrieked. "David Floyd shut up and sit down."

"Tell your mama to shut up," I shouted at her.

"You idiot," she scowled, and sat back down. "What's he doing in here anyway," she whispered, but loud enough for me to hear. "This is for smart kids."

She found my vulnerability and hit me where it hurt most. "I bet I can slap the smart out of you," I said not thinking.

Right at that moment, Mrs. Hassenback looked up from her desk up front and said, "David Floyd I warned you that I would not tolerate your thuggish ways. I want you out of my class right now."

"What about her?" I asked knowing darn well she wasn't about to put the coach's daughter out with me. "She said all kinds of stupid things about me so why don't she have to go too?"

"Because you are always a trouble maker and will always be one. You'll never pass my accounting class because you don't have the ability. And you'll never amount to anything in life. Once a loser always a loser."

I had made it to the entranceway, but when she said that, I stopped and looked back at her.

"I'll not only pass your class, but someday I'm going to get a Ph.D. in accounting because you don't have one and probably could never get one." I hurried out of the room and started toward the principal's office again prepared for licks.

Mrs. Hassenback screamed at me. "You are out of this class permanently. If you want to try to pass you will have to do it from Mr. Cervenka's office."

She wanted me to fail not only her class but also in life. There is no way that woman should have ever been allowed to teach because of her contemptuous attitude toward students. For that reason my determination remained steadfast and strong. My failure would provide her a perverted kind of satisfaction. As I marched to the office I had one other goal now other than basketball and that was to pass her class.

Despite my determination I undoubtedly would have failed accounting if not for the support I received from Melissa Bass, a young white girl who came from the other side of town, away from the poverty stricken east end. Her father was a judge, but unlike Stacy she did not flaunt here status. Melissa was dating my brother Levi. In fact, they were practically engaged. When he first started dating her, Melissa's mother found out, came up to the school and created a scene. After a while, her mother grew used to the fact that she might have a black son-in-law and accepted him. But at that time, there was plenty of turmoil.

After class Melissa hurried down to the principal's office and caught up to me just as I was leaving. I looked at her and started to walk away. I never thought Melissa liked me. I knew she dated my brother, but many of his friends didn't like me. They all claimed I had a big mouth, in fact they called me "Mouth of the South.' And that was okay with me because I didn't like them either. Levi always dated white and I never did. I was attracted only to black girls. So I paid no attention to Melissa when she called out.

"David, Mrs. Hassenback really is a mean person. I really don't like her and I don't think many of the students like what she did to you." She created the bond with me and I knew at that point I must re-consider my feelings about her. She reached out to me and the least I could do was respond.

"Yeah, I know. I didn't do anything to her to be kicked out of class that way. And it was really that snob Stacy's fault," I said as I stopped, turned and faced her.

"David, I'm going to help you pass accounting," she whispered. The office clerks listened to student conversations hoping to hear something controversial enough to tell the principal. We both would have been kicked out of Hassneback's class if she knew. "I'll meet you after school and give you the material we covered in class. I'll even help with the answers." She looked all around as she continued to whisper. "Nobody can know about this. My mother would kill me if she knew I was helping Levi's brother pass accounting."

I could only stand there silently and listen to Melissa. People, especially white people with the exception of Mrs. Williams, never helped me. Melissa was willing to put it all on the line for me, and for that I came to admire and respect her. She provided me with class notes everyday and then on test day, I was allowed back in the classroom to take tests, and we derived a way for her to share the answers with me. We did this for the entire year and I managed to barely stay above the minimum required to graduate.

At the end of the year, Mrs. Hassenback's class was the only one in question. If I didn't pass it, I wouldn't graduate. So on senior skip day, all the graduating class skipped school and went down to the beach and partied. I sat outside Mrs. Hassenback's classroom while she and Mama added up my cumulative average for the year. Earlier in the week she told me that if my average equated to 69.999 she would still fail me. Essentially she told me that I would get no breaks from her. That infuriated Mama when I told her, and she insisted on being there while my final grade was computed. I sat outside on pins and needles waiting for the outcome. In-house suspension or licks did not match the anguish I felt. After a half hour, the teacher marched out of the classroom and murmured, "You passed," and kept walking. No congratulations or good luck in the future as she had said to the other students. Mama followed her out of the room, smiled and said, "We beat her, you graduated, lets go home." During those past thirteen years from kindergarten through twelfth grade, I experienced many ups and downs. That day represented an up, but very soon, after graduation, the downs would again attack my life and almost destroy me.

CHAPTER 24

———◆·❖·◆———

Nine! I didn't want to believe I scored only a nine on the ACT given that the first 5 points are free for just signing your name to the test. Three weeks after taking the ACT my answer finally arrived in the mail. I retrieved it out of the box and ran back into the house where Mama waited also on pins and needles. Heading into the house I momentarily thought back to that Saturday morning at Brazosport High School cafeteria where all the students congregated for the exam. My close friend Thomas took it the same day and sat directly in front of me. He kept turning around glaring at me, picking up my nervous anxiety and fears of the outcome. The look on his face told the whole story. After twelve years of dodging the bullet we both knew the bullet had finally caught up with me. I could no longer manipulate the system. No one would be there to help me with the answers because I couldn't read. I struggled with every question. Again, Thomas would turn around and he desperately wanted to help his childhood friend, but could do nothing. When the test ended we walked out of the cafeteria together.

"How you think you did?" he asked

"Not too good, I don't think," I replied.

"Damn, David I wanted to give you some of the answers, but the monitors were all around us."

"Yeah, I know."

We exited the cafeteria and a boy who I'd seen around campus but didn't really know, walked up and got right in my face.

"David Floyd, why you taking the ACT? You're not going to college are you?"

"You better bet I am," I snapped at him.

"Yeah, right," he snapped right back at me.

I stood next to Mama in the living room and stared at the glaring number nine tormenting both of us. I finally plopped down on the couch and buried my head between my hands.

Mama patted me on the back and said, "Don't worry you applied to other schools. Maybe one of them will let you in."

My sorrow quickly turned to anger. It all seemed so unfair. The ability to read had nothing to do with basketball. I had no plans to be a scholar or even an outstanding student. My future lay in the NBA and San Angelo was the last necessary step to getting there. I wasn't good enough to earn a tryout with the pros right out of high school, but with four years of college ball and good coaching, I would be ready. San Angelo was going to deny me that opportunity because of a test. I had to figure out how to turn this around, to get it back on track in my favor. If there was no answer, there was no future for me. I refused to accept the possibility I would spend my life in Freeport, constantly revisiting the myriad negative memories it held for me.

Days passed and I did nothing but mope around the house. I had applied to other schools and expected to receive notice of their rejection also. No one would accept me with a score of nine and my very low grade point average. To break the monotony I went to Lincoln Par and played ball with J.B. and any other "ballers" down there. Mama was getting tried of me hanging around the house, Ronnie and James wanted me to hurry up and go somewhere so they could finally have the bedroom to themselves. They both were Freeport Intermediate, Levi in the navy and Nicole in elementary school.

By the middle of June, speculation came to an end as I received a letter of acceptance from Lamar University in Beaumont, Texas on a provisional basis. Mr. Smedley, the Vice-Principal at Brazosport, helped me fill out an application for admission and financial aid at

Lamar just in case San Angelo failed to admit me. In fact, he did all the work for me. I had to take all remedial classes and could not even try to walk-on as a basketball player because of Proposition 48, which required all athletes to maintain a certain grade point average and score a passing grade on entrance examinations. That was devastating, but I had no other option. In late August I headed for Lamar College and my first experience as a college student. It would be a disaster for me.

I arrived in Beaumont by Greyhound Bus and then caught a city bus to the campus. My financial aid was still pending so I didn't have a dorm room or money for food or other daily necessities. Fortunately, two friends from high school, Benny Backman, Jr., an outstanding football player and Michael Wright, who ran track and played on the basketball team with me, agreed to let me bunk with them until my aid came through. I also depended on Benny for food. His father, Benny Backman, Sr., who happened to also be a shrimper by trade, but one who took his responsibility to family seriously, sent his son a monthly stipend. I was able to eat regular meals most of the time because one man cared what happened to not only his son, but me also.

Benny, Sr., was pretty regular in sending the money, but sometimes it didn't arrive on time, and I was forced to panhandle. I had a couple favorite streets in downtown Beaumont where I stood during rush hour and begged for money. I usually hustled enough change to buy a McDonald's hamburger, fries and a coke. On some occasions, businessmen in suits would challenge my reason for begging.

"Hey boy, you sure you're not strung out on drugs?" a man dressed neatly asked.

"No sir," I answered. "I'm a student at Lamar and haven't gotten my financial aid money yet. I want to eat."

"Yeah, well, I know a lot of you boys are just trying to hustle to buy drugs."

I wanted to pull the cup in my outstretched hand back and tell him where to go. But he could help me. I bit my lip, pulled my pride back and kept begging.

"Sir, I have never done drugs, don't like drugs, and I just want to eat."

"Why doesn't your family help you?" he asked. "Why doesn't your father send you some money? After all you're trying to better yourself by going to school, seems like he would want to help."

"They don't have no money. That's why I'm on financial aid. I just need a little money to get through the day." I again thrust the cup toward him.

He gave me a hard, cold stare but went in his pocket, pulled out a dollar bill and tossed it in the cup. "I hope you're telling the truth. I'd hate to know my money is going to support a drug habit."

"I can assure you it isn't," I said as he turned his back to me and walked away. I stayed in that spot until I collected five dollars, then hurried off to feed myself, knowing I would do this again until Benny's money arrived from his father, and ultimately I would receive my financial aid.

I was a real neophyte as a college student. So dumb I didn't know I had to buy textbooks for my classes. They allowed me to take history and psychology along with my remedial reading class. I also had a physical education class. I felt foolish one day while walking back to the dorm with Joanna Rogers. She was in my history class, lived in the same dorm I stayed in and played basketball. She had her history book tucked under her arm. I was curious so I asked.

"Where'd you get the history book?"

She looked dumbfounded. "What do you mean where'd I get the history book? I bought it in the bookstore, silly."

"Why'd you buy it?" I continued this embarrassing line of questioning. "I didn't buy one."

"You have to buy a textbook, David."

"You mean I have to buy a book for history?"

"Not only history, but all your classes."

"I never knew that and nobody ever told me," I said.

Suddenly Joanna broke out laughing, but she touched me gently on the arm, stopped and said, "I'm sorry David, but everyone in college knows you have to buy books for all your classes, except P.E. and sometimes you might have to get a book for P.E. also. No way you can pass your classes without books. You'd better get over to the book store and get them before you flunk all your classes."

"How much do they cost?"

"A whole lot."

We'd reached our dorm and Joann patted my arm. "A whole lot," she repeated.

I headed toward my room with her three words reverberating in my mind. I didn't have money to eat. How was I going to get enough to buy books? And if I did get them, I couldn't read but a few words inside the pages. I was struggling along, and it really didn't look good for me.

After classes I always headed over to the gym where the head coach allowed me to shoot around with the team. I played inter-squad pick up games with them. The players under scholarship were impressed with my ability. The coach promised to let me tryout for the team once I cleared probation and was in compliance with Proposition 48. They had a pretty good team and, along with me, would have challenged for the division championship. But that was not to be that year or any other year in the future at Lamar. I failed all my courses with the exception of P.E. and history. The history professor gave me a "D" even though I should have received an "F". He gave me the "D" because I visited his office all the time and that convinced him I was trying.

Two of my closest allies in my struggle to survive that first semester were the Smith twins, sisters to Kevin Smith an outstanding Dallas Cowboy defensive back. They often provided me with food and financial assistance when I had nothing, and that was most of the time. I often had nothing even after I began receiving financial aid. After the financial assistance kicked in my problem stemmed from having to help Mama back home. She struggled trying to feed and clothe Ronnie, James, and Nicole. Just when I received a check, she would call complaining that the lights were about to be turned off or they didn't have enough food, and this went on continuously. I automatically sent one half my financial aid to her and tried to survive on what was left. At the first of the month, I ate well, but by the end of that month I was broke and begging. That's when the Smith twins always came to my rescue.

I stood outside their dorm room located right below mine, knocking on their door. I was hungry and wanted to see if they had any leftovers, and anything I might be able to cook.

"Who is it?"

"It's me, David."

After a brief interlude the door swung open and one of the girls said. "Hey, what's up?"

"You know what's up. I'm hungry."

"Yeah, all the time," she retorted.

"Come on, don't you guys have anything?"

"No, but we do have a potato you can cook." She went in the cupboard and got the potato.

It was a nice size and I figured I could cut it up and make French fries. Now if I could find someone else with some kind of meat or cold cuts, I'd be set for the evening.

"Thanks," I said and opened the door. "I'm so hungry I can't hang around and talk." I closed the door and trotted back to my room.

I cut the potato into long, thin pieces and tossed them into the frying pan filled with hot grease. I figured while they cooked I'd visit a couple friends down the hall and salvage something from them. I headed out the room with the fries cooking well.

My friend had some leftover ground round and I could make a hamburger to go with the fries. I thanked him and turned to leave. Benny, Michael and I had no furniture in our apartment. We slept on the floor. We didn't have a television, so when I saw *Good Times* playing on my friend's set, I lost all track of what I should be doing. It felt good to sit down on a couch, settle back and watch a little television, especially with my favorite actress center stage.

An hour later I heard Benny shouting my name outside the door. I jumped up and swung the door open. "Hey man, what's going on?"

"You left the stove on and whatever you were cooking burnt up and now it's full of smoke. It stinks like hell in there."

"Oh shit," I shrieked, and ran down to our apartment with Benny right behind me.

I yanked the door open and was inundated with smoke. I quickly closed it and we ran down the hall to call the fire department. Pandemonium broke loose as students ran from their rooms and to the closest exit. I heard the sirens from the fire engines as Benny and I followed the other students out of the building. As I ran out of the building, I thought what a price to pay for relaxing in front of my friend's television while admiring Thelma.

Damage to the apartment amounted to fifteen hundred dollars and Lamar put a hold on all my records. Despite failing all but two of my classes I was still eligible to register for the spring semester, but first I would have to pay the fifteen hundred dollars. I went home to Freeport and decided not to return to Lamar. I was out of school, with no job and that created serious problems for me at home.

CHAPTER 25

⸻

I spent a lot of time hanging around Brazosport High School when I got back from Lamar. J.B. was now a senior and the star of the basketball team. I hung out with him when he was not in class. It was a violation of school rules for ex-students to enter the building so I hid from the monitors. One morning a hall monitor caught me walking a young girl to class.

"David Floyd, what are you doing on school property?" he snapped at me.

"I don't know," I replied. I really didn't know why I was there nor did I know what I was doing.

"I suggest you vacate these premises immediately or I will call the authorities."

This happened to be a teacher I never had but didn't like me at all. A couple times my junior year, we had run-ins, and he meant what he said. He would happily have me arrested. In fact there would be a celebration in the teacher's lounge. I hustled out of the school and went home.

Mama waited for me in the living room. She had that expression of disgust and anger only she could display. Something was wrong and it had to do with me.

"David, what are you doing hanging out up there at the high school?" She tore right into me.

"I don't know," I said sheepishly. "I ain't got nothing else to do, so I was up there talking to J.B."

"Ain't you and J.B. talked enough for the past fifteen years that you don't have to be up at that school bothering them folks? One of the vice-principals called me today out of courtesy. Told me that if they catch you up there again, they going to have you arrested."

"Mama, they're just talking. They ain't going to do nothing."

"All these years, David, and you ain't never been arrested. Now you going to wait till you get out of school to go to jail," she said just as if she didn't hear me.

"Mama, I ain't going to go to jail," I reiterated with emphasis.

Tears filled Mama's eyes, her expression changed, voice mellowed.

"David, this is breaking my heart. All the struggle we have been through and now look at you," Mama paused to catch her breath. Her voice choked and she wiped her eyes. "I know I did wrong by you when I'd leave you at Mama's and go off to Florida. But David, I was young and thinking about myself. I never realized how I was hurting you. Then I did stop going."

"Mama, I…"

"I don't want to hear what you got to say right now," she interrupted me. "I don't want you to end up like a lot of these young kids. I don't want you to turn out to be nothing." She again stopped for a moment. "Look at you, don't have a job and just hanging around here. I really believed you would do more with your life just like Levi."

Watching my Mama cry brought a sense of shame. I couldn't do this to her. The two of us had fought some battles like the time I tried to stomp on her foot, but I loved her, if for no other reason than she was Mama. The same way I loved my Dad even though he disappointed me on numerous occasions. I had to do something to make this right. I had to find a job.

Next morning I got up before Mama and walked three miles to one of the most popular restaurants in town. Rick, who I'd known for years, owned On the River Restaurant. I caught him as he parked his car.

"What's going on Rick?" I asked. We shook hands and walked inside.

"Not much, how about you? I thought you'd be playing ball somewhere?" he said.

"I had a few set backs, but I'm still working on it."

"What brings you around this early in the morning?" he asked.

"I need a job, Rick." I got right to the point. "I need to help Mama with some of the bills, and I have to do something other than lay around the house."

"You need to be in school, David," he scoffed. "You have so much potential I hate to see you waste it hanging around this place." Rick was an avid Brazosport High basketball fan and knew what a great job I did helping our team to win division my senior year. He knew my ability in creating a winning atmosphere and wanted me to take that ability outside Freeport. But I needed a job because Mama cried and that was not acceptable.

"I know, and I plan to return to school and get my degree in accounting, but I have to work right now."

He walked over and opened his office door. "I'll see what we can do. Drew, can you come in here for a minute," he called out to his manager. Instantly I had second thoughts. Working under Drew was not my ideal plan. We didn't get along at all. My instinct told me to get out of there, but Mama's tears told me to stay.

The following Monday I started work at the restaurant under Drew's supervision. We didn't care much for each other, and it wouldn't be long before our relationship went sour. For starters I dreaded the work he assigned to me. I worked nights bussing dishes from the tables and mopping the floors after the restaurant closed. They expected the restaurant to be squeaky clean before I left that night. I could never satisfy Drew. He complained constantly.

"David, get over here and bus these dishes off this table. They been sitting here and we got customers waiting."

I rushed to the table, removed the dirty dishes and cleaned the top.

Before I could get those dishes to the back he called out, "There's another table over here and the floor is dirty. Looks like somebody dumped half the food on the floor. Get over here and get this up."

I seemed to be going in all directions at the same time. The more he pushed me the angrier I got.

"Drew, man, why don't you back off a little? I'm doing the best I can," I finally said to him.

"That's not enough," he snapped. "You got to speed up your pace. Tables have to be cleaned so customers don't have to wait too long. We don't want them to leave and go somewhere else."

"Yeah, like there are so many choices in Freeport," I whispered while hurrying to clean another table. I wanted to throw one of the dishes at his head and walk out. But I remembered Mama's tears and took his abuse.

One night I showed up for work, and my cousin Previn, the same boy who busted my mouth at Lincoln Park, was there, working as a cook. I had suggested Rick give him a job, but I never thought it would be one better than mine. I was irate. That night I slung dishes, was rude to the waitresses, and pouted the entire night.

Next day I showed up early while Rick was still there. There was no need for me to talk with Drew. I had to talk with the owner and let him know I was not happy. Previn had a better job and made ten dollars an hour while I only earned $4.50. I also had to let him know how Drew treated me. He kicked his feet up on his desk and heard me out.

After I finished he swung his legs back off the desk, got up and came over to sit next to me in the other chair.

"I figured you might want that job and that's exactly why I didn't give it to you," he said. "And I know Drew is being tough on you because I told him to."

"Why? What did I do," I asked somewhat in disbelief.

"It's what you didn't or are not trying to do," he replied. "I didn't give you the cook's job because I thought you would become too content with it. You'd settle for a cook's job at ten dollars an hour and that would be the extent of your ambition, and I wasn't going to let that happen. You have too much talent and ability to settle for working here and going nowhere." He reached over and placed his hand on my shoulder. "Previn doesn't have your ambition or talent, so that job is good for him and it's not for you."

He shifted around in the chair. "And I told Drew to make your life miserable every minute you spent on that do-nothing job of bussing dishes and mopping floors. I want him to make you miserable enough that you'll run to the nearest college and enroll. I won't let you be content with this. Previn, yes, you, no."

Rick walked around and sat in the chair behind his desk. "Now go back to that minimum wage job, take the shit until you finally make up your mind to do something about it, and I know you will."

As I started bussing the dishes, I realized that someone, other than Mama, cared about me. At some point I would have to accept Rick's advice and do exactly what he suggested. Ironically, that point came late in the evening just before we closed.

Three young white men, two who I recognized from Brazosport High, the third I didn't recognize, came in just before we closed and ordered dinner. The place was practically empty and I was ready to start cleaning the place, but now couldn't until they finished eating. I stood back in a corner with a white apron wrapped around me, and a mop in my hand. One of the young men kept staring over at me. I figured he probably knew me from the basketball team and was telling his friends of my outstanding play on the court.

The three of them finally got up to leave and I hurried over to clean the table. The young man who had stared at me, turned back and this time pointed his finger in my direction. I heard him say to his friends.

"See that guy over there cleaning our table." The other two looked back at me and he continued. "Man he was one hell of a basketball player last year, but look at him now. Cleaning our dirty dishes. That's what happens to their people." They all chuckled, headed down the stairway and out of the restaurant.

My first inclination was to attack him just as I did in the past. But I fought it off. After mopping the floors, I hurried out of the restaurant determined to visit with Mr. Smedley, at Brazosport High the next morning.

My mind was now made up. I would go back to school, learn to read, and not only get a Bachelor's degree, but a Ph.D. In the future my mother would only cry tears of joy for my accomplishments. I could do it simply because any individual who endured what I had over the past years, possessed a mindset to achieve the impossible.

Mr. Smedley sat and listened as I explained my intentions to him. Every once in a while he smiled, especially when I expressed my determination not to be stopped by anything or anyone. He saw a new person in me and liked it a whole lot.

"So you want to get a Ph.D. in accounting?" he asked.

"Yes sir, no doubt. I will get a Ph.D., not I want to."

"You can't read David." He gave me a hard stare. "How you going to go from a nineteen year old boy who probably shouldn't have graduated from high school to a Ph.D.?"

"With great determination and your help," I said.

"You know I'll do anything I can. What do you need from me?"

"Right now, two things. Help me choose the best college for me, given my problem with reading and help me fill out the financial aid package like you did before."

"When do you want to get started?"

"Right now, right this minute."

Mr. Smedley strolled over to his shelves of college catalogues, lined up neatly and in alphabetical order. He took three out, came back around his desk and sat next to me.

"Let's take a look at three Texas colleges I think best suit you, and that's all I can do today," he said. "Tomorrow we can work on the financial aid package."

"Okay with me," I concurred. I'm sure he picked up the sheer determination in my tone.

"What about basketball?" he asked as he opened the catalogue from Texas College, an all Black college in Tyler Texas. "The colleges I'm going to suggest do not play NCAA basketball. This might be the end of your dreams to play in the pros."

His words hit me like a sledgehammer to the head. All my life I dreamt of a professional basketball career, but now it was time for a reality check. Basketball always served as compensation for my failure to read. Now it was time to let it go. I had to give up my crutch and make a serious commitment to overcome my handicap. My day had come to make realistic decisions about the future and it did not include basketball, but it did include reading.

"I'll have to let it go, Mr. Smedley," I said solemnly. "Don't get me wrong, I'll always love the sport. But it's not designed for men 5 foot 8, but men 6 foot 8. Accounting is designed for anyone with a will and determination. That is the new David Floyd."

A smile covered his face and he continued, "Paul Quinn in Waco is another possibility for you and then there is Huston-Tilloston in Austin. Take your pick, and tomorrow we'll go to work to make this happen."

The next day I let him know my choice was Huston-Tilloston because it was closer to home. I believe he would have preferred me to pick Texas College because it was his alma mater, but accepted my choice. We then filled out the financial aid package. Without aid there was no way I could attend Huston-Tillotson. My record was following me and I still owed Lamar fifteen hundred dollars for the damage caused by the smoke.

Since going to work for Rick, I had given most of the money I made to Mama for bills. That also changed as I put most of it into a savings account. Before I could get any additional aid I had to clear that outstanding debt at Lamar. That soon became a problem. As fast as I gave Mama money she spent it. Now I had to stop doing that because I had to pay off my debt. Over the next four months I saved twelve hundred dollars. Within that next month I'd have all fifteen hundred and could pay Lamar. But Mama had different plans for my money.

One morning she woke me and nonchalantly said, "David I need three hundred dollars for the light bill. If it's not paid today, they're going to turn them off."

I rose up in the bed and said, "I can't do that. I almost have enough to pay off Lamar, and I'll be eligible for financial aid at Huston-Tillotson."

Mama had never heard me say "no" to her. When she asked, she expected to receive.

"What do you mean, you can't do that." Her voice shrilled. "You have to do it. We can't be in here with no electricity."

"I can't help that, Mama. I'm not going to give you the money I need for college. I can't let you do that to me."

"What? Are you crazy or something, boy? I need the money to keep the electricity on for your brothers and your sister."

"Mama, please I'm too close. You can't ask me to give up now."

"You ain't giving up shit," she shouted. "You'd better give me that damn money."

I hated letting Mama down, but there was no way I could give her any of the money I'd been saving for almost five months. Even at my age she could beat me, curse me, and I didn't care. That money was my ticket out of Freeport, and come hell or high water it would serve that purpose only.

"You little Black bastard, I can't believe you're going to refuse," Mama screamed. She hit me with her balled fist and I simply turned away from her.

"Mama, I'm not going to do it. Now if you want me to leave, I'll go stay with J.B."

Mama glared at me for a very long moment, then turned, walked to her bedroom and slammed the door behind her. She understood that I would not be dissuaded from my mission. After another month I had the fifteen hundred dollars needed to pay off Lamar

University, and then received a financial aid stipend for Huston-Tillotson.

With my financial aid papers and the application for admission to Huston-Tilloston, I was now prepared to start my life outside Freeport. On a Monday morning when students were scheduled to register for classes, I boarded a Greyhound Bus in Freeport with a transfer in Houston and started out on a new chapter in my life. The old David was left behind, and the new one headed out, determined this time to achieve the goal of a Ph.D. in the years to come.

PART II

CHAPTER 26

I arrived at the Greyhound Bus Depot in Austin at 10:30 AM and caught a cab. With one duffle bag containing all the clothes I owned, my financial aid papers and application for admission to the college filled out, the Yellow Cab dropped me off at the front gate to Huston-Tillotson. I felt both exhilaration and apprehension. My heart raced as I walked up to the guard station.

With the exception of fighting and basketball, most exercises in life were difficult for me. I had limited knowledge of the world outside of Freeport, and could only read at the second grade level. My family life had been dysfunctional with men in and out of our home like flies. Those who should have nurtured me were a grandmother who often told me as a young child that I was black, ugly, and therefore of little value to society, and a mother, who, only a few days back, cursed me out because I wouldn't give her my school money to pay the light bill. From that world, I was entering into one that I knew very little about, but knew I must conquer it or my life would, as Langston Hughes poetically put it, "fester like a sore and dry up."

The January sun seemed hotter than usual. From the one semester at Lamar, I knew I must locate the registration office. I approached the guard inside the booth. He glared at me as though I was from outer space.

"Where would I find the registration for new students?" I politely asked.

He looked at my duffle bag and then at me. He gave a slight smirk and pointed in the direction of a brick building to the right of where we stood. "Second building on the right."

"Thank you," I said and headed in that direction.

As I got closer I saw a long line stretching around the side of the building. I strolled to the back of the line, stood behind the last student and asked. "Is this the registration line?"

"Yeah, kind of long isn't it?"

"Sure is," I agreed.

"And it's moving kind of slow. Be prepared for a long wait. I already been out here over an hour."

"That doesn't sound like fun."

"It isn't," he replied and turned his back to me.

I took that as a strong hint he didn't care to engage in conversation. That was unfortunate because I wanted to pick his brain about the college, the professors, and students so I'd know what to expect. I switched my focus from him to the campus. It was small, very small. The entire campus appeared to be one-fourth the size of Lamar.

A number of students, who probably had already registered, wandered the grounds with their parents. Many parents stood in line with their sons or daughters. No one was there with me. It reminded me of my first day in kindergarten when Levi and I made that trip to O.A. Fleming alone. Mama was in Florida and Grandma at work. The conditions and location had change, but the empty feeling didn't.

I choked back tears and fiddled with the eleven dollars I had tucked in my pocket after purchasing the Greyhound ticket and paying the taxi driver. That was all the money I had. The duffle bag across my shoulder contained my entire wardrobe of three tee shirts and pairs of underwear, four pairs of socks, one pair of cutoff shorts, and I was wearing the only pair of shoes I owned, run down penny loafers purchased at the Goodwill store before I left. Standing in that line, at the end of which lay my future, I felt empty and useless. My entire life was consumed with poverty, and being at Huston-Tillotson, with no support from family, either financially or psychologically, I was scared. Was all this my fault, or Mama's, or did fault lie somewhere else?

Suddenly, loneliness and self-pity gave way to fierce determination to succeed. The focal point of my drive had always been to never give up, like scoring that one basket on Uncle Lynn, or enduring Bobby's vicious whippings, and of course, Mrs. Hassenback's comment that "I'd never amount to anything." How should I measure my fear of loneliness and apprehension of a new existence in the context of past experiences?

I finally stood in front of the man registering students for classes.

"Your name," he said without looking up. A notebook of green bar computer paper loaded with names, sat on the table in front of him.

"David Floyd," I said almost in a whisper.

I watched as he leafed through the pages, finally stopped and read the names. He turned the page and then turned back again, doing that a couple times.

"That's interesting," he mumbled. He spent another half-minute studying those pages. "Did you attend Huston-Tillotson last semester?" he asked.

"No sir, I didn't."

"So you're a second semester transfer?"

"What's that mean?"

The registrar stared up at me with a slight frown. "It means you're entering college in the spring semester and not the fall when most students enter."

I took my duffle bag off my shoulder and set it on the ground in front of me. "Yes sir, I guess so. Is something wrong with that?"

"Most students start in the fall, but no, there is nothing wrong with it," he answered. "But there is a problem because I don't have you listed as a registered student." He paused, looked another place in the large notebook, and then looked back at me. "When did you send in your application for admission?"

"I have my application with me and it's all filled out."

"You didn't submit your application for admission?"

"No, I didn't. I thought I could do that when I came up here. I do have my approval for financial aid."

"That's only half the process young man. Financial aid means nothing without first being admitted to an institution."

"So what does that mean?"

"It means you are not admitted to this college and you'll have to wait until the fall semester to be admitted."

My legs weakened under me and I almost fell to the ground. He couldn't be serious. I thought back to Lamar and realized that Mr. Smedley had done all the work to get me admitted. He had evidently sent the application in early, and I didn't even know it. I just showed up at registration and chose my classes. I thought that was all I had to do this time too. Now, this man sat there and told me I couldn't attend Huston-Tillotson when classes began in a couple days. I had to get into college; there was no other option. I had to convince this man to bend his rules and admit me. I didn't even have enough money to get back home.

"Sir, you have to let me register," I pleaded. "You see, I can't go back home, in fact I don't have enough money to get back home." I pulled out two five dollar bills and the one, and shoved them toward him.

"There is nothing I can do," he said. "I have no record of you, and as far as this school is concerned you just don't exist. I'm sorry." He sounded sincere.

I heard students behind me grumbling. Someone in line shouted, "Come on man, hurry up. It's hot out here."

His complaint caught the attention of the registrar. He closed his book and said, "I'm really sorry, but there is absolutely nothing further I can do. The only person with authority to admit you now is the president."

"Where is he?" I asked.

The man pointed to a large building across the grassy mall. "In that building. When you get inside turn left and you can't miss it."

I hoisted my bag over my shoulder, turned and walked away. One single voice from a student in the line shouted, "Good luck."

I entered Dr. McMillan's office apprehensive of my future at Huston-Tillotson, even before the semester began. I was about to ask the president to do me a favor. No principal of any school I attended ever did me a favor. To the contrary, they always made my life miserable. Why would this man in charge be any different? My knees wobbled, my heartbeat increased, my fear of failure took over.

Memories of standing under the basket and the coach telling me I had to touch the backboard to make A team returned. Should I turn and walk away as I did that day? I'd rather abandon this pursuit of education than face rejection. But then I also recalled Mama's tears and her fear that my life was doomed to failure, just another lost black man in the mire of the east end of Freeport. Suddenly I felt a new thrust of energy, and with great reluctance I approached Dr. McMillan's secretary. I could see him in his office to the left.

"Good afternoon, m'am, I need to see President McMillan," I said.

"Do you have an appointment?"

"No m'am, I don't."

"What is this all about?"

I noticed Dr. McMillan staring at me over the top of his glasses for a moment before he returned to his writing.

"Well, m'am, it's kind of a long story," I started. I set my duffle bag on the floor. "I came up here from Freeport to go to college, and stood in line to register for a couple hours. When I got to the front, the man told me I was not registered to attend Huston-Tillotson, and that I would have to register first and return next semester, but you see, m'am I can't wait that long. I got to get…

"Wait, slow down," she interrupted me. "What do you mean you're not registered? You didn't apply for admission by the deadline date back in November."

"No m'am, I didn't know I had to apply early. I thought I could give you my application when I got here." I dug in my pocket and pulled out what was now a rather crumpled application. "Mr. Smedley at my high school helped me fill out the application for financial aid, and I also have that paper work approving my aid with me. I now pulled out that document and placed it on her desk. "And you see, I got to get admitted because I don't even have enough money to get back home. I got eleven dollars to my name."

I pulled out the money and also placed it on her desk. "When the man told me I had to already be admitted, and there was nothing he could do, and the only person who could help me was Dr. McMillan, I hurried over here. 'Cause I just got to get admitted today."

"Just a minute," she said, got up and disappeared in Dr. McMillan's office, closing the door behind her.

It seemed an eternity before that door swung open and she walked back out. She smiled and said, "Dr. McMillan will see you."

His office was massive, elaborate and reeked of authority. He had a large oak executive desk, with a high back executive chair. Plaques and awards hung from the walls. The ambiance was both impressive and intimidating to a boy who grew up in delapidated houses with holes in the floor.

Dr. McMillan removed his glasses and leaned forward on his desk. "How can I help you young man?"

"I need your permission to register for classes." I felt nervous energy burning through me. I was actually talking with the president of the college. "The man outside at the table told me the only way I can get into your college is if I see you. He said something about I didn't apply ahead of time and that only you could let me in." I was beginning to feel a little foolish having to repeat the same story three times, revealing my naivete.

"Why didn't you apply?"

"Honest, sir, I didn't know I had to. I applied for my financial aid and got approved. That's all I thought I needed." I showed him the financial aid papers. "See sir, I got them right here."

He took the papers, glanced at them and handed them right back to me. We stood staring at each other and that's when I broke down. Tears freely flowed down my face. Again, my legs buckled and I placed my hand on the edge of the chair in front of the desk to keep from falling.

"Sir, you just got to let me in. I can't go back home because there is nothing good for me. I'm trying to get out of that life." I paused to wipe the tears. "Everyone and everything has failed me but I kept on fighting. I don't want to end up as just another statistic either in jail like a lot of my friends or dead like my cousin and Don and Moppie." I don't know why I called those names. Dr. McMillan knew nothing about their deaths or my past.

He continued to stare at me, and I knew he was not touched by my story. Why should he be, and why did I think he would care for a boy who didn't know enough to get admitted to the school before showing up to register? He must have thought I was some kind of ghetto fool. Assuming I had failed, I lifted my duffle bag and prepared to leave.

"I'm going to admit you on a special provision," Dr. McMillan said.

He pulled some papers from inside his desk drawer. Stunned, I stood there while he filled them out and handed them to me.

"Take these to the registration desk. They'll have to set you up to take some tests in order to determine what classes you should take. It is simply a placement test. We need to test your skills in reading, writing, and math." He stood up and glared at me across his desk. "You said you wanted a new life and a new start. This is your chance. Huston-Tillotson is giving you that opportunity. Don't let the university or me down."

I stuffed the papers in my pocket. This time tears of joy flowed down my face. "I won't sir, I promise you."

"Drop by from time to time and let me know how you're doing."

"I will sir, don't worry." I hurried out of his office and the building.

For the next four years he might have come to regret telling me to keep him informed as to my progress. That was something I had no problem doing.

CHAPTER 27

The bright Texas afternoon sun shined down on me when I walked outside after receiving Dr. McMillan's approval to enroll, and I took it all in. I glared directly up into the bright rays and for the first time in a long while, I smiled. I was a college student and this time I would make it work for me. Energized by the sun and Dr. McMillan's signature, I headed back to the registration line that was now even longer than when I first arrived on campus.

With my spirits soaring I took my place in the line and engaged the young lady in front of me in conversation.

"This your first semester?" I asked

"No, I'm a sophomore, my second semester," she said.

The young brother in front of me, then joined in. "What are you?" he asked.

"What do you mean, what am I?" I asked.

"Are you a sophomore, freshman, first semester or what," she answered. "I don't ever remember seeing you on campus and this is a pretty small school. Everybody pretty much knows everybody else."

"This is my first semester," I replied. "In fact, this is my first day on campus."

"You weren't here in the fall?" the young lady asked.

"No, I wasn't."

"That's kind of different. Most people start their college career in the fall, not the spring," the young brother said.

"Oh well, I guess you can say I've always done things different." I wondered about a school so small everyone knew each other. What is it they would get to know about me and just how would

I fit into such a small, rather cliquish school. It wouldn't take me long to find out.

After standing in that line for two hours with the hot sun burning down and no cover from its rays, I finally reached the front of the line. The man who first helped me smiled and said, "See you got it done. Good job."

"Thanks," I said. "What do I do next?"

"The first thing you must do is to take an assessment test, because we don't know exactly where you should start?"

"Do I do that today?"

"Yes, you do. You need to go to the assessment office back in the building where the president is, but on the second floor. Go do that now, and then they will let you know what classes you're eligible to register for."

With all paperwork now in place, I started back across the grassy mall and into the building. Climbing the stairs to the second floor, I thought how much more thorough Huston-Tillotson seemed to be over Lamar University. They never did any of this at the university. I thought it might be due to Huston-Tillotson being a Historical Black College and the administration taking more interest in its students.

Whatever the reason I took the examinations, and the results were as expected. I was required to take remedial reading, writing, and math. I also took a survival class. It turned out to be a valuable lesson on how to succeed as a college student.

One final chore I had to do that day was to get my housing in the dorm. Now registered, I headed to the housing manager's office. With considerable pep in my step I bounced into the manager's office. The man sitting behind the desk looked up at me, but I spoke before he had a chance.

"My name is David Floyd. Dr. McMillan told me to come over here and get my housing. I have financial aid, but it hasn't arrived yet. Here are the papers from Dr. McMillan giving me permission to get a room."

"I'm Reverend Lewis head of student housing," the man said as he picked up the papers I had laid on his desk, and examined them. He then looked up at me and smiled. "Okay, let me see what I have." He looked behind him at a wall filled with keys and numbers above them. He pulled one down and turned back to me. "You'll be in Dormitory A and Room 140. All I need now is the $28.00 deposit for the key."

"Reverend Lewis, I only have eleven dollars."

"You came all the way down here with eleven dollars?"

"I did have a little more, but I had to pay the cab fare from the Greyhound Bus depot."

"How do you plan to make it?"

"I got financial aid coming and I can pay the difference when I get my first check."

"That won't be necessary," he said and thrust the key toward me. "Just don't lose it because I won't be able to give you another one."

"No sir, I won't."

The dorm was filled with students returning for the second semester. They had parents or friends there to help carry in their belongings. One young girl hurried up to her dorm room door, opened it while an older man carried a small refrigerator inside. Further down the hall another man carried a small television inside a dorm room, followed by a very cute young girl. All around me students chattered and laughed with family helping to get them settled in. Where was my support base, my family sharing this joyous time with me? Levy was in the navy and Mama didn't have enough money to get my two brothers and sister to Austin. I was once again alone, but I fought back the tears and feeling of depression. I was in school, moving forward with my life and that's what mattered.

My roommate was a rather oddball guy. I'd never known a black who rode skateboards, and that's all he cared to do. I'd never known a black with a pompadour hairstyle, with it all sticking up in the front, like a return to the late 1950's. I'd never imagined a black

Elvis Presley would be my roommate. Turns out I couldn't have found a better person to room with because he was never there. I essentially had the place to myself. Torry was his name, and we got along just fine because we seldom saw each other. I figured out what part of the room he occupied and then claimed my small niche. I put the duffle bag in a small closet and put the sheets on the bed. It had been a very long day for me, and I was exhausted. I fell down on the bed and drifted off to sleep with a broad smile on my face.

The next morning after breakfast, the first person I met was Mrs. Valerie Curry, one of the counselors. I was at her office when it first opened at nine. I sat waiting for her to finish reviewing my test scores.

"You've already signed up for remedial reading and writing as well as remedial math," she said. "You also have the required survival class. I think that is enough for your first semester. She put the papers down on her desk. "I now need for you to declare a major or would you prefer to wait until after you complete the first semester of remedial classes?"

"No m'am, I know what I want to major in."

"You do?" She looked surprised

"Yes m'am, I'm going to get my degree here in accounting, and then I plan to keep going and get my masters and Ph.D."

Mrs. Curry glanced at my test score again and then up at me. "Are you sure?"

"Never been more sure of anything in my life. I had an accounting teacher who kicked me out of her class in high school and told me I'd never amount to anything in life. I told her I wouldn't only amount to something, but would do better than her in accounting, and get a Ph.D."

"Isn't that a rather strange reason to major in a subject?"

"It might seem that way to some, but it's exactly what I'm going to do."

She wrote my major on a document, slipped it into a folder and said. "Whatever floats your boat. You're all set for classes tomorrow. Good luck."

I strolled out of Mrs. Curry's office and out of the administration building feeling the magnitude of what I had accomplished in two days. I showed up at Huston-Tilloston with a duffle bag and eleven dollars. In a day, I was admitted to the school, with full financial aid that covered my tuition and living expenses. I didn't want to wait until tomorrow. I wished the classes would start right then at nine-thirty in the morning. I was already a year behind my high school graduating class. I had to catch up. But first I relished my accomplishment. A young man reading at the second grade level made it back to the university. That alone was an incredible feat, but not quite enough for me. I still had a major battle before me, but I was ready to take it on.

CHAPTER 28

H aving settled in for a second chance at college life, I began classes and found I was confronted with the same nemesis that plagued me since first grade. Remedial reading brought old memories of students laughing because I failed to read my lines when called upon. It brought back memories of fighting because of the teasing, and trying so hard to succeed that I would actually get sick when I failed. I never imagined that I would be called upon to read in front of the other students in college.

It happened the second week of class. Mrs. Roder, the instructor and a wonderful person who helped me immensely, called on me to read a paragraph from a fourth grade reader.

"Tttthhhe bbbboooy wwwho…"

"That's okay, David," Mrs. Roder said. "We'll come back to you. Relax and realize we are all friends in this class."

But we weren't all friends. My reading level was the very lowest and when I tried to read, just as it happened in elementary and intermediate school, college students laughed. The irony is that they were also in a remedial reading class. Vicky Clay, also a freshman and from San Antonio, Texas, was the most vicious of all my fellow classmates. One day after class, she couldn't get over to the student lounge fast enough just to ridicule me. Not only did she make fun of my inability to read, but also attacked my dress, especially the shoes. Vicky pegged me with the nickname of Pealo, because my penny loafers were so run over.

She strolled up to a group of students, sitting in chairs at a table playing cards, and announced, "Pealo is a trip, can't read worth a damn. Here he goes in class, 'bbbbeeecccaussse tttthhhey ddddiddn't'…"

The other students broke out laughing.

"How'd he do it?" a girl sitting at the table asked for a repeat performance so they might get another laugh at another person's problem.

Vicky was now on a roll. She had everyone's attention as they stopped playing cards and looked directly at her. I stood in the background trying to smile, but all the time hurting inside. I was the same David admired in high school as the star athlete, and now I was being derided by this absolutely ugly human being.

She continued, "I thought I was bad. I read like Einstein compared to David. I don't believe he can read a kindergarten book."

"Hey Pealo, she sure talking about you," one of the young men sitting at the table spoke up. "You going to let her talk about you that way?

"Vicki, what you think Pealo will do first, learn to read or get some decent shoes?" The third person at the table chimed in.

I had enough. I turned and hurried out of the student lounge. I couldn't hang around and listen to the taunting, it hurt too much. Back in high school I escaped from the teasing by fighting. I didn't care who you were, Kikki and Tanya, J.B.'s sisters or Hayward Barnes, the boy Ronnie busted in the head on 'nigger trail", I would start swinging if you made fun of me. What I had discovered, however, was that fighting never changed my condition. After the violence I still couldn't read. Instead of fighting now I turned and walked away.

When I reached my dorm room I lay on my bed and cried incessantly. I couldn't stop crying because the teasing hurt so badly. I recalled the conversation I had while standing in line to register. Huston-Tillotson was a very small and tight community of students. Vicky was trying to set me up as the fall guy within that community. The one person everyone could use to get a good laugh, relieve their anxiety and pressure. I prayed I could last the four years, and that the badgering would not run me away.

After a couple weeks of the laughing and vicious teasing I decided to sit down with Mrs. Roder and discuss it with her. We met in her office. Instantly, my eyes filled with tears.

"What is it David?" she asked. "What's bothering you?"

"It's the reading exercises in class," I said.

"I know, it's the laughing and snickering isn't it?" she knew exactly what was bothering me. "I try to control it as best I can, but they're so immature."

Unlike most of my teachers throughout elementary, intermediate, and high school, Mrs. Roder really cared. She was black, and I thought that was the difference. I'm not sure I would've made it without her. I offered a solution to the problem.

"Mrs. Roder, there was a time in my life when I would've fought every one of them laughing. I would've come out swinging, but I've matured beyond that point."

"That's good David. That makes you the better person." She walked from behind her desk and took a seat next to me. "How do you want to handle this? I don't want you to be uncomfortable in class. You'll never learn to read that way."

"What if you don't call on me in class?"

"David, you have to do the reading exercises. That's the only way you'll learn."

"Could I do it privately with you?" I asked.

Mrs. Roder sat there silently for a moment obviously thinking through the situation. I prayed that she would allow me to meet after class and read to her privately. I almost got what I prayed for.

"I tell you what we'll do," she finally said. "Instead of meeting with me after class, you'll meet with Ms. Phillips, my assistant and read to her. You still must come to class and please do not miss any of your scheduled meetings with Ms. Phillips.

I choked up and again tears welled up in my eyes. The faculty at

Huston-Tillotson was becoming my best friend, not the students, but the faculty. They cared about David Floyd, and that was a totally foreign experience for me.

"Mrs. Roder," I stood up and fought back tears, "that is something you'll never have to worry about. I will be here on time and ready to learn."

"Good, David. I know you will." She smiled at me as I turned and walked out of her office.

Ms. Phillips selected the kindergarten reader, *Buttermilk Bill and the Train* as a starter for our sessions. It was the same book Mrs. Silva, my fifth grade teacher, tried unsuccessfully to get me to read. Ms. Phillips chose this book because I told her I enjoyed trying to read it back in the fifth grade, and it was one Mama read to us years ago. I also told her that every time I stumbled on a word, I wanted to go back and start all over again. It took me three weeks to finally read it from cover to cover without stuttering or stumbling over words.

I was doing satisfactory work in the other remedial writing and math classes. One valuable lesson I learned in the Survival class was time management. We were told that every hour we spent in class should be matched with three hours of study time. I stretched it to four hours, religiously giving each class four hours of my time. I never missed and sometimes would go longer than four with the reading. After classes I took the city bus over to the University of Texas library and checked out books under an inter-college loan program. I read books on history and self-improvement most of the time. Words I didn't understand I would write down and immediately go to the dictionary and look up the meaning. I was so dedicated to study that I practically had no social life at all. That is, until one afternoon when I wandered down to visit Curtis Green, one of the only friends I had on campus, in his dorm room. That is when I first met Kim.

A pretty, dark-skinned young sister, with plenty of nerve and personality, I fell for Kim the first time I saw her. She was on campus with her friend, Rochelle Baker, who was dating Curtis at the time.

That day my brain was like mush from six hours of constant studying, so I took a break. When I walked in I spotted Kim sitting on the bed talking with Rochelle.

"Who is that?" I asked Curtis.

"Kim. She's Rochelle's best friend. I guess from your staring you want to meet her."

"You darn right I do."

We went back into the bedroom, the introduction was done, and I sat there the rest of the afternoon talking to this beautiful black princess. She told me she was eighteen and planned to attend Huston-Tillotson in the fall. Later on in the afternoon, we went down to my dorm room. I'd forgotten that earlier I had washed my few pair of underwear and they were hanging up in the room. I quickly retrieved them and shoved them in the dresser drawer. We laughed, and from that time on, she became my constant companion on and off campus until I found out she was only 17, still in high school and had been skipping school to hang out on campus.

Because of the number of times she'd missed class, she was classified as a high school freshman, when she should have been a junior. I was furious with her and threatened to break off the relationship unless she changed her attitude about school.

When Kim found out how serious I was about education, instead of hanging out at Huston-Tillotson she went to class. I didn't want to lose her because she was the first girl I ever loved, but she had to finish her education in order to be with me. I would catch the bus to her high school and find her car in the parking lot just to make sure she was there. She was always there and we were back on track with our relationship.

My progress in the four classes pleased me to no end. As we neared the end of the first semester my reading level improved to fourth-grade. Kim became real important in my progress. We spent hours in the dorm room working on my reading drills. She held up flash cards, and I pronounced the word and identified it in the book I was reading. I then had to explain its meaning in the sentence where it was found. Slowly, I was conquering my demon and it felt good. I smiled every time I thought I might make it. I might run this race and win. I owed it all to Mrs. Roder, Ms. Phillips and Kim.

CHAPTER 29

I walked out of my classroom having finished the math final exam. I held my arms high in the air and shouted, "Yes, I finished my first semester of college." Students walking along the grounds stared over at me, but I didn't care. I passed all my remedial classes and in the fall I could take a normal course load. I no longer would be pegged by the nature of the classes I attended. Kim waited for me outside. I ran up and threw both arms around her.

"I did it," I shouted.

"I know you did." She smiled.

I took her hand and we headed off campus going to a movie and a few hours of relaxation. Our last three months had been so tense, with her trying to help me with reading and then finishing her own classes, that often we would be at each other's throats. Now we would put all that behind us for a few days and just enjoy each other.

I decided not to take any summer classes that first year, so I had to vacate my dorm room. I figured I'd take off for home for a week and then come back and find a new place to live. Since I didn't get financial aid when not in school, I'd also have to find a job when I got back. I probably could have gone back and worked for Rick at Restaurant on the River, but I didn't want to spend that much time in Freeport. That chain was now permanently broken and I only wanted to visit Mama and Grandma. I knew I could find some kind of work in Austin. I took off that Friday after my final examination and headed home.

Fatigue hit me hard when I arrived back in Freeport. I slept most of the first day and all that night. While at school I never had time to get tired. All semester I adhered to my 1 to 3 rule and sometimes stretched it to 1 to 4. With four classes I was in the library or studying in the dorm for sixteen hours a day. Curtis would often tell me I was going to suffer from burn out. But those two words had no place in my vocabulary. Hard work paid off, but now at home for a week I could allow for a little down time.

Well rested after that first day I now was ready to get caught up on everything happening in Freeport since I left back in January. Nicole was in elementary school and doing well. Evidently she inherited some of Bobby's smarts. Little James was anything but little. He had grown to be a muscular young man and was the starting defensive end on Freeport Intermediate football team and definitely on his way to getting a football scholarship. He was flat out good as a player.

Most of my attention focused on Ronnie. He had dropped out of school, and word on the street was that he dealt drugs. He fell prey to the trap and I figured it was only a matter of time before the system got him because drug dealers either went to prison or died. Neither of those options was acceptable to me, and at the right time, I planned to discuss it with him.

That second day Mama prepared a feast and invited all the family. My two aunts, Uncle Ronnie and Lynn, as well as the entire crew of cousins, including Previn, came by that day. Grandma didn't make it. She wanted me to come to her, which I definitely would do before I left. I was anxious to tell her about attending a Historical Black College, about my first semester and of course about Kim. Mama got the whole story the afternoon I arrived and before I crashed.

With the entire family there I was reminded of the Sunday dinners at Grandma's house when we would all show up, Mama would get angry, and we'd leave, usually before eating. There was no arguing this time. Instead it was like a mutual admiration society. I believe Ronnie was the most elated. He couldn't stop patting me on my back and telling me how proud he was and that, if there was anything he could do to help me, just let him know. I accepted his accolades with mixed emotions. He was my brother and I loved him, but he had given up and quit. He had dropped out of school and now was selling drugs. That saddened me and also made me angry that he had let his life slip into such a state of degradation.

After the family had eaten and congratulated me for my successful first semester then left, Ronnie and I sat alone on the porch. It was the perfect time for me to challenge his lifestyle. It had to be done with finesse.

"Hey man, what does sitting on Mama's porch remind you of?" I asked.

"I don't know for sure. What's it remind you of?"

I leaned forward in the beat up lounge chair that leaned to the left. "Remember how Mama would have all of us out here just dancing and having a good time while we watched everybody else going to church."

"Oh yeah, I remember that. There was one song she loved to play. What was it?"

"*Ain't No Stopping Us Now.*"

"Man, David you sure could dance. Do you still dance up there at the university?"

"No, brother, I don't have time for that kind of thing no more. I'm about the business of studying."

"Speaking of studying how's your reading."

"Coming along real good. I'm so glad I'm at a black college with mostly black teachers. At least at Huston-Tillotson they really care." My thoughts went to Ms. Williams at Brazosport. I couldn't be unfair. She was white and she cared. "Don't get me wrong, there were a few caring teachers at Brazosport, but for the most part, they didn't care one way or another what happened to you if you weren't from a middle class family and if your parents were poor. And let's face it, we were really poor."

"We're still poor, David. Things ain't changed. You lucky man, you were able to get out of here just like Levi. You both escaped."

"You can do the same, Ronnie. You just have to change your lifestyle and mostly believe in yourself."

"Man, ain't nothing I can do. I dropped out of school 'cause I got tired of people looking at me like I'm some kind of oddball or freak. So now I do what I can to make a little money and help Mama."

"But what you doing has no future and it's wrong. You selling drugs, and drug dealers either go to jail or end up dead. Is that what you want for yourself?"

"Man, don't worry. Ain't nothing like that going to happen to me."

"Yeah, the famous last words of most drug dealers."

"There ain't nothing else I can do, David. You don't seem to understand the life I've had to live since I was five and overweight."

"There's a lot you can do, but first you got to stop using weight as a crutch for your failure. Your biggest handicap is in your mind." I paused for a moment. I had to make my brother understand he was his worst enemy. "Ronnie all these years I used basketball as a crutch. I didn't have to worry about my learning disability because I had a future in the NBA. So like I had to give up basketball as an escape from reality, you got to give up using your weight. Man go back and get your GED, and then come on up to Huston-Tillotson, and I guarantee you'll look back at all this nonsense and get a good laugh that you fell prey to this trap."

Ronnie suddenly got up and walked from one end of the porch and back, all the time hitting his balled fist in the palm of his hand. He finally stopped and stood right over me.

"Man, I just don't have a damn choice, David." His voice rose. "All I can do is hustle to help Mama. And I'll help you if you want me to."

"Ronnie, there is no way in God's world that I'll accept money from you. Don't ever offer it to me, and don't let Mama know where you getting that blood money from."

Ronnie sat back down and momentarily covered his face, then looked up and smiled. "I know it's wrong, brother, and I don't like it no more that you do. But right now I ain't got no choice. I'm caught in this trap of a place and the only way I see me getting out is in a box. I hate this shit."

Mama stepped out on the porch. "You boys come on in here and help clean the kitchen. James already done started."

Ronnie's words were unnerving and frightening. He had given up, and I didn't know how to turn him around. He had allowed the ugly side of our existence to win out and now was drowning in the squalor. He was dealing drugs, had minimum education, and worst of all, suffered from diabetes. We both got up and headed back inside the house. There was no need for me to say anything else. A chasm had developed between us and I began to doubt it could be reversed.

It was mandatory that I get down to Grandma's the next morning and spend some time with her. She was used to me attending to her needs and just sitting with her more than any of her grandchildren. I had always showed up to wash her dishes, clean the house, and run errands. Despite the pain she caused me as a child, I loved and respected her. Now that I was older I understood why she had such a negative perception of me. Since we looked a lot alike, she being very dark with the same features as I had, she disliked herself. The older she got, the less important that all became, and I believe she came to understand how irrelevant skin color was. Because I was always there for her, that eventually defined the nature of our relationship. She finally had a man in her life she could depend on, and I cherished that responsibility to her. Going home for the first time wouldn't be complete if I didn't spend some time with her.

She was sitting on the couch reading her Bible when I walked into her house about noon. She smiled at me, patted her hand on a spot next to her and said.

"Come and sit over here David."

"Yes m'am." I hurried over to the couch and sat next to her. She appeared relaxed, almost subdued and when she spoke it was reflective and a lot of recalling the past.

"I'm very proud of you David." She patted me on my thigh. "I've always believed in you and knew you could accomplish anything if you put your mind to it." She paused and a smile spread across her face. "Out of all Wanda's kids, you were always the most aggressive and ambitious. And out of all my grandchildren, you're the most attentive to me. I thank and love you for that."

This was not Grandma talking. I had to ask, "You all right, Grandma?"

"I'm fine baby. Just as fine as I can be."

Grandma turned and gave me that "deer in the headlights" look.

"Wanda should've never had all those different men over you kids," she said. "It was wrong, and them men was not good for you all."

"Whatever, Grandma, it don't matter now."

"It does, son, and I've talked about it to her. She knows the damage, especially that fool Bobby, did to you. And she knows the damage she did when she would run off to Florida all the time. She should've been here with you all." Grandma paused for a moment as if the next words were ones she knew she must say. "I know I didn't treat you all that good either when she left you here with me. But David I loved you as much as anyone else. Some of the things I said I shouldn't have, but Grandma was hurting too. I want you to forgive me for the times I made you cry. Can you forgive an old foolish woman who really is proud of you? I know you're going to soar to high places. Grandma only hopes she can live long enough to experience it."

My sight blurred from the tears that filled my eyes. I wiped them away. "Oh Grandma, it ain't nothing. I know you love me." I could think of nothing more to say. "You need me to do anything for you?

"No baby, just sit here with Grandma and let me enjoy you before you go back and get all that education. Don't let nobody stop you, cause David Floyd can accomplish anything he sets his mind to. You look like me, and you're strong like me and like your Mama. You know all three of us look just alike. We some beautiful people, ain't we David?"

"Yes, we are Grandma." I laid my head on Grandma's shoulder and this time I didn't wipe away the tears.

Two days later I packed that same duffle bag and caught the Greyhound back to Austin. My first visit home had been good for me and especially good for Grandma. I can imagine how long she had wanted to say those things to me, but waited for what she considered the proper time. I spent a lot time with her those last two days. She had said things that day that people usually think about as they near the end of this life. That bothered me and I kept asking if she was all right and how her health was holding up? Grandma assured me that she didn't plan to leave here until she got the word that I had graduated from college. With that reassurance, I rode back into Austin ready to take on the next challenge, and that was to finish my degree in three years.

CHAPTER 30

When the bus pulled into the depot, I saw Kim parked outside waiting for me. She sure looked good. We'd only been apart for a week, but I missed her so much, I couldn't wait to hug and hold her tight. I was the first off the bus, ran up to the driver's side of the car, she rolled down the window and I spoke first.

"What's happening?" I said and planted a kiss on her lips.

She smiled and said, "Not much. What's happening with you?"

I hurried to the other side and climbed in the passenger's seat. "I'll tell you all about it." I gently rubbed my hand up and down her arm. Her skin was soft and felt good to the touch. I really did care for my young, beautiful princess. I was confident I'd met the love of my life, and someday she would be my wife and have my babies. The latter came sooner than I expected.

Since I had to give up my dorm room before I left for Freeport, while down there I'd made calls back up to Austin seeking another place to live. I called practically everyone I knew who had a place and might be wiling to rent me a room. I'd made up my mind that I'd never live on campus again. I preferred to spend as little time as possible with the Huston-Tillotson student groups. I pretty much had it with being the brunt of their jokes. I avoided Vicky Clay like the plague.

A senior I had met that first semester, Kelvin Rayme, agreed to allow me to share one of the two bedrooms with another student, Ronnie Sloan, in his Point South Apartment. It was really a nice place, in fact the best living accommodations I had during my three years at Huston-Tillotson. Kelvin also had a roommate, Derrick Bonner.

Kim took me to my new living quarters, which was far on the south side and a long way from the college. When we got there I dropped off that same duffle bag with all my belongings, talked with Kelvin and met my new room mate, Ronnie Sloan, also a freshman, and then took off to spend some time with Kim. I was settled in. Now all I needed was a job, since my financial aid was cut off in the summer.

The next day, I got up early and took off looking for work. I decided to look around the area near the college. That way, I wouldn't have a long way to go after classes. I also refused to put a job before my classes and studying. Therefore, I sought work at places I could quit if they attempted to interfere with my schooling, and move on. That same day I found a job at Church's Fried Chicken, right off the campus.

George Coleman, a young brother I met playing pick-up basketball games in the college gymnasium, worked at Church's. Some of the other students had nicknamed him Chicken George because of where he worked. Working in a fast food joint was not exactly what I wanted to do but it was convenient.

I convinced Chicken George to introduce me to Joe, the manager. I found out he was looking for a cashier. Joe and I hit it off right away. He gave me the job working six hours per day, seven days a week during the summer. In the fall, when I went back to school I worked a lot less hours. But Church's would be my primary job until 1994 when I left for Bentley College.

Even with the job at Church's I was still short of money needed to pay my rent and eat. It was July and financial aid would begin again at the end of August. Somehow, I had to figure out a way to survive. Since paying rent was the number one priority, I had to use my wits to eat the days I didn't work at Church's. On my day off, I hung around the more exclusive and expensive restaurants in downtown Austin. One of the places was Don McClusky's Steak House. I strolled by the restaurant and stared inside at the patrons dressed up, sitting straight up and engaging in conversation.

The tables were covered with lace tablecloths, candlelight served to enhance the ambiance, and waiters were dressed in tuxedoes. The patrons were always smiling and seemed to be content with life. I wondered, while staring inside, why life was so unfair and what my family and many other families just like mine had done to deserve such deleterious lives. The discrepancies were so blatant, and the people inside didn't seem to care. It angered me that they led such silver spoon lives, while I couldn't get a spoon at all. I hung around until the restaurant closed at ten o'clock, then went to the back where they tossed out the scraps. I found the un-eaten cooked potatoes, took them out of the trash and ate them. That would be my supper.

The next day I'd go all day without eating if I wasn't working, make my way over to the restaurant and again retrieve the cooked potatoes out of the trash. For over a month I ate out of the trash bin at Don McClusky's Steak House. The very last time I made a promise that someday I would be able to walk through the front door, sit at a table next to those rich, happy people and also enjoy the ambiance and the food at one of the best restaurants in the city.

Between my struggles for survival I found time to practice reading. My progress that first semester with Ms. Phillips built a new confidence in me. Now I wanted more. All the barriers were removed, and nothing stood between my goal and me. I usually closed at Church's when I was able to work, get up the next morning spend some time with Kim, and then have her drop me off at the University of Texas library where I would read for at least four hours. One afternoon as we drove up Chacon Street, on the way to the library, I looked directly into the face of my past.

I shouted so loud I frightened Kim.

"Turn around! You got to go back."

"Go back where?" she asked having recovered.

"Back up to that bus stop." I turned and stared back at the man sitting on the bench.

"Why? I have to get to work."

"I don't care, just turn around and go back."

Kim made a U-turn in the middle of the block and drove back up Chacon. "What's going on?" she asked with some irritation.

"That's Bobby, Nicole's daddy, sitting back there at that bus stop." I pointed to Bobby Robeson sitting on the bench. He looked disheveled. His clothes were raggedy and dirty. Many homeless people would spend hours at a time sitting on the bus benches along Chacon Street. I never imagined, the many times as we drove up that street, I would one time see the man I detested most in life. Now I was going back to check on him.

"Why would you want to see him?" Kim asked. "Ain't he the one that used to beat you?"

"What do you mean, 'why do I want to see him?'" I shot back at her. "That's my sister's father, that's why."

"Whatever," she said and pulled over to the curb.

I got out, and with no hesitation strolled up to this man who at one time I was deathly afraid of. His head was bowed, and he didn't bother to look up when I approached him.

"Hey, Bobby," I snapped at him.

His head jerked up, and his body pulled back in a defensive posture. He glared at me, and a slight smile spread across his face.

"David, is that you?"

"Yeah, it's me. How you doing?" I don't know why I asked that question. It was quite apparent he wasn't doing well.

"I'll be all right," he said. "I'm down on my luck right now. But I'll be up and back on my feet real soon. What you doing up here?"

"I'm a student at Huston-Tillotson College."

"Boy, that's good. I knew you could make it. You was always the smartest."

For a moment we could do nothing but stare at each other. I felt uncomfortable seeing him in this condition. I couldn't return his compliment because he wasn't doing well. And I wasn't going to tell him that he looked terrible.

Instead I asked. "You been eating and you have any money?"

"No, David, I've been trying to find work, but it's just real hard times for me right now."

I dug in my pocket and pulled out the only money I had. "Here take this five dollars." I handed him the money. "I'd give you more, but that's all I got."

"You'd give me your last money after the way I treated you?" He placed the five dollars in his pocket.

"You're my sister's father, and I'm doing it for her." I hesitated for a moment, then turned and got back in the car.

Kim drove off, and I didn't look back. That was the last time I saw Bobby. He died several years later after that encounter.

CHAPTER 31

I was elated and energized when college resumed the first week in September. I took a full load, five courses, since I had successfully graduated beyond remedial studies. I felt a strong sense of pride with my chest stuck out. I was no longer considered a remedial student, and even though I could only read at the fourth grade level, it wouldn't be long before I out-performed the other students in my classes. I was determined to make Vickie Clay eat her words. Unlike high school, my friends no longer had to sneak answers to the quizzes or take notes for me.

Even with my financial aid, I kept the job at Church's. Joe and I had developed a close relationship. He trusted me to work the cash register and knew I would always be on time and never try to beat him out of money or food.

One day in late September Kim came in the restaurant and asked for a piece of chicken. She was tired, hungry, and had missed lunch, rushing over to be with me. I guess she figured I'd be willing to give her at least one piece of chicken free, and that would be no big deal. She was wrong.

"Kim, I can't do that," I told her as she stood across the counter with a shocked expression.

"What do you mean, you can't do that?" she fired back. "David I missed lunch to get over here to be with you and you're not going to give me a piece of chicken, not even a wing?"

"Not even a wing," I said standing my ground. "I was hired to work the cash register, not give away food."

"Food!" She shrieked. "What is one piece of chicken?"

"A piece I don't have the right to give away. Joe hired me because he trusts me not to cheat or steal from him. I'm not about to betray that trust." I couldn't understand why Kim failed to see that Joe had to be careful whom he trusted. Many times he'd hired Huston-Tillotson students, offering them the opportunity to make some extra money. And many times they fed their friends from school, and after a while that cut into his cost.

"What if I ask him and he says it's okay. Then will you give me a piece?" She asked with sarcasm. "Is he here?"

"Yeah, he's back there working the window."

"Would you call him, please?"

This all seemed ridiculous to me. What was her point? It's not like I owned or even managed the place. I was hired help, and according to my thinking, I had no right to give anything in the store away. It was only one piece of chicken and in the larger picture it would not affect their bottom line. But what Kim failed to recognize is that if all employees were able to give away food, someday it would cost them. I stared hard at her trying to figure out why she wanted to push the matter far beyond where it should go. And her anger was something I'd never seen before, at least not at this level. Soon it would all fall into place.

"Joe," I called out. He didn't answer, but instead made his way from the window to where we stood.

"Go ahead," I said to Kim feeling quite foolish.

"Never mind!" Kim shrieked and turned to walk away.

"What's wrong Kim?" Joe asked

"It's really nothing." Her voice choked.

Could a simple piece of chicken be that important to her?

Joe gave me a very hard stare and his voice softened as he turned to Kim. "What is it?" He paused, but Kim didn't respond. He then turned to me, and his voice hardened, "What did you do to her?"

"She wanted me to break the rules. She wanted me to steal."

Joe looked at me with a perplexed expression this time.

"I'm hungry," Kim explained. "I didn't bring any money with me, so I simply asked him for one lousy piece of chicken, and he acted like I asked him to rob the place."

"What?" Joe walked back to the large container and took out three pieces, came back over to us, and handed them to Kim.

"Thank you," she said softly, then hurried over to a table by the window and sat with her back to me.

"What's wrong with you, David?" Joe asked.

"Excuse me, but it you decide to give out free food, well, you can do that."

He placed his hand on my shoulder. "I understand where you're coming from, and I appreciate your honesty. But sometimes it's okay to bend the rules."

"Not in my world," I retorted. "But I don't understand why she got so upset. She's been doing a lot of that lately."

Joe stepped back away from me and smiled, "You really don't know?"

"No sir, I don't."

"I believe this evening you need to have a serious talk with Kim. I can't say for sure, but I've been married ten years and have four kids. With each one, my wife's behavior during pregnancy has always been the same. I swear I saw that same behavior in Kim. You need to talk to her."

"I'm pregnant, David," Kim blurted out. We sat on the bed in my room at Point South. It was early in the afternoon when she arrived at the apartment and the first thing she did was run to the bathroom. As I heard her inside I knew what Joe said was true. Mama had done the same every time she was pregnant. When I asked, she gave me the answer with no hesitation.

"What are we going to do?" I asked.

"I ain't getting rid of my baby," she shouted and jumped up.

"No, I wasn't talking about nothing crazy like that. You right, you ain't going to kill my child." I took her hand and pulled her back down on the bed, sitting close to me. "You think I'd ever ask you to do something as crazy as that?"

I could feel her body relax next to me.

I pulled her face close to me and kissed her. "How are we going to make it is what I wanted to say. You're a senior in high school, and I'm in my first year of college. It's going to be rough."

Kim sat up straight and I could feel her body stiffen.

"What's going to be rough is telling Mama," she said.

"I'll be with you when you tell her," I promised.

Kim laid her head on my shoulder, and I accepted her more now than ever before.

"My Mama had to raise five kids all by herself. She got very little financial and no emotional support," I said as I reflected back on Mama's struggles. "None of the men really helped her. James' dad did when he was in town, but most of the time he was gone. My Daddy wouldn't even buy me a pair of tennis shoes when I really needed them, but he could buy a round of drinks for a bunch of drunks." I paused and wrapped both arms tightly around Kim, who was crying. If possible I would have melted her right into me. "It's all right. We'll be all right," I promised. "You'll never have to go through what my Mama did."

"How am I going to tell Mama?" she asked.

"We'll do it together."

"I can't do it at home. I got to do it in public so she can't go off on me too bad."

"Is she at work right now?" I asked.

"Yeah, I dropped her off before coming over here."

"Let' do it now, right in front of all those customers."

Kim sat straight up and thought for a moment. "You going with me for sure?"

"You bet I am." I stood up, held my hands out for her to take, and pulled her off the bed. "If she's going to be angry, it's going to be with both of us. It did take two to tango." I smiled and she smiled back.

"Mama is not going to be too nice about this. I have to work up the nerve and I want to do it today," she said and then stopped. She pulled me back down on the bed. "Just hold me, David, please." Tears flowed freely from her eyes, and at that moment I would have done anything for her. We stretched out, I held her close, and without talking, we listened to Patti Labelle sing sweet love songs. We knew each song was meant for us only because at that moment we were the only three in the entire world, just Kim, our baby, and me.

It was a little past one o'clock in the afternoon when we walked in Grace's Homes Style Cooking, a restaurant that catered to the lobbyists and government employees near the state capitol. Kim's mother was a waitress ad was standing near a table of six taking their order. The restaurant was still crowded and we stood at the hostess' station trying to get Mrs. Brown's attention. Verna Mae Brown was a vivacious person with a great personality. I didn't know her that well since I'd only been dating Kim for about seven months and didn't spend much time at her house. Our relationship was built around Kim coming to visit me. School, and work kept me so busy I didn't have a whole lot of time to socialize other than the time I spent with Kim.

The two of us moved to the side as more customers came in and approached the hostess's station.

"This is perfect," Kim whispered to me. "There's a lot of people in here, so Mama can't make too much of a fuss."

"Kim, you're fooling yourself," I said while watching the hostess escort the customers to an empty table. "You got to go home sometime."

"I know," she replied.

"You're scared aren't you?"

"Yes, I am. You'd be to if you really knew Mrs. Vera Mae Brown. She ain't going to be happy."

"Together we'll be all right," I assured her. I took her hand and held it tightly. Finally, Mrs. Brown glanced over at us and headed our way.

"We're getting ready to find out if we'll be all right." Kim squeezed tightly on my hand.

"What's wrong?" Mrs. Brown asked as she approached. "David, how are you?" she asked then looked directly at Kim.

Maybe I was being paranoid, but her expression and tone told me she already knew what was wrong. "Kim, what's wrong with you? Why are you and David here at this time of day? Shouldn't you be in school and David, shouldn't you be at work?"

"Yes m'am," I said.

"Mama, we have to talk to you," Kim said.

Mrs. Brown's eyebrows furrowed and lips pursed as she looked at Kim and then at me.

"What have you kids done?" she asked. "Come on over here and sit down." She led us over to an empty booth. We sat down, but she didn't. "I have to check on my customers. I'll be right back, and this better be important to come on my job." She hurried back over to her customers sitting in the booth.

"You still think it's going to be all right?" Kim asked.

This time I didn't answer. Maybe this was a bad idea. We should have waited until she was home and relaxed. But we were already there and this needed to be done. Mrs. Brown strolled back over where we sat and took a seat in the booth next to Kim.

"You kids hungry?" she asked.

"No m'am," I said even though the aroma of fried chicken, candied yams, and fresh rolls triggered the hunger pains in me.

"No, Mama," Kim said. "But I do have something real important to tell you."

"What is it?" she snapped practically before Kim finished speaking.

"Come on Kim, I have to get back to work so tell me what it is."

At this point I was totally zeroed out. I no longer wanted to be there. I wanted to get up and run out. But that's what my Daddy did, and that's what the kind of men I grew up around did. I wanted no similarities to them. I had escaped that mentality and would never be drawn back into it.

"Mama, me and David are going to have a baby," Kim blurted it out.

There was a long pause and it seemed an eternity. I wanted Mrs. Brown to do or say something because the silence was not a normal response to Kim's announcement.

"What do you mean, you and David are going to have a baby?" she asked. "You're going to have a baby, not David."

"Mrs. Brown I know you don't think...."

"Quiet, David," she cut me off. "Why did you come down here on my job to tell me that you're pregnant?" she asked. "Are you sure you're pregnant?"

"Pretty much so," Kim said.

Mrs. Brown stood up. "Well, you two figure out what you're going to do, and Kim I'll talk with you this evening at home." She finished and walked away.

"I'll come over also," I said in an attempt to keep my commitment to Kim.

"No, David," Mrs. Brown heard me, stopped and turned around. "I need to have this conversation with Kim, and I need to do it with the two of us." She finished and continued walking away from us.

Kim and I said very little after leaving the restaurant. She drove me to Church's, and I wanted to say something about this private conversation Mrs. Brown wanted to have with her daughter. What was the real reason for excluding me? I really did like and respect Mrs. Brown, but she'd better not try to make Kim abort our child. I really needed to be there when she had this motherly talk, but that was beyond my control. I was still an outsider to the family. I had to say something to Kim. I had to make my position very clear.

"Don't you even think about an abortion," I blurted out.

She took her eyes off the road for a moment to glare over at me.

"What makes you think I'd even think about doing that?" she asked.

"I don't know," I replied. "Just a whole lot of crazy thoughts messing with my mind. " I leaned over and kissed her on the cheek as she pulled in front of Church's. "Let me know how the conversation goes."

I watched as she drove off. Kim and I were now joined together by a baby not yet visible to the eye, and that union would last for at least the next eighteen years. That seemed like a long time, but I was ready to be a father, no matter how difficult our road would be.

CHAPTER 32

From the first time we met, there was no doubt that I would love Kim. And now I loved her even more because she was carrying my child. My life would change drastically with the responsibility of fatherhood, but I was determined to be the best father possible. Daddy had never been there for me and I would use him as an example of what not to do. I sat on the side of the bed in my room and reflected back on the time at the dock when Mama had to force him to even acknowledge that I was standing right next to him, and the time he chose to buy a round of drinks at the Blue and White rather than give me money to purchase a pair of tennis shoes. I also recalled the vicious beating he gave me for quitting baseball. There was nothing positive I could recall about our relationship.

For years, his absence allowed me to create a fantasy father who measured up to all the standards I felt important. At one time I imagined him as a doctor, another time an astronaut, and then as a professional basketball player. I saw me sitting in the front row at the Houston Rockets games and cheering my father who scored the winning points. My dream of a fantasy father helped me make it through the hard times we experienced in our home.

This would not be the case with my child. He or she would be in my life all the time even if, for some reason, Kim and I didn't make it together. I loved my father but I didn't like him, and that is a heavy burden for any child to carry. I was determined that my child would not only love me but like and appreciate my accomplishments in life, and my dedication to him or her. It would be a rough road for the next few years. Staying on top of my studies and taking care of a family would be a challenge, but no bigger than the ones I had confronted all my life with a reading disability and a home life that had been anything but normal. Speaking of family, my thoughts wandered to Mama. I had to call her. I could only hope that she'd share in my joy, something she very seldom did. I hurried out into the kitchen where the only phone in the apartment was located, snatched it up and dialed her number.

She picked up and before she could say hello, I shouted,

"Mama, you're going to be a grandmother. My girlfriend Kim is pregnant." There was a brief silence and I wasn't sure what I'd hear when she finally responded. I braced myself for the worst. But Mama responded in a manner I never expected.

"Are you ready to be a father?" she asked.

"What ya mean?" I was lost for words. How do you ever know when you're ready for that kind of responsibility? I assumed that you just accept it and move on. I answered as best I could. "Yeah, I guess I am."

"David," she snapped. "If you have to guess you're ready then you're not." Mama paused as if to let her words of wisdom sink in. "You're going to have to drop out of school."

"What do you mean?" I now snapped. "I'm not dropping out of school."

"Yes you are. You got to find yourself a job and take care of your child."

"Mama I don't have to drop out of school to take care of my child. That is something I will not do."

"David, you ain't going to be no dead beat dad, not taking care of your child like your no-good Daddy and all these no-good lazy ass black men in Freeport." Mama was yelling at me.

"Mama just relax." I tried to calm her down. Her history with a bunch of irresponsible men was a long one, and she'd always blamed her father, who had also been quite irresponsible, for the hard life she and her siblings had suffered. "If there is one person I will not be like, that is my Daddy. But if I drop out of school, I'll never be able to give my child the best. Mama, I'm going to do both things. I'm going to take care of my child and how many others that Kim and I might have, and I'm going to graduate from Huston-Tillotson." I had to pause for the emotional charge I felt. I was choked and didn't want Mama to know I was about to cry. "I watched you cry too many years, and I would never do that to Kim."

"I'll pray that you really do mean that David, and cry if you don't."

I couldn't hold back the tears, and it was difficult talking. "Mama I have to go, but I'll call you in a couple days and let you know how we're doing."

"Just a minute David." She refused to allow me to escape this emotional overdrive. "Have you told her mother?"

"Yes we did."

"What did she say?"

"Told me she wanted to discuss it alone with her daughter. When I see Kim in the morning I'll know more." I cut my words short and to the point. This prolonged discussion was torture.

"Okay then call me tomorrow, and let me know what she said. And remember David, just 'cause you got her pregnant don't make you no man. What'll make you a man and a father is what you do after that baby is born. Now go on, 'cause I know you want to get off this phone."

"Yes m'am," I said and we both hung up.

I hurried back into my room and stretched out on the bed. I placed my hands behind my head and stared at the ceiling. This was one time I was glad no one was home. I needed this time to reflect on the pregnancy and Mama's words. My thoughts took me back to Freeport at least fifteen years. I clearly saw the holes in the floor of our bathroom and jumping over them to get to the toilet, the dirty bath water, and the beef tip stew. We had a rough time making it from day to day, but I didn't blame Mama. I blamed those sorry men who loved to dip into the pleasure palace, but did not want to accept the consequences that went along with the dipping. My Daddy had sixteen children and none of us knew each other. Chances were he never took care of any of them. I was sure some good came out of having him as a father, and that would be an example of what not to do as a father. Again tears filled my eyes as I thought about Mama. Were all those relationships she had based on a mother's love for her children. She needed financial support, and got it the best way she could. Five different fathers, and not one of them was worth a damn. She had deserved better, and because she didn't have the best, I would see to it that Kim did. It was late and I needed to study. I was also exhausted and needed to sleep. My thoughts were racing way beyond the material in a book. My concentration wouldn't stay focused, so I climbed in the bed, turned on my side and drifted off to sleep.

Next morning as I stepped out of the apartment to catch the bus to school, Kim pulled up to the curb. Why wasn't she at school and had something happened to the baby? I rushed to the driver's side and swung the door open. "What's wrong, why are you here and not in school?" I shouted

"Calm down," she said. "Nothing's wrong."

"Why ain't you in school then? We already had this discussion about cutting classes." I hurried over to the other side, opened the door and sat in the passenger seat.

"I couldn't go to school after what Mama said to me last night," she said and tears filled her eyes.

I felt a little guilty when I saw the tears. "What happened Kim? What did she say to you?"

"She said that you will leave me even before the baby is born. And if you do last until the birth, you'll be gone in a month. Is that what you going to do to me David? You going to leave me with this baby to raise by myself?"

"Kim, I'd never do that to you. Please believe me. I will never abandon a child of mine." I leaned toward Kim and kissed her on the cheek. "I told you what my Mama had endured all these years. I measure life through Mama's tears, and I'll never cause another human being to suffer as I've watched her."

"You sure?" she asked and smiled.

"Yes, absolutely, positively sure."

"Thank you, David."

"Thank me for what? Being a man?"

"Not that, but reassuring me that my first impressions of you weren't wrong."

"Well, they weren't, so now you got to get to school."

"I can take you over to Huston-Tillotson first."

"No you can't. It's way out your way. I'll catch the bus like I do everyday."

"You sure?"

"Just as sure as I am that you will never have to worry about me not being there for you and our baby." I got out of the car and watched her drive off. I felt good because I knew I meant every word I said and the promises I made. She would know that David Floyd was a good man as defined through Mama's tears.

CHAPTER 33

———◆•◆•◆———

Throughout this entire emotional roller coaster I never lost focus that studies were paramount in my life. I didn't put them before Kim and my child to be, but I had to keep my eyes on the prize. My reading had improved considerably, but I still stuck to my schedule of meeting with Ms. Phillips. Half way through the fall semester she tested my reading comprehension, and I'd advanced to the fifth grade reading level. That was improvement, but not sufficient for my needs. I wanted to be at the same level as any second semester freshman. And I wanted to graduate at the same time as my high school graduating class. They had an entire year's jump on me since I spent my first year wasting a semester at Lamar, and just bumping around Freeport for the other semester.

My single-minded drive to meet all the deadlines I set for myself irritated Kim. She participated in the Zenith Program, an accelerated high school study plan to assist students who had fallen behind their class to catch up and graduate on time. Both our schedules cut into the amount of time we could spend together. And when we did find time to be together, I expected her to help me improve my reading comprehension.

The pregnancy, her accelerated school program and my insistence that she help me had her on edge all the time. Arguments between us increased to the point it seemed that's all we did. She would show up at my apartment, and within five minutes we would be at each other. When we fought, I do not believe we were angry at each other but, instead, frustrated with our situation. We were two kids about to be parents, but we weren't financially or mentally prepared for that kind of responsibility. Kim was only seventeen and was struggling to graduate on time in June 1991. The overwhelming pressure I put on myself triggered my depression, and now I had the additional responsibility of dealing with Kim through her mood swings and emotional outbursts.

I did, however, recognize that Kim carried the greater of the burdens. She was carrying a child for a man who was only a freshman in college, was working at Church's Fried Chicken, and worst still, read at just a little above the fifth grade level. What kind of confidence could she possibly have in me when she was literally helping me learn to read? I wasn't sure just how much my promise "to take care of her and the baby" she really believed. When she went into one of her tantrums, I tried my best to take all this into consideration, but sometimes it was very difficult. The tantrums would eventually cause serious problems in our relationship, but they never deterred me in my commitment to always take care of my child.

Living so far away from campus and Church's caused some serious problems in my time management. I had so many hours in a day to complete a list of chores. I lost too much time sitting on the bus, even though I did manage to practice my reading. It soon became clear that I needed to move closer to the campus, but not on campus. I needed to find students seeking a roommate, which I was able to do through Chicken George. One day at work he told me that he and some other guys had found a house right off campus. It was old and raggedy with no furniture, but big enough for all five of us. Splitting the rent five ways reduced the amount I had to pay from what it was at Point South. The place reminded me of houses in Freeport. It was a shotgun structure and when you opened the front door, you could see straight through to the back door in the kitchen area. It had two bedrooms to the right of the living room and in the kitchen there was a pantry area for canned goods and other groceries.

I had gotten to know all four of my new roommates quite well, especially Chicken George, so I figured we'd have no problem getting along. John Paul, a friend from West Columbia, Texas, had originally rented the house his freshman year, and welcomed all the additional financial help he could get. He occupied the first bedroom off the living room for himself. I had the second bedroom. For some reason, they all agreed I wouldn't have to share it with anyone. That was probably because Kim was pregnant and they wanted to allow us our privacy. And they were only there to clean up and change clothes. They spent most of their time at their girlfriends' apartments and dorm rooms. Kim had to come to me, if we expected to have any privacy. So I had the bedroom, but without a bed. In fact, no one had a bed. We only had a kitchen table and four chairs in the entire place. Kim and I made a pallet on the floor in my room. We spent many evenings there with her tutoring me in reading.

Chicken George and Melvin Williams slept on the floor in the dining room whenever they slept over. Our fifth roommate was Derrick Bonner who slept in the pantry off the kitchen. Late at night we could hear Derrick swatting at the rats that invaded the pantry late at night. Those rats that often wandered into the living room and once into my bedroom, were as big as the ones we had in Freeport. I was used to them as were the other guys, but Kim wasn't.

No one was home one night when Kim and I got there a little after eight o'clock. When we strolled through the front door I hit the light switch and nothing happened. The electricity had been turned off. I was furious and actually couldn't believe they'd failed to pay the bill. The only light in the front room came from the streetlight out front and it helped us get around in the living room. I remembered that John Paul stored some candles and matches in his room. Kim stood by the front door while I navigated my way into his bedroom, found the candles and matches. The light from the candle made it possible to get around areas right in front of me. I grabbed Kim's hand and we slowly walked to my room and made it over to the pallet on the floor. We then stretched out with backs upright against the wall. All the time I held the candle because I didn't have a holder to put it in. Kim finally spoke.

"David I want to go home," she said. "This is kinda scary."

"Why you scared?" I asked. "We don't have time to be scared. We gotta do my exercises for an hour."

"David, you don't think we going to do any reading exercises in the dark?" Kim shrieked.

"Yes I do. We got the light from the candle. That's all we need." While holding the candle with one hand, I pulled out the book I was reading along with the flash cards.

"This is madness." Kim curled up with her legs tucked under her. "Ain't no telling what might come in here. I want to go home."

"Please Kim, I can't break my schedule." I pleaded with her. "We can do it, just try."

Kim took the flash cards, I opened the book and we began the exercises. We were doing fine for about a half hour and then it happened.

"David, did you hear that?" Kim asked.

"What?" I heard it but didn't want to get distracted from our exercise. "I didn't hear anything."

"Aaaah," Kim screamed and jumped straight up.

The candle gave off just enough light that we both spotted a fat, hairy rat with an ugly long tail. The rat had just made it into the room when Kim screamed. The noise scared the creature, and it jumped straight up, came back down to the floor, scurried around in circles for a moment, then turned and left the room. Kim ended up in the corner with her back against the wall and arms wrapped around her body.

I jumped up and rushed over to the door. "I'll close it, and we can finish," I said.

"I'm going home David." She started toward the door and then stopped in the middle of the room. "I'm not going out there by myself and without some light," she said.

"Okay," I finally conceded, took her hand and guided her out of the room and to the front door. "We'll get the lights back on tomorrow," I assured her.

"You'd better 'cause I ain't going to be sitting up here in the dark." I walked Kim to her car and watched as she drove off.

The next day we did get the lights turned on. But I had to confront my roommates because they had a very nonchalant attitude about paying bills, especially the utilities and rent. Because I spent the most time in that rat-infested place I insisted that they hustle their share of the money. This time they came up with their share but it wouldn't be long before the lights were turned off again.

The problem we had getting everyone to come up with their share of the utility money carried over to the rent also. Chicken George was the major culprit. He never had his rent money and at the first of the month he always disappeared until the fifth when he figured we'd already paid for the month. I covered his share for a couple of months, but then tired of his antics. By the middle of October the lights were off again. The landlord was chasing us for the rent, and we were all at each other's throats. Finally, the day before Halloween we all met at the house, with the lights off and with an eviction notice. We agreed to move out the day after Halloween. The rats would be our excuse. We felt no obligation to pay October's rent since we had complained on many occasions about the rats to the landlord. He refused to take any actions.

We had very few clothes and no furniture except a stereo. We could be totally out of there by November 1, but Halloween night we threw a party in the dark. We did have our party and we did vacate the premises that very next day.

Chapter 34

Through our collective ingenuity, skill, pleading, and a lot of luck, the four of us found another house and convinced the landlord to rent it to us. John Paul didn't go with us, but instead moved in with his girlfriend. It was a two-bedroom place about a mile from campus that was, for me, walking distance. Melvin and Chicken George shared one bedroom while Terrence and I shared the other one. Terrence was elated that he no longer would have to sleep in a makeshift room and fight off the rats in the pantry. Kim was also happy that she wouldn't have to visit me and the rats. It was a perfect set up for me because Terrence spent most of his time at his girlfriend's apartment and I had the room to myself most of the time.

Our major problem in the other house was that Chicken George never had his part of the rent as well as money for other bills. We let him know up front that he could only live with us if he pledged to carry his share of the financial burden. He made that promise. Still I had my doubts that he would actually come through. But he was a friend, and we had to give him another chance. Out of the three of us, I was the harshest with him, and on a number of occasions we were close to throwing blows. For some reason Chicken George hadn't assumed his responsibility as a man. It was like he believed he had a right to live off others, and we had a responsibility to let him. Partying and spending money on foolishness was out of the question with me. For years I had watched grown men squander money on whiskey and women at the Blue and White Café. I didn't want to live like that and certainly did not want a roommate who thought and lived that way. I backed off him, however, when he promised to do better than what he had in the past. I knew only time would tell.

In between these struggles I managed to keep my eyes squarely on the prize. I was like a laser beam with my progress compared to my fellow students who'd been with me in my initial remedial classes at the school. I kept to my formula for studying. My second home was the University of Texas library. Once I finished all my homework, then I would practice my reading. Kim was still using the flash cards as a prop for learning. The fall of 1990, I took my first accounting class and that turned out to be the greatest challenge that semester.

Mrs. Curry, my counselor, taught the Introduction to Accounting I. She was the only instructor at Huston-Tillotson that I believe did not care for me. It was nothing like the disdain Mrs. Hassenback showed toward me, but with a coldness and smugness that seemed to tell me that I had no business in her accounting class. I had barely made it through remedial math my first semester, and during my initial counseling session with her, she questioned why I was majoring in accounting. Essentially she viewed me as a remedial student who would never rise above mediocrity. The difference was that I knew I was bound for success and carried myself in that manner. She wanted me to show humility while I projected pride; she wanted me to recognize my weaknesses as such, and I gave her a heavy dose of strength.

Our first confrontation in the classroom exploded over a very basic accounting principle pertaining to credit and debit in customer's bank accounts. I would count deposits as credits, and withdrawals as debits. I must have frustrated Mrs. Curry on many occasions as she constantly instructed me on the proper way to make the entry. For some reason I had the toughest time comprehending that relationship. It took me practically the entire semester to finally grasp it, and that was with much difficulty.

Despite our many battles I do believe Mrs. Curry was happy that I finally began to understand the basic principles of accounting. I earned a "B" in her class. Most rewarding was that I did it myself. It was no longer a case of teachers passing me just to get rid of me or other students providing me with answers. This was all David Floyd. That second semester I really came into my own as a college student. I was no longer taking remedial classes, but instead was a competent college student. However, I still could only read at the fifth grade level.

In December when the semester ended I had one full year of college instruction behind me and was feeling mighty good. My reading ability, thanks to Kim and Ms. Phillips was constantly improving and in five months I would be a father. Starting my sophomore year, I set my goal to graduate from Huston-Tillotson in three years and then move on to graduate school. I had made up my mind that I would do graduate work somewhere other than in Texas. I would take Kim and my child, and together we would move on to bigger and better opportunities. Basketball was a distant memory as was Mr. Waniack, Mr. Westbrook, and any other distractions from my past.

With my confidence in the classroom sprouting like fresh, new flower blossoms, I was now ready to step back into campus life. During the fall of 1990, I received three different credit cards in the mail. At first I thought it must be a mistake. After all, I had no established credit, received financial aid from the school, and earned a mere pittance at Church's. No competent lending institution would provide me with a perfectly good credit card for my use. But they were in my name and the accompanying letter clearly stated I had three hundred dollars credit to use anyway I felt appropriate. With all three I had a total of nine hundred dollars. It seemed too good to be true, so I decided to put it to the test.

On one occasion when I headed over to the University of Texas campus for my three hours study in the library, I stopped at the

Gap clothing store right off campus. I deliberately went by that very store on my trips to the University because they had some of the best clothes I'd ever seen. And these clothes had the original price tag on them, and if my credit cards were legitimate, I would have the luxury of removing those price tags for whatever I decided to buy.

I entered the store with apprehension. Finally, after I browsed for about five minutes, a store clerk approached me.

"These are really some sharp looking shirts," he said. "Just got them in yesterday." He pulled a light blue shirt from the rack and placed it in front of me. "This one sure would look good on you."

I took the shirt from him and held it up to my body.

"Come on and look at yourself in the mirror," he said.

I followed him over to the full-length mirror and stared at the shirt against my body. I could visualize strutting down the streets of Freeport, and marching right into the Blue and White and everyone staring at me. I imagined Mama, Grandma, and the entire family patting me on my back for my fine selection. And most important, I visualized the students in the lounge on campus opening their mouths wide, amazed as to how magnificent I looked in my pretty light blue shirt with new matching slacks and shoes. And the best part was that I could now afford all of them with my new shiny credit cards.

"I'll take it," I said. "And I also want to buy some pants, underwear, socks, and maybe new shoes if you all have what I like." My words were strong and powerful with plenty of clarity.

"Let me take you around and see if we can find exactly what you want," the clerk said as he led me to the section where slacks were hung in rows. "Take your time, pick what you want, and I'll ring you up when you're finished."

I spent over an hour and a half picking different items. When I finished, I collected all of them, walked to where the salesman waited patiently and dropped them all on the counter.

"Ring them up," I said with all the confidence of someone who did this on a regular basis.

He took each item, found the price tag and rung it up. With each ring of the cash register, my anxiety grew. I wanted to lean over the counter and see how much I had spent. When he finished, I shifted my weight from one foot to the other, burning off nervous energy.

"Will this be cash or credit card?" he asked.

I fumbled in my pocket and pulled out the first card. I handed it to him, held my breath, and looked down at the floor. What if I was turned down? What if all those cards were fake and the letter a hoax? That would be embarrassing because I'd have to carry all those clothes back to the rack and every customer in the store would know why. Again I shifted my feet. What was taking so long? The salesman looked at me and smiled.

"Sometimes this machine can be real slow. Must be a lot of people out shopping today."

I said nothing back to him. I wasn't in the mood for idle chatter. I was about to confront a major embarrassment and didn't want to hear any nonsense about a slow machine.

Just at that moment when I knew my heart was going to come up through my throat, the register printed a receipt. I'll be damn I did have all that credit. My body relaxed, my feet no longer shifted, and I smiled.

The salesman stuffed my clothes into a large store bag. I signed the receipt and instead of going to the library that day, I hurried back to the apartment and started trying on new clothes. I couldn't wait to see Kim so that she could catch a glimpse of the new David.

———◆◆◆———

CHAPTER 35

Emboldened with a newly found pride I began to spend more time on campus. I now possessed plenty of clothes and, most important, new shoes. Even though the students still called me Pealo, I no longer fit the image associated with that name. The new David Floyd held his head high and strutted across campus. However, the new clothes and shoes represented vain David, while the real person was taking a full load of regular college classes, constantly improving his reading ability, and was about to be a proud father.

The vain David took another bold step and decided to pledge. I was starting to buy into many of the less important and somewhat superficial aspects of college life. A fraternity was one of them. There was only one that I would even consider pledging and that was Kappa Alpha Psi. I picked that fraternity because my old friend, Kelvin Rayme was a Kappa. During that brief period in the fall 1990 that I shared an apartment with Kelvin, I learned a great deal about Kappa men through him. Since I had such high respect for him, I wanted to belong to the same fraternity in which he was a member.

Students interested in pledging Kappa were invited to a smoker in March 1991 held in the Administration Building on the third floor. This was the same building where I first met the President of the school and where I also took reading instructions in the basement of the building. Now I stood proudly in a third floor classroom determined to pledge Kappa and become a member of one of the most prestigious Black fraternities in the country. That had to stand for something.

The Kappas congregated in the classroom right next to the one we occupied as potential pledges. The brothers had twenty chairs lined up in rows of seven for the members of the fraternity and then a chair in the front of the room facing toward them. In that seat, the potential pledges would sit to be questioned. I timed one of the students who went into the interrogation room. He was in there about fifteen minutes. I knew that was how much time they would spend with me when I was called in. After the tenth person was escorted into the room, my nerves were on edge. Would I be the last one to go which meant I endured the longest wait?

Finally, with only two of us left, they called my name. As I strolled into the classroom and took the seat facing the brothers, I assured myself this would be a piece of cake. Little did I know this would turn out to be one of the most disappointing and humiliating encounters I experienced at Huston-Tillotson. A number of the fraternity brothers did not like me and were determined to make certain I never became a Kappa. The leading antagonist was Osie.

"Why you want to be a Kappa?" he asked almost before I sat down.

"Because of the principles Kappa Alpha Psi stands for," I answered.

"I believe you lying to us," a brother said.

"Yeah, I agree," another brother added. "That's not why you want to pledge. You think it makes it easier to catch girls and get yourself a little poon tang. Ain't that the reason?"

"No, not at all," I replied. "I got a girl and I'm only interested in getting my degree and then moving on to get my masters. I'm determined that someday I'll have my Ph.D. within the next five years."

"And how are you going to do that?" Ossie asked. "I understand you had to take all remedial classes your first semester. Did you pass them?"

"Of course I did." I glared at him. I didn't' like the direction this interview was going. Why were they asking me such confrontational questions? It finally hit me. They had no intention of bringing me on line. They were simply pulling my chain. The next question confirmed my suspicions.

"David, if you were out in the woods with the esteemed President of our fraternity and he got bit by an extraordinary poisonous snake right on the tip of his penis, would you willingly suck the poison out to save his life?"

I couldn't believe the question. They had to know my answer.

"With all due respect to the President, he would just have to die."

They all busted out laughing. For a moment their laughter took me back to my past and visions of students laughing as I struggled to read flashed before me. The derision emanating from these men was not what fraternity life was supposed to be all about. Had I been terribly mis-led about the values and principles of Kappa Alpha Psi? These so-called men were not much better than the less educated kids back in Freeport. I sat there patiently and waited for these grown men to stop acting like juveniles. Finally the lead brother said.

"You're finished, Floyd. We'll let you know our decision within a week."

The other brothers in the room said nothing more. They just sat with smirks on their faces. I hurried out of the room, down the stairs and out of the building. The evening air felt wonderfully fresh and clean, unlike the stuffiness in that room on the third floor of the Administration Building. There was no doubt the Kappas would turn me down and I only had to take a day or so to condition my thinking for that rejection. What they didn't know was that you never turn David Floyd down. My determination was too strong to succumb to their rejection. If they didn't accept me this time, I would wait until next year and re-apply, and the year after that until I won. Becoming a Kappa was important to me, but not quite as important as beating that particular bunch of brothers at their own silly game.

A week later I did receive the rejection letter. The reason they gave was my lack of extracurricular activities on campus. They claimed they were seeking men who dedicated their free time to participating in school activities. Providing me with a reason for the rejection was their mistake. Now I knew exactly what I had to do in order to remove their excuse. Once I did that, I would be back next year sitting in that same chair. It was not so much about becoming a Kappa, but about winning instead.

I tried extremely hard not to let my disappointment show, but failed miserably. It took a much larger crisis than their rejection to make me realize that it was all relatively insignificant. The crisis involved Ronnie and drugs. Melvin woke me up at three o'clock in the morning.

"David, you have a telephone call," he said as he yawned.

"Damn, Melvin, tell whoever it is that I'm asleep and I'll call them back in the morning." I turned my back to him and covered my head with a pillow.

"Come on man," he insisted, "I already told them that, but they insisted that I wake you up."

"Is it Kim?"

"No, I think it's your brother, and he said it's awfully important."

I rose up in the bed and my thoughts went to Mama. Had Bobby showed up back in Freeport and finished the job? Was Mama dead? I climbed out of bed and headed toward the kitchen counter where the phone was located.

"Yeah, this is David," I said.

"Ronnie got busted by an undercover cop," James said. "He's in jail for selling drugs and Mama said you'd better get down here to help him out."

My body froze and I squeezed the receiver. Flashes of my last conversation with him sitting on Mama's porch captured me for a moment. I had told him drug dealers either end up dead or go to jail. There is no storybook and happy ending in the life of a drug dealer. And now it had happened to him. I couldn't picture Ronnie sitting in a jail cell for very long. It was much too confining for him. I had to get down there right away. I wasn't quite sure what I could do, but at least I would be there for him.

"David, did you hear what I said?" James asked, anxiety building in his voice.

"Yeah, I heard you. How is Mama holding up?"

"How do you think?" James sounded irritated with me. "She said you'd better hurry up and get down here."

"I'll be there in the morning," I said and hung up.

One rule I'd always kept and that was never to miss a class. I viewed attending classes in the same manner as going to work. College was my primary job, but now I faced the prospect of missing work for a few days. Only Mama and Ronnie had the power to make me break this rule. One of them was in trouble and I had to go. I threw a few clothes in a suitcase, explained to Kim what happened, had her drop me off at the Greyhound Bus Depot and was on my way to Freeport.

No one seemed to be in a state of panic when I arrived at Mama's house five hours later. Ronnie had been bailed out with money collected by Mama from other members of the family, and was at home when I arrived. I was a little disappointed in the nonchalant attitudes Mama, James and even Nicole had, since my brother had led me to believe this was an emergency to end all emergencies. They greeted me like nothing at all had happened.

"How's school?" Mama asked as I met her in the kitchen. James was sitting at the kitchen table, Nicole watched television in the living room, and Ronnie wasn't home.

"I'm doing just fine," I said.

"And how's Kim and the baby?" she asked.

I was baffled. Why all these other questions and no concentration on Ronnie's problem? Was Mama concealing her emotions from me? She had done that in the past. We never knew what bothered her because she always kept problems from us. Mama was always the protective mother hen guarding her babies against the abuses of society as she saw them. The fact that Ronnie might be locked up for a number of years in prison, and she not able to take care of him as she had done all these years, had to bother her. She was now diverting attention from that major concern by asking me what I considered rather trivial questions at a time of crisis.

"David, did you hear me talking to you?" she snapped.

"Yes, Mama, Kim and the baby are fine."

"Remember what I told you about being a good father to your child."

"I never forget, Mama, and I plan to be a good father."

"I just don't know how you expect to keep going to school and take care of your family."

"With a great deal of difficulty, but I will get it done." Mama was close to going on the attack against me, which was a strong indicator that the Ronnie situation was eating at her. I needed to push it a little.

"Mama, why you so concerned about me when we should really be talking about Ronnie?"

"He'll be all right," she said. "No way my baby's going to go to prison. God wouldn't put that kind of burden on him."

"If you're so sure and not worried, why'd you insist that I get down here right away. I had to miss classes and that's something I just don't do."

"He's going to be all right, but he needs you because the two of you always been close and looked out for each other. Even though you fought all the time, one thing I always knew was that you wouldn't let anything happen to each other. Now you need to tell him that and make him feel better. Make him feel that everything's' going to be all right." Mama sat down in one of the kitchen chairs and leaned her elbows on the table. "That boy just can't go to jail. He won't make it in there." Mama's voice choked like she was about to cry. Before it had been the men in her life that caused the tears, now it was one of her own sons. I wondered would she ever get a break?

I sat down in the only other empty chair. James and Nicole remained quiet. "Ronnie broke the law, and for that, he might have to pay a heavy price. You know darn well in this county they love to put black men away.

"It wasn't nothing but some little bit of marijuana. Why all the fuss?"

"Because it's against the law, Mama," James now chimed in.

"You and Nicole go to your rooms." She scowled. "This ain't no conversation you all need to hear."

"Aw Mama," Nicole moaned. "We ain't no babies and we know what's going on."

"I know you do, but I don't want you involved, now get on out of here."

I was surprised how both of them complied with Mama's wishes. Nicole headed to her bedroom and James shot out the back door. Like me, they knew Mama was tearing apart inside, and needed no additional stress from them.

"I'm so grateful to God that I got you and Levy through high school and out of here without any trouble and no problems with drugs," she said. "I feel sorry for these poor young kids today. Ain't nothing good here in Freeport, just a lot of trouble, even in elementary school. Oh God, I hope he ain't been selling no drugs to school age children."

"I doubt that, Mama," I quickly answered. "Ronnie has a moral compass like all of us, and it wouldn't allow him to sell to kids."

"Well, you know him best, so I'll take your word for it." She got up and headed for her bedroom. "I got to rest. All this makes me tired."

I sat there alone in the kitchen wondering just what I would say to Ronnie when I saw him. He needed my support, but I struggled with giving it to him. I thought I knew him quite well, but evidently I didn't. When I told Mama he wouldn't sell to children, I never believed he would sell to anyone, so I couldn't be certain he hadn't reached that low level of dealing. I could only hope he hadn't. What I did know about him was he allowed the weight problem to win. I also wondered if it would do any good to re-visit that issue. Being over weight was not only the burden he bare quite badly but also the crutch he leaned on to give up on life. Quitting school and dealing drugs meant he had given up, and it was only a matter of time before it would all be played out for him.

He smiled when he finally walked through the back door and spotted me still sitting at the kitchen table.

"Hey, brother, what you doing down here?" he asked. "You give up on school or something?"

"No way," I answered. "Mama asked me to come down here 'cause you got yourself in a little trouble."

"Oh that ain't nothing. You could've saved yourself a trip. They ain't going to lock me up."

"How can you be so confident?" I asked.

"Be serious David. Look at me. I weigh four hundred pounds and they know darn well I wouldn't be able to last in prison. My public defender already told me they going to give me a pass because of my handicap. They going to spank me on the hand a little bit, but I believe in the long run, they'll let me go. Put me on probation or something."

"You ain't worried?"

"Hell yes, I'm worried. Man I'm looking at over ten years. I don't want to spend another night in jail, let alone ten years." Ronnie paused and looked down for a moment. "And David you got to know I'm sorry for the shame I done brought on Mamma and the family."

"Why you commit a crime if you don't want to do time?" I asked.

"Man, don't' nobody want to do time. But some of us don't have the education to make good money no other way. Hell, I don't want to flip burgers at McDonald's no more than anyone else. So this was an easy way for me to make big money real fast."

"Yeah, big money real fast that won't last."

"Hey big brother, I know that now, but please spare me the lecture. Let me take you over to the River Restaurant and buy you dinner. Lets not deal with this, it's too depressing."

"Not with blood money." I really did want to go back to the restaurant so I could let Rick know how well I was doing and to thank him for his concern he had expressed about my future. But I refused to take money from Ronnie, not even in the form of a dinner.

"Why you being so self-righteous?"

"I ain't being self-righteous, but aren't you a little concerned that this same money you going to use to treat me to dinner, might put you away for ten years or more?"

"I already told you I'm scared. What more you want from me?" Ronnie jumped up, went over to the sink and poured himself a glass of water.

"I want you to stop doing these crazy things that make Mama cry," I said. "She worries about you, and when she worries, I worry, and I don't like that."

"I'm sorry man, but I got to live my life as I see fit. Now this drug thing was a bad idea. If I don't go to jail ain't no way I'll keep doing this. I couldn't if I wanted to. Freeport is too small, and if I got back out there in the game, the narcs would know in no time."

"So you finished with it."

"I got to be, David. I don't see where I got a choice."

"Are you doing it because you know it's wrong or because you got caught?"

"Don't take me down that road, David," he grumbled. "I already told you I'm finished. You don't need no more information than that."

He was right. That's all I needed to know. His reason for giving up the drug game didn't matter just as long as he would do it and not cause Mama the worry and the tears. I walked over to where he was standing and grabbed his hand.

"Give me your word and your hand." I grabbed his big, fat hand and squeezed it.

Ronnie smiled, something he didn't do that often. In fact, as I thought back over our childhood, he hardly ever smiled, just cried all the time.

"How long you going to hang around?" he asked.

"Your court date isn't for a couple weeks, so I can't stay that long. But I'll come back for the trial if I can."

"Don't bother, it ain't no big thing. I'll be in and out in no time 'cause they just ain't going to send me to prison."

"I sure hope not." I walked back over to the table. "Not for your sake, but for Mama's. I don't think she could last knowing you were locked up. She'd spend every moment you did in that place with you."

"I know, and I'm sorry man. I'll make it up to her."

Ronnie actually said he was sorry for something he did. In all our years he'd never apologized because he considered it a sign of weakness. I had to get out of Freeport on that positive note, but I had one other thing to do. I contacted my Daddy and insisted that we talk. He had spent his entire life running away from me, but he couldn't run this time. I was now in control of the kind of relation-ship we had between us, and as such he would talk with me about his failure to be a father.

Daddy was renting a small room in a boarding house down by the docks. When he opened the door and let me in, I was struck by how much he'd aged. Daddy looked tired and grimaced a lot like he was constantly in pain. Little did I know at that time the cancer had begun to eat away at his body. The fire was gone from his body, and his words were slow and lazy. This was not the same man who'd beat me with a rope that day on Grandma's porch.

"Hey boy, how you doing?" he asked as he waved me into his

room. The only place for me to sit was on the unkempt bed. I sat at the edge, and he sat next to me.

"Been a long time since I seen you, boy," he continued. "I hear from Shorty that you now in college and studying to be some kind of accountant or something. Is that true?"

"Yes," I replied. There was no enthusiasm in my voice because I didn't get a warm feeling about him. "I'm going to be a father. You're going to be a grandfather in about four months." I don't know why I volunteered that information. It wasn't because I felt he cared. This was a man with nineteen kids all spread along the Gulf. He probably had a dozen grandchildren, so what would one more mean to him?

"That's good, David. If it's a boy, you going to make him David the Third?"

"I don't know about that. Kim might have something to say about the name." I cringed when he suggested that my son might be named after him. I loved Daddy, but he did not deserve that honor.

"Your first boy got to be named after you. That's what I did. How you think you got the name David?"

"Yeah, Daddy, how many of your other kids are named David also?"

"I don't know. Why you ask?"

"Do you know the names of all your children?"

"What kind of question is that? Hell yes, I know all their names."

"And when's the last time they been to see you or you been to see them?"

"I don't see none of them at all. Only one I see is you."

"Daddy, you don't see me. You've never seen me." I felt disgusted with him. I thought back on the time when we saw him at the dock when he just arrived from Florida. Mama had to force him to acknowledge my presence.

"What's wrong with you boy? You act like you angry or something. Is that why you came by here, to tell me off?"

"No, Daddy, I don't want to tell you off, but I want you to face up to the fact that you never served as a father to me. You just plain didn't seem to care."

"How you know how I felt?"

"I guess I really don't know, but I can only go on your actions, and they were absolutely terrible."

Suddenly Daddy got a burst of energy, rose up and stood over me. He'd balled his fist and pulled his arm back. I jumped up also and stood over him.

"I don't think you want to do that Daddy. I'm no longer that young boy you beat with the rope on Grandma's porch. I don't take no more beatings. So please sit down and hear me out. You owe me that much."

He sat back on the bed and I did the same.

"You know what it's like to have a father who never acknowledges your birthday, never buys you anything for Christmas and embarrasses you by getting sloppy drunk and falling out on the street."

"What you talking about. I ain't never fell out on the street."

"You were so drunk you don't even know it happened to you. I found you one night so drunk you'd pissed in your pants and a bunch of white boys from my school had surrounded you and were taunting you. I had to break through them and take you back to the boat."

"I hope you beat their asses for laughing."

"That's not the point, Daddy. You embarrassed me to no end." I paused and took in a deep breath, then released it. It helped calm my nerves. This was like therapy, and I had to get it all out right then. I might never get another opportunity. "Only once in my life did I ever ask you for something and you turned me down."

"I don't remember. What was that?"

"I know you don't," I said, "but you'll know today. You recall me coming into the Blue White one day and asking you for money to buy new tennis shoes because I'd just made the school basketball team and everybody had new shoes, so I wanted them too."

"I don't remember any of that. Why you keep bringing up all this old shit now?"

"Because I want you to know how much you disappointed me and that I'll never do that to my children. What I learned from you was how not to be a parent."

Daddy's head drooped and his back slumped just like a defeated man. He looked pathetic and for a moment I felt sorry for him. But I did not regret what I'd said.

"I wouldn't want you to be like me either. You going to be better than me. Times have changed, David. You black kids got plenty of opportunities that we didn't have when I was coming up. I'm sorry, and I hope that someday you'll find a way to forgive me."

Now my head drooped and tears filled my eyes. "I've already forgiven you Daddy. Through all the bad you've done to me, I still love you and would do anything in the world for you. But you just had to know how I've felt all these years." I stood up and placed my hand on his shoulder. "I need to go, Daddy." I gave him a piece of paper with my telephone number written on it. "If you ever need me, call and I'll be here for you."

He looked up at me and tried to smile. "Thanks," he murmured.

"I'll let myself out Daddy," I said.

He didn't bother to get up. My last memory of him would be with his head bowed and body slumped, sitting on the edge of a bed. He claimed that we had better opportunities than his generation. That was probably true, but Daddy never tried to be anything more than an alcoholic. That defined his life and all his relationships. The two men closest to me, Daddy and Ronnie, allowed their weaknesses to control and ultimately defeat them.

CHAPTER 36

———————◆◆◆◆———————

I left Freeport early Monday morning. Mama and James drove me up to Houston to the Greyhound Bus Depot. I would arrive back in Austin at ten thirty in the morning and be at the campus for my afternoon classes. The three of us said very little during the fifty-mile ride. I stared out the window at thecountryside, admiring the rapid growth taking place in Lake Jackson, south of Freeport, all the way up to Houston. For the first time I thought of Freeport as a relic. A place where progress took place at a snail's pace if at all. Fewer people visited the beach area, usually opting for Galveston. The life blood for the city was still the shrimpers. If that ever dried up only welfare, drugs, and crime would be left. Someday, I thought, I would get Mama out of there. Move her to Houston, Dallas, or even Austin. I knew also that someday I would write about Freeport and especially Mama's tragic life there. The town had made her hard on the outside, but within her frail body was a sensitive woman who had been denied the opportunity to grow beyond the boundaries of that city. One day, however, she would be the beneficiary of my determination to succeed.

The confrontation with Daddy was gratifying, almost therapeutic. My father had always existed as an albatross around my neck. I finally had the opportunity to confront him with the myriad of unresolved issues between us. When I challenged him and felt victorious, the burdens were lifted, and I was free of the many years of fear that had always defined our relationship. When he stood up with a balled fist, I'm not sure I would have fought back if he had swung. But in that situation if I'd gotten the mindset to hit him, I know I would have destroyed the poor man. All the years of pain, fear, and embarrassment would have poured out through my two fists. Thinking back on that tense moment, I'm glad he didn't challenge me.

I could now return to Austin with my last Freeport burden lifted. I smiled knowing I had accomplished two challenges. I dealt with Ronnie and Daddy, and clearly let them know their complacency was detrimental to them, and I had moved far beyond where they still resided, within a stagnant existence.

Kim was her usual cantankerous self when she picked me up in front of the bus depot. I waited for a half hour before she finally arrived and that put me in a foul mood. Waiting in front of a Greyhound depot is not my idea of fun. Despite our bickering with each other she was really looking cute in her maternity dress. Her skin had a radiance to it, and her body had filled out nicely. I liked how beautiful she looked, but was just too mean to tell her so. Her complaints and my stubbornness would define our relationship until after the baby was born.

The last few months of her pregnancy had turned out to be pure hell between the two of us. We were young, not used to the incredible responsibility of parenthood, and still really getting to know each other. Kim was a homebody, wanting nothing more than to spend all her free time with me. I didn't really mind that at all, but I still wanted us to go out and enjoy ourselves. I was beginning to feel caged in and I didn't like that at all.

Catfish Station was a local jazz club located right in the middle of the black community in Austin. Every Friday night they featured their own version of Showtime at the Apollo. It copied closely the format of the original Apollo amateur talent search in Harlem, New York. Local talent would display their ability every Friday night. Some of the performers received raving applause from the crowd, and others were booed off the stage. I volunteered to act the role of the Sandman, who dressed in old raggedy clothes, would come on stage and sweep the booed talent off the stage with a broom. I didn't get paid, but it brought me lots of attention, something I still craved as a carry over from Freeport.

Kim refused to go with me on Friday nights. She complained incessantly about my leaving her to go to the club. Our arguments were heated. We went at each other like two pit bulls with neither of us backing down. Not only did I go to Catfish Station, I started going to parties on campus. Despite the fact that Kappa Alpha Psi turned me down as a pledge, I still went to their parties. One evening, just as I walked out the house on my way to a party on campus, she drove up.

I got to the car before she could get out.

"Where are you going David, you knew I was coming over?"

"I didn't know for sure you were coming this evening," I said not totally truthful. I knew she came over every night. I was just trying to get out of there before she showed up.

"I come every evening, David," she snapped. "Where you going anyway?"

"Over to the Kappa house for a couple hours."

"Why you just going to leave me and the baby? And why you want to go around them people? They don't like you."

"You can come and go with me if you want to. It'll be good for you to get out and party a little."

She slammed the palm of her hands against the steering wheel.

"Kim, calm down. You're going to hurt the baby."

"Why you care? All you care about is your precious fraternity."

"Don't say that Kim. You know I care about my baby. Why you acting like this?"

"Because all you want to do is run the streets," she shrieked. "You make me sick." Kim rolled up the windows and took off down the street.

Our relationship was almost at rock bottom. I don't think either one of us wanted to end it, but we didn't know how to save it. If there was ever a time that counseling could have helped, it was with the two of us, but neither one of us was mature enough to consider that possibility. Most important to me was my commitment to be in my child's life. It was clear that the two of us might not make it, but she would never have to worry about me not being around. I would always be there for her and our child. As the arguments intensified and the relationship worsened, I prepared for the break up. It happened one day at her mother's house.

As usual we had been arguing about something irrelevant. Both our tempers were running at a very high pitch. It was April, and Kim was less than a month from delivery. Added to that burden she was also studying to graduate from high school that same month. Pressure was mounting on her and she took it out on me. In all fairness to Kim, I don't think I was as understanding of her condition as I should have been. We finally broke it off on her mother's front porch. As usual it had to do with her perception that I was hanging out and partying too much.

"David, is this how it's going to be after the baby is born," she shouted as we climbed the steps to her front door.

"Only reason I go out is because all you ever want to do is sit around the house. Hell, Kim I work all the time, go to school and study all the time. I need a little release time."

She opened the front door, walked inside and said, "Well if you need party time, don't include me." Without looking back she swung the door shut.

I had put my hand on the frame to keep her from closing it. When she swung it closed, it penned my hand against the frame and practically broke it.

She looked back and I believe wanted to apologize, but instead, slammed the door shut this time locking it from the inside.

I walked the six miles back to my house near the university. It gave me a lot of time to think. When Kim had first told me she was pregnant, I pledged to be with her all the time, but now we were apart. She had become impossible to get along with and always wanted to fight. Was it my job to be so understanding of her condition that I should accept her verbal abuse, which came fast and furious? I didn't want to lose Kim, but I didn't want to keep her if it meant a constant barrage of verbal attacks.

My resolve not to stay involved with Kim was tested the very next day. She showed up at the house in the morning and wanted to work things out. But at that point I couldn't do that with her. The abuse was too hurtful. All my life I had lived in an environment dominated by some kind of abuse. My Daddy, Bobbie and even Mama had used me as their punching bag over the years. Now that I was out of that environment, there was no way I would take it from Kim. We talked for about fifteen minutes, and then she left. I wouldn't see Kim for a week. In the meantime, I began to hang out over at the University of Texas campus with Melvin and a couple other guys, and that is when I met Tina.

I believe I temporarily got sucked into a brief relationship with Tina because of the volatile past few months with Kim. It was refreshing to talk and be with someone not arguing and hollering at me all the time. At first we started out only as friends, but it soon escalated to more than that. After a couple weeks I was spending all my spare time over at Tina's apartment. When we weren't there, we spent time at my place and that is when all hell practically broke loose.

We were lying on the floor in my room when Kim knocked on the door. She knew my schedule and figured I should be home about that time. She was right. I was home, but she was wrong assuming I was there alone. She banged on the door for about ten minutes. Tina and I stayed on the floor. It was my luck the way the house was constructed she couldn't see into my bedroom through the window. We only had to wait her out. It seemed as though her knocking would never end.

I felt bad knowing that she was carrying my baby, may have needed me for something, and I wasn't there for her. This was the lowest point in my life. I really cared for Kim and only liked Tina. I was being selfish, but felt that Kim had forced my hand because of her constant arguing.

We waited there on the floor for at least another fifteen minutes after the knocking stopped. I then hustled Tina out of the house, and never brought her back over there.

After that scare, I practically lived at Tina's apartment. One night, however, I decided to give it a break and stay home by myself. As fate would have it, that was the night Kim's water broke. It was a little after two o'clock in the morning, and I'd just drifted off to sleep after studying for over five straight hours. When I heard the knock at the door I didn't want to get up. But I was the only one in the house, and at that time of morning it could be an emergency. As I walked into the living room and to the front door, I peeked out the window and saw Kim leaning against the house. She was struggling to keep her balance. I hurried and opened the door, went outside and put my arm around her.

"Come on, David, it's time," she screamed at me.

I slammed the door shut and helped her down the steps and back to the car. Her mother was driving and when we both got back in she took off toward Saint David's Hospital. We said very little on the ride to the hospital. I think Mrs. Brown was aware of the tension between Kim and me. I could almost read her mind thinking this was the beginning of my abandonment of her daughter even though I was in the car accompanying them to the hospital.

At the hospital, Kim was rushed right into delivery. I went in with her. Unlike my Daddy, I planned to be there when my child was born, and planned to be the first person other than the nurse to hold my child.

The doctor examined Kim and decided to induce labor. That didn't work right away, so he and the nurse left Kim and me alone in the room. I found a spot on the floor and lay there. I was so hyper there was no way I could go to sleep. Every fifteen minutes Kim would rise up in the bed and cry out my name. Each time she called me I jumped from the floor and held her hand until she was able to calm down. Periodically, the nurse would come in the room and check on her. With each visit she would say that Kim was getting closer and closer to delivery. Then she would be gone and it would be Kim and I alone waiting for our child to decide to enter our world.

We finally saw the doctor again that morning. It was close to ten o'clock when he came in and examined Kim. It seemed like less than a minute and he was gone again. I was getting frustrated and angry. Why couldn't he do something? A few minutes after he left the room to get coffee, it all happened. Kim felt the baby moving so I ran out of the room and got the nurse. She came back in, and less than five minutes later she was holding my son. I cut the umbilical cord, took him in my arms, and rubbed our skin against each other. I was told that if a father rubs his skin with his son right after birth, they would have a strong bond. I wanted that with him, something I never experienced, and it was absolutely mandatory for me to have.

We named our son David Alexander Floyd, Jr. I did not have the identical name as my father, since his middle name was not Alexander. So therefore I was the senior and my son junior. That worked well for me since I had no desire to have my son named after my father. He didn't deserve that kind of respect and honor. David Alexander started with me, and that's the way it should have been.

The semester had just ended when David was born, so I devoted all the time I wasn't working to being with him. That caused some serious problems between Tina and me. We were spending very little time together. Actually, a week after David's birth, I had moved in with her because my roommates and I had been evicted from the house. The problem again was with Chicken George, who never seemed to be around when rent was due. We were all tired of covering his part of the rent and instead decided to move and not live together again. I needed a place to stay and Tina's was the most convenient. Right after her classes ended at the University of Texas, she planned to go home for the summer, but first we had to decide on the nature of our relationship. She initiated the conversation one evening after I returned from spending most of the day with Kim and little David.

"You know I'm leaving in the morning for home, David and we haven't spent anytime together at all," she calmly said to me.

"I realize that, but I've been spending all my time with my son."

"And with Kim."

"I guess you can say that."

"You still really care for her don't you?" she asked

"Yes I do."

"In that case, I think we need to end this and when I come back for the fall semester, I'm going to move back on campus." She paused and then handed me some papers. "This is the lease I have here, you can keep the place until it's up. If the landlord questions you, just tell him I'm gone for the summer and will renew the lease in the fall when it's time."

"You sure you trust me to make the payments and not mess up your credit?"

"Yes, I do, David," she answered. "If there is one thing I believe I've come to know about you it's that you are responsible." She lightly kissed me on the lips. "I'm gone in the morning, good night."

That night was the first time I slept in what was supposed to be the room I was renting from her. We both knew it was over, and even though it may have been nice to have one more night of ecstasy with her, we restrained.

I had, in my mind, renewed my relationship with Kim. I needed to be with her all the time, so that I would be there for my son. I refused to be a long distance daddy. David would never have to imagine what his Daddy did, or where he was at any given time as I did all my life with my father. My goal was to be right there with him, despite the realization that reconciling my differences with Kim would be quite a task.

CHAPTER 37

In the fall of 1991, I began my second semester as a sophomore at Huston-Tillotson. My life had changed considerably since I first arrived in Austin over a year and a half ago. I had matured a great deal. I was now a father, and gladly accepted that responsibility with enthusiasm. I carried a full load of classes to include Composition, Chemistry, Intermediate Accounting, and Personal Finance along with Health. I was still working at Church's and finding time to improve my reading skills. I could only hope I wasn't digging a hole too deep to get out of if necessary.

I wasn't sure how long I would be able to keep Tina's apartment at Fountain Terrace. Since there was only me, I agreed to let Chicken George move in with me. He agreed to pay half the rent, but given his past track record I had serious doubts that I'd ever see any money from him. I wasn't sure how long I'd be able to stay in Fountain Terrace, but I would stretch it out as long as possible. I had no choice; there was no other place for me to live.

Kim had graduated from high school. In fact, she marched with her class two weeks after David was born. We never discussed marriage at that point in our relationship. It didn't seem appropriate since we had broken up just a month before David's birth. She had a job at Shortstop Restaurant as a waitress, which meant I had to get over to her house, pick up David and take him to school with me. Together, we'd catch the bus to the campus, and he would actually go into classes with me. The instructors were understanding and had no problem with that arrangement as long as he didn't cry. I got a lot of help from the female students who constantly fussed over David. After class I'd hustle over to Shortstop Restaurant and hand David over to Kim, who got off work early in the afternoon. Through this rigor, I maintained my grades and continued to practice my reading. I could now read seventh grade level books with relative ease.

Everything was working out well, and then Chicken George reneged on paying his rent in the month of September. There was no way I could pay the entire amount given the additional cost of David's food and other necessities. I refused to allow anyone else to pay for him. From the beginning I made it known my son was my responsibility, and that meant all costs incurred from his needs. We were evicted at the beginning of October. I had no place to live, so decided to sleep in the park and clean up the next day at Kim's house. I did this for two weeks and finally, Mrs. Brown found out I was sleeping in the park and felt sorry for me. She allowed me to stay at her house, with the understanding I would sleep on the couch. I lived with them until the spring of 1992 at which time I got an apartment in the Elmridge Apartment Complex, which was essentially public housing.

Since I had every intention of pledging Kappa again in the spring, I had to correct the one reason they used to turn me down the prior year. Their excuse was due to my lack of participation in campus events. What better way to participate than to get elected to a position in the student government? When elections were announced in the fall of 1991 I ran for treasurer and easily won. After all, who could possibly out talk me?

With my election to the student government, I was fully entrenched in campus life. Little David participated with me as I took him to government meetings and continued to take him to class.

By spring 1992 my life had settled into an orderly routine. I moved into the Elmriridge Apartment Complex. The apartments were close to school and Church's Chicken, so I cut down a lot of travel time and had that additional time to study. My longest travel time was over to Kim's house to pick up David. However, within three months of moving into the new apartment, with no roommates, that all changed. I adamantly told Chicken George no when he had asked to move in with me, and this time, he wasn't the one who I took in.

It was a warm spring night in March when I left Kim's house and caught the bus back over to my apartment. Once home I spent a couple hours studying and decided to turn in when the doorbell rang. It could only be one person, and that was Kim. I had no other visitors. I opened the door and she stood there holding David.

"David, our house burned down," she screamed.

"What?"

"Yes, right after you left. The entire house is gone. I don't know what I'm going to do."

"Where's your mother?" I asked.

"With friends. She wanted me to stay with them also, but I told her no. I wanted to be here with you. This is where me and David belong, with you. You promised I never had to worry."

"Come on in," I said and took David from her.

"We lost everything. All our clothes and everything for David," she shrieked.

I put an arm around her while holding David in the other. "You all going to stay here with me," I said. "Slowly as a family we'll get everything back together again. I got a little cash and we can buy you some things tomorrow and get some things for David. We're going to be all right."

Kim started crying with head buried on my shoulder. She didn't say anything at all, but her tears told the entire story. All I needed to hear was her sobbing and our problems from the past year were gone. When Mama had cried there wasn't much I could do, but now I was in charge, and I could help wipe away Kim's tears. That is exactly what I set out to do. We would become a family, living in the Elmridge apartments for the next four years.

I often wondered how long it would take for Mama and my family to visit me in Austin. It finally happened in March, a couple months after I moved into my new apartment. Mama decided it was time to see her first grandchild, so she, along with James and Nicole, drove up on a Friday afternoon. Ronnie, who had received two years probation for the drug charge couldn't leave Freeport. His health was also failing him. The diabetes was getting progressively worse. James stayed with Kim and me, while Mama insisted on staying with Mrs. Brown in her new apartment she'd moved into since the fire. Over the years they became close friends, and I can imagine they shared many conversations about me.

One day, after they had gone back to Freeport, Mama shared one conversation they had, and it made her feel proud. Mrs. Brown told her that she'd doubted my sincerity and believed I would abandon Kim leaving her with a baby to raise on her own. In addition, she told Mama that she was not in a financial position to help Kim and just didn't know what she was going to do after I did my disappearing act. She prayed many nights that I would live up to my commitment and I had done just that. Not only did I take care of David's financial needs but I was also there to help raise him. Mama said she thought her chest would burst with pride. I had done something to make Mama proud of me, and that made my own chest burst with pride.

A year had passed since the Kappa's had embarrassed me and now it was time for pledge season. I was prepared for the brothers I knew wanted me to fail again. We met in the same place, and again they waited until the very end to call on me. Somehow they had to come up with a different excuse than the one from last year, since I was definitely entrenched in school affairs as treasurer for the student government.

It didn't take long to find out what they had conjured up this time. I sat again in front of the brothers, and one of the seniors initiated the charges.

"David, it's been brought to our attention that you cursed out one of your instructors. Is that true?" the brother asked.

I gave them an inquisitive look and said, "I have never been disrespectful to any of my instructors. Which instructor was it that I supposedly cussed out?" I asked.

"We heard it was Mrs. Harris," Osie replied and in doing so set his own trap.

"That is interesting," I said, "because if you had looked through the packet I prepared for this occasion, you will find a letter from Mrs. Harris recommending me for admission to the Kappa's. Do you want me to show it to you?"

"No, that won't be necessary," Osie snapped.

Kelvin had showed up late for the meeting, but was there in time to hear the exchange between Osie and me. He now spoke up.

"You brothers been messing with David since he attempted to pledge Kappa last year. It is time for this nonsense to stop. First, the fact that he would even come back and consider Kappa speaks highly of him. A lot of brothers would have quite frankly said 'fuck you' after the way you treated him last year. And my second point, if you knew this brothers background and what he has gone through to reach this point in his education, you would consider it an honor to have a brother of his quality wanting to pledge Kappa. You either vote him on line, or I'm going to national and let them know you are discriminating against a brother who will bring honor to our fraternity. Now I suggest you get on with your business and vote this brother on line."

Evidently Kelvin's words had an impact on the others. They voted me on line, and I began my pledge period to become a Kappa. Even though Osie and the other brothers who didn't want me in the fraternity had voted to allow me to pledge, they were determined to break my will before I crossed over and became a brother. They had made it clear that I would not ever be a Kappa. The method used to break me down was paddling. They would beat me until I bled and then beat me some more. One night I came home so bloody, Kim threatened to call the national office in Philadelphia, Pennsylvania and complain. I talked her out of it. What these brothers didn't know is that I was used to beatings. My life with Bobby prepared me for this very day. If at ten I could endure his vicious beatings, I knew darn well at twenty-one I could endure anything these men dished out.

Osie wasn't the worst of the brothers beating on me, even though he was quite bad. There was a brother named Dustin who was just plain sadistic. He slapped one of my fellow pledges so hard we could hear him whimpering. It made my blood boil. One night he was beating on me and I turned to look back at him.

"My whole life prepared me for this. You can't break me, not now or ever," I said.

The beatings continued for the entire nine weeks. But in the end I didn't break and crossed the burning sands as a Kappa man. Enduring the beatings and making it into the fraternity gave me a feeling of accomplishment. I was no longer Pealo, with the raggedy loafers who could barely read, and who had been laughed at by the other students. I was now teasurer of the school government and a member of one of the most prestigious fraternities in the country. Most important, at the end of the semester I was moving on to my junior year, and quite confident that by next year I would graduate. It was time to start looking at graduate programs at other schools.

CHAPTER 38

Mrs. Maria Goodrich, the graduate school admissions officer at Bentley College in Boston, Massachusetts, will probably never forget me. For months I called her every day about my admission to their graduate program in accounting. During my junior year at Huston-Tillotson I began to seek out graduate programs. I narrowed my choice down to either Wake Forest, Texas Tech, or Bentley. My preference was for the latter since it was located on the east coast in Boston, one of my dream cities when I was young.

In the summer of 1992, I doubled up on classes. My goal had always been to graduate in 1992, the same year my high school graduation class was graduating from college. I knew that was an impossibility, but I could get the job done by the summer of 1993. It only meant I had to study harder, take more classes and still find time for my son and of course Kim. That same summer I went to work for MCI company selling memberships over the phone. They had a prewritten script that you simply read when talking with a potential customer. With the help of Kim I memorized the script. Kim had also gotten a job with University Credit Union so our financial condition had improved considerably. Our lives had taken a turn for the good, but I still was aware that I needed to keep on improving my reading skills. Whenever we found some time, either during the day or late at night, Kim worked with me, still using the cue cards. I was now reading at the eighth grade level, but knew I would have to soon take the Graduate Management Aptitude Test if I expected to be admitted to any graduate program. We kept this routine until summer 1993 when I finally graduated from Huston-Tillotson.

There is a reason why Mrs. Goodrich will never forget me. I finally narrowed my choice of graduate schools to Bentley. When I made that decision I began a relentless barrage of telephone calls after I submitted all the paper work for admission. I faced two major problems; 1) my grade point averaged at graduation from Huston-Tillotson was only 2.90, and 2) my GMAT score was a low 375. Neither of these would qualify me for admission to one of the best business schools in the country. But like all other things in my life, I knew this would not come easy. My strongest characteristics were my determination and stamina. Throughout my life I had heard the word "no" so often that it lost all meaning to me. "No" simply meant that I had to try harder. I was going to be a student at Bentley and no one would stand in my way. My incessant telephone calls began in the summer of 1993 right after I took the GMAT. I called at least three times a week. Mrs. Goodrich's biggest mistake was providing me with the toll free number to the college. Sometimes I would just call to wish her a happy day, or to ask about the weather, but always with the purpose of keeping David Floyd's name on her mind. Once I called to inquire about her health. We would always end the conversation with her telling me she'd gotten no word about my admission from the committee.

Right after graduation I was hired by the City of Austin Auditor's Office. Bob Kellogg, the man for whom I worked, became my mentor. I began to get first hand experience as a public accountant. The pay wasn't that great, but along with Kim's income, we made enough to keep food on our table and take care of our son.

I believe Kim would have been content for me to just work for the City of Austin and not go on for my advanced degrees. We talked about how we would handle our situation when I got accepted to Bentley. Kim did not want to move to Boston. She was only nineteen and did not want to be that far away from her mother. We agreed that she would stay right there, continue to work at the credit union, and of course raise our son, while I went back to Boston for the two years it would take for me to complete my studies for a masters degree.

I waited with great anxiety for Bentley to contact me with the good news. With each passing day, my mood became more irritable than the day before. Finally, in the early summer of 1994, the school contacted me with the news I had been accepted for the fall semester of 1994.

My joy was cut short from a telephone call I received from home. Mama informed me that Grandma had died of a heart attack.

Mama had called me on Wednesday, but we couldn't leave until that Friday. Kim and I both had to wait because of our jobs. And we also had to wait until Rich McGiver, who was playing basketball for the University of Texas could go, because he was our transportation. That was, for me, the roughest and most difficult trip I have ever taken. I hadn't talked that much with Grandma since we had our reconciliation discussion in 1990. In fact, I hadn't been home for a couple years. I would call Grandma and talk with her periodically, but I never knew she was sick, and it came as a shock when I got that call from Mama.

I remained reticent all the way down to Freeport. I was tuned out to the others in the car. I couldn't accept the reality of Grandma's death. Despite all the years she had treated me badly, I still loved her, unequivocally. My consolation was our last conversation back in the summer of 1990 when she apologized for the abusive comments she'd made over the years about my dark complexion. Even though she'd favored Levi, I knew then that she loved me. There is no doubt I loved her, and making it through the ordeal of her funeral would test both my mental and physical stamina. I was preparing for the most difficult day of my life.

We went straight over to Aunt Faye's house when we arrived in Freeport. That's where the entire family congregated Friday afternoon for a family cookout. It is a black family tradition to have lots of food at the designated home where the bereaving family congregates. Aunt Faye's backyard was crowded with Grandma's church family, neighborhood friends, and all her children and relatives. Walking outside I caught the aroma of barbequed beef and chicken both cooking on the grill. Folks were standing in small groups drinking beer, sodas, and some stronger substances. They were recalling old memories and making new acquaintances. Family squabbles and bickering are all put aside for the sake of the deceased person, and with Grandma that was especially true since she'd always been the strength of our family.

I ran over to Mama and hugged her as tightly as I ever had in life. At that point I lost emotional control and cried with my head on her shoulder. Mama could only pat me on the back in her effort to reassure me that everything would be all right. She kept saying over and over again that Grandma was now in a better place as if she was trying to convince herself.

I broke from Mama's embrace and went to each of my brothers and hugged them. That may have been the first time in our lives that we had ever hugged. I also found Nicole and hugged her. I do know it was the first time we as siblings had shared that much emotion among us. With each hug, we assured each other that Grandma was now in Heaven or with Jesus, or resting in the strong and powerful embrace of God.

But despite all these soothing words, I couldn't help wanting Grandma back in her small house, sitting in her living room watching one of her many favorite television programs. I longed for the Sunday family dinners once again, even though they always turned out disastrous for us. I'd even settle for one of Grandma's insults if she could just come back from that mysterious place that follows death. I was being selfish because I didn't want to share her with God or Jesus. We all needed her much more than either of them because all my life she'd been the strength of our family, the glue that kept us together as a family. With her gone, that would all change. I just knew we would never capture that unity again in this life. That made me sad and brought a constant flow of tears from my eyes.

That evening Grandma's wake was held in a small town twenty-two miles from Freeport. It was held out there because that was the closest black mortuary to Freeport, and our family was related to the owners of the funeral home, E. Viola and Sons. The entire family went to the wake with the exception of Ronnie, Kim, Little David, and me. I just couldn't see myself sitting around in a funeral home staring at Grandma's body lying in a casket. It would be sufficiently difficult the next day at the funeral so I didn't need this additional stress. We went back to Mama's house, and Ronnie and I sat and reminisced about Grandma. That led to memories of our lives in the cramped living quarters, with various men and all the struggles we endured under Mama's roof and her rule.

First Street Emmanuel Baptist Church was packed when our family entered the sanctuary and marched down the center aisle to our reserved seats in the first four rows on the left side of the church. Kim, Little David, and I were seated in the second row right behind Mama. The casket containing Grandma's body was placed right in front of us. It was closed but would be re-opened at the end of the service for a final view by family and others, some friends and some simply spectators.

I glanced at both sides of the pews and saw familiar faces that took me back through my troubled years in Freeport. I realized how far I had come over the past four years. Very few people in that crowd would have thought I would earn a college degree in accounting. In fact, most of them would have bet I'd be in prison by now; another victim of the young black man's struggle for survival in a world where the odds are stacked against him. It all made me grateful that I had beaten those odds.

The Full Gospel Choir, in full regalia, stood and with voices sounding like angels from Heaven, just as if God had sent them to us to soothe our pain, broke out in chorus, "*Precious Lord take my hand. Lead me on lest I stand.*"

Mama had been able to hold back the tears, but when those angelic voices greeted us with the reassuring words of such a powerful song, she could no longer control her emotions. With audible sounds of grief, she began to wail. I was sitting in the row right behind her and her expression of sorrow affected me. I also began crying and Kim put her arm around me for support.

Reverend Richardson finally took the podium and offered a minister's usual words of comfort. He was no longer the pastor at First Emmanuel. He had moved on to minister another church in Corpus Christi, Texas. Mama, Aunt Faye and Aunt Clevella had made a special request that he come back to Freeport to officiate over Grandma's service. That's exactly what Grandma would have wanted. She loved her minister, and we all knew something would have been missing if he hadn't preached her home-going celebration. He did the job we expected of him.

He began the sermon by telling a story about the passing of a city leader in Corpus Christi and the opening of a new bank building. The florist sent the flowers and cards meant for the bank to the church where the funeral was being conducted. When the family read one of the cards meant as a welcoming of the new bank it read, "congratulations on your new home." He then tied that to Grandma moving on to her new home, which was in a better place, and that God had reached His powerful hand out to her to welcome her home. He reassured us that she was happy and content. He made us feel that death was a good thing and a far superior state of existence over this life. I reached the conclusion if death represented all the pleasant and good things described in his sermon, then he had to be right. Grandma was content and happy. That brought a slight smile to my face.

We had all settled down and relaxed our nerves when they opened the casket for a final viewing. And I lost it. We had to sit there while the entire congregation marched in front of the casket. Some people would just keep going and then others would stop and stare. Some would remain quiet as they moved on and others would break down and cry. The crying affected me as I felt my emotions moving up through my body to the point I couldn't control any part of me. Finally, when it was time for the family to get up and make that last walk my legs practically failed me. When in front of the casket I fell to my knees, clinging to the side. I stayed there until my uncles pried me away and helped me back to my seat. Regardless of what Reverend Richardson preached about, I didn't want Grandma over there at that new place. I wanted and needed her still here with me.

Once the last of the family members had viewed Grandma's body, the funeral director closed the casket and the pallbearers carried it out to the hearse. Kim, Little David and I got into one of the three family limousines and proceeded to the cemetery right outside the city limits. Grandma's plot was near her daughter, Marilyn Ruth who had been murdered years ago, as well as Patrick's, who committed suicide right in Grandma's house. The dirt to cover the casket was piled off to the right and camouflaged with a green canvas. Chairs were lined up next to the open hole in the ground for the family. They were shaded with an awning. Friends and visitors stood behind the chairs. Mama took a chair right in front as Reverend Richardson said a few words, asked everyone to stand and offered a final prayer asking God to accept his "faithful and loyal servant into his eternal Kingdom" with the proverbial praise, "well done my obedient servant."

Once it was over, and everyone piled into a limousine or other cars to leave, Ronnie and I stayed behind. We watched the men lower Grandma's casket deep into the ground and then cover it with dirt. Two hours later when we finally left the cemetery I was exhausted and in no mood to socialize at the family gathering still going on at Aunt Faye's house.

The next day we left Freeport, and my thoughts turned from despondency to the joys of leaving for Bentley University and quest of my second goal, a Masters Degree in Accounting.

CHAPTER 39

———◆◆◆———

Kim cried all the way to the airport and kept crying as she and Little David accompanied me to the gate for United Airlines Flight #228 from Austin to Boston, Massachusetts. Little David was three years old, and Kim had him dressed in a white shirt with short black pants. I kept his hair cut close to his scalp and he looked a lot like me. As I gave the gate attendant my ticket and proceeded toward the plane, I could hear my son call out "Daddy, Daddy." I didn't want to leave Kim and Little David behind but from the time Bentley notified me that I had been accepted to their graduate program, I begged Kim to go with me, and she refused. My financial aid and the little money I got from Bentley was enough to sustain the three of us for the next two years. However, Kim couldn't break away from her mother and sisters. She preferred to stay in Austin and continue working at the credit union. I could understand her emotional ties to family. Boston was a long way from Austin, and I wasn't sure how well I'd make the transition. But I had to; Kim didn't.

From my window seat on the plane I saw the two of them standing at the window inside the terminal. Little David had his head pressed against the glass. Kim waved in a slow side to side motion as the plane taxied toward the runway.

Once they were out of sight, I relaxed back on the headrest and closed my eyes. What on God's earth was I doing? Here I sat on a jet plane preparing for takeoff to Boston and a temporary home for me at a university ranked in the top twenty for business schools. My academic skills did not match the quality of competition I would confront at Bentley.

A young man sitting next to me exacerbated my fears when he asked why I was going to Boston. I answered that I was to attend graduate school at Bentley University and that my major was accounting.

"Man, you must be awfully smart," he said. "That's a really hard school. I know a lot of people who dropped out or flunked out 'cause they couldn't cut it."

I chuckled to myself. If he only knew. I was now reading at the seventh grade level, finished my undergraduate work with a 2.97 GPA at a college not ranked at all, and scored only 375 on GMAT. I was far from being smart. This could easily be the end of the line for me.

Bentley had a cab waiting for me, and the driver held up a sign with my name on it when we entered the baggage area at Logan Airport a little after four o'clock in the morning. That impressed me and gave me a feeling of importance. I climbed into the back-seat of the cab and relaxed while the driver headed for Waltham, the Boston suburb where Bentley was located. Thoughts raced through my mind at astronomical speed. I hadn't slept much on the plane, but I wasn't sleepy at all. We went under the tracks for the T train. I watched as it pulled out from its stop, and heard the rumbling of the wheels against the track as we went underneath the plat-form. That was the first time I'd ever seen a metro-rail. That form of transportation was not popular in Texas. The driver pointed in the direction of Harvard Square telling me that's where the his-torically famous university was located. We drove between the large skyscrapers in the downtown area. As a country boy from Texas, I began to feel that I might be in over my head.

When we arrived at Bentley the housing office was closed, but the manager had left my dorm key with the security guard. My roommate had just gotten up when I unlocked the door and went inside. Dizho was a brilliant Chinese student studying as part of a foreign exchange program. We hit if off right away. Our biggest problem, however, was communication. He spoke Chinese and proper English and I spoke a lot of broken English and slang. His contact had been with Blacks from Africa and not America so he found my dress, mannerisms, and language much different from Africans. We were a good match because we learned from each other. He was intrigued with Black Americans and followed me around quite a bit, while I was impressed with his study habits and began to copy him. We remained roommates for the two years I was at Bentley. He insisted it be that way.

The first day of classes proved my initial suspicion was right. I was in way over my head. Students in my entering graduate class were pure pedigree for the Bentley academia rigor. Sitting in the classroom, I was surrounded with the elite. The student to my right had just graduated from Harvard, to my left from Massachusetts Institute of Technology, behind me from West Point, and in front from Stanford.

Nevertheless, when it was my turn for an introduction, I proudly announced I was a graduate of Huston-Tillotson and in unison the entire class responded with a resounding "where?" They assumed it was located in Houston, Texas and I corrected them with a little information about my alma mater. They all, including the instructor, wore perplexed expressions. The instructor asked.

"Why did you come all the way back east to go to graduate school?"

"Because I wanted to attend an outstanding school with an outstanding accounting program," I answered.

"What about the University of Texas?" he continued his questions. "It has a very strong business school."

At this point I was registering mixed messages, but didn't want to misread the reason for his questions. I couldn't help noting I was the only black American in the group. However, I fought the temptation to attribute racial motives to his questions. I accepted that he was simply curious as to why I would come all the way back east when an excellent business school was right there in my backyard.

"I wanted the opportunity to experience living on the east coast," I said. "And the opportunity to live in one of the most important historical cities in America."

Evidently my answers satisfied him because he asked me no further questions. Neither did my fellow classmates, but after that I noticed that they were only lukewarm towards me. I surmised that they assumed I was a product of affirmative action, and if not for being black would never have been admitted to Bentley.

Their snobbish attitudes became even more pronounced whenever the class was confronted with a problem that called on each of us helping to find the solution. At the beginning of the semester we all exchanged telephone numbers (in 1994 there we no emails). While trying to solve the problem no one called me. It was awhile after that I discovered they had a number of study group sessions and I finally did get the answer. I had to do it on my own. I was not welcomed into their clique.

I began to worry because we had a major group project coming up in a couple weeks and I was concerned that I might be stuck without a team and if put on one, they would resent me. Once assigned a city, we as a group had to conduct actual performance audits to determine how well they utilized their available resources. It was no small task at all.

The week before the assignment, we had our first examination. I studied night and day for that exam. I solicited help from my roommate, and also had a young tutor who was an absolute whiz in accounting. Because of their assistance I maxed the exam. Our instructor made a public announcement to the entire class that for the first time in his class a student had gotten a hundred on his exam, and that student was David Floyd.

I wished for a camera at that moment to capture the shocked looks on the other students' faces. The student from little Huston-Tillotson in Texas outscored all of them on the exam. After that, they no longer viewed me as the affirmative action token in the class. When the professor told us to join teams for the performance audit project I had no problem getting on a team. Just as I had done with Vicky Clay and the Kappa's, I won again.

Even with that minor accomplishment, I still knew I was way over my head. Nothing in my background prepared me for the rigors of a university like Bentley. I took advantage of every tool available to me, from individual tutors, to labs and professors during their office hours. I also emulated Dizhos study habits. Whenever he went to the library, I was right behind him. He would spend up to six and seven hours every day in the library and I would be right with him. Once he accused me, jokingly, of being his shadow, always following him around. But he had the best study habits of anyone at Bentley, and so I took my lead from him.

I never missed an opportunity to meet one of my professors at his office if there was something I didn't understand from the lecture. I practically drove my Advanced Economics professor insane I was at his office so much. There was one particular economic concept I just couldn't comprehend and that was the difference between the change in demand and the change in quantity demand. He used every possible example to drive the concept home, but it wasn't registering with me. He would get frustrated and finally say, "let's take a break and walk away from this until another time." And that would frustrate me. I didn't need a break, I needed to understand that concept. I wanted to stay right there in his office but he was looking for a way to get me out. After numerous frustrating sessions, I finally got it, and most importantly I received a B in his class.

Unlike in the past, I earned that B. Nothing was ever given to you at Bentley. Unlike Huston-Tillotson, Bentley professors had no sympathy for your struggles. They didn't care if you were married with a family or just single and a slow learner, everyone was treated the same. You had to keep up to stay with the fast pace of the class. After one semester I was glad that Kim had decided to stay in Austin. I needed all my time to keep up with the classes, and any distraction would have been devastating. By the end of that first semester, I was proud of my accomplishments. Because of my hard work, my fellow students finally accepted me. They willingly brought me into their elite eastern Ivy League clique. What they didn't know is that, at no time, did I want to be included. I only wanted to be respected.

With the combination of financial aid from Bentley and federal student loan money I was able to send both Kim and Mama money, pay all my bills and fly home to Austin every other month. Despite all the help Bentley gave me, for some reason, I began to view my relationship to the college and the student body, from a racial perspective. I was the only black in my class of 45 and strongly felt that the other students assumed the only reason they admitted me was because I was black. I resented them for that reason and walked around campus with a huge chip on my shoulder. I was also making a major adjustment of spending most of my time in a white world. During my school years in Freeport I went to school with whites, but once the day was over we had no further contact. At Huston-Tillotson, the college was black, but at Bentley, with the exception of a few undergraduates, the school and culture was white. In Freeport I failed to recognize the blatant racism that existed in the city and the schools. At Huston-Tillotson my self-esteem had been destroyed, because I blamed me for all my weaknesses, I allowed a student like Vicky Clay to tease and make fun of me. Finally at Bentley all the anger, built up over the years, exploded.

My first confrontation occurred in the stairwell of the dormitory next to mine as two of my newly found black friends, who were undergraduates, and I made our way down the stairs. Just as we got half way down, three white football players started up. It was about nine at night and they were loud and appeared to be drunk. As they got close to us one of them, the quarterback on the team, shouted.

"Y'all niggers get out the way."

I came to an abrupt stop, as did my two friends. We did not move as they approached us.

"Back in Texas we drag white boys down the stairs and into the basement for using that word," I snapped at him.

"Well in Massachusetts, they don't do anything but move out of the way."

I prepared for the rumble assuming the brothers would back me up. They didn't. Instead they backed down and moved out of the way. The quarterback and I eyeballed each other as they passed by. A week later the quarterback came up to me and apologized. I accepted his apology, but at the time I had been ready to go to blows.

The second confrontation happened while I was standing in the food line in the cafeteria. A young white student, who looked to be an undergraduate, grabbed a tray and got in front of me.

"Hey, bro," I said. "I was already in line and you need to get behind me."

"Sorry, I didn't see you," he said to me, but kept moving forward in the line.

I tapped him on the shoulder. "Slow down buddy, you need to get in line behind me."

"I don't think so," he said and kept moving forward.

Without really thinking, I pushed him from behind. He fell forward out of line, but when he regained his balance, he started back toward me. Before our scuffle got out of hand a cafeteria worker stepped between us. After a brief moment's reflection I realized I was about to fight in the university cafeteria. I needed to get a handle on my behavior. But it just got worse on the basketball court in the school gym.

I played intramural basketball games on an all-black team, and our competitors consisted of all-white teams. The competition got intense, and we complained to the referees how they wouldn't call blatant fouls committed by the other team against us, but if we just touched our opponents, we were hit with a foul. There was no doubt in our minds that the discrepancy was based on color. We complained, but there was nothing we could do the stop it.

One time I called a meeting of all the black students to plan a protest march against the basketball team and coach. A young black ball player, John Spriggs, should have received a full scholarship. John was a really good point guard, much better than the white player who did receive a scholarship. We planned to protest all the games for the entire season.

The administration asked Dr. Earl Avery, the only black administrator, to talk with me since I was perceived as the leader of the protest. He intervened and convinced us that a protest was not a good idea. Dr. Avery told me that my name kept coming across his desk for the wrong reasons. He explained that I would never make it through the program and chances were good I'd end up suspended from the school if I kept down the path of always being angry. And he was right. I was on my way to getting expelled if he hadn't intervened. Dr. Avery became my mentor for the remainder of the time I was at Bentley, much in the same manner as Coach Wallace had back in intermediate school.

My anger was a result of my low self-esteem triggered early in life when I could not read. Dr. Avery helped me to curb that anger and realize there was a greater prize waiting for me once I graduated from Bentley. I listened to him and began to recognize the magnitude of my accomplishment that lay right before me. Anger shouldn't be the emotion that controlled my behavior, but instead a determination to finish my course work at Bentley and then move on. Anger was for that group of men who couldn't cope, and fell victim to their own insecurities and low self-esteem. At one time I didn't like myself, but as I prepared to become a graduate of one of the nation's most prestigious business schools, I had all the reason in the world to like who I had become. Dr. Avery helped me to reach that point in my life.

After that initial meeting with Dr. Avery, I was at his office practically everyday. He really did help me keep my eyes on the prize and the most important lesson I learned from him and my experience at Bentley was that not every black person was my friend and not every white person my enemy. The quality of the person as a human being was the most important consideration in judging others. I had lived among many scoundrels in Freeport and they were all black. As I neared completion of my two-year program at Bentley, I adopted the Martin Luther King, Jr., philosophy, and that was to judge individuals by the content of their character and not the color of their skin.

I grew a great deal as a man at Bentley and most important, after two years of struggle, I prepared to leave that institution with a Masters Degree in Accounting. It had been a real struggle. The most difficult class was Ethics in Accounting. I took it my second year, and it more than any other one class, started me on the way to an ulcer. But I endured and won.

CHAPTER 40

The last two months of my second year at Bentley, I began to receive job interviews from major corporations. In March 1996, Cargill Corporation flew me and fifty other applicants from other schools to Minneapolis, Minnesota for a series of interviews. I arrived just as the weather was changing so it was not exceptionally cold. They put us up in a swank hotel, something I was not used to. We spent the entire day going from one interview to another. I believe I impressed their management and felt confident I would receive a job offer.

That evening after all the interviews were over and we had eaten dinner, the men in the group decided it was time for a little relaxation. We all decided to go to a nightclub for a couple of hours. I agreed to go along, assuming it was a regular nightclub. We piled into a couple of cabs and took off. When we arrived, I stared up at the billboard outside the club. It was lit up in bright red letters with one word over and over again, "Girls! Girls! Girls!"

I started out of the cab with the others. "What kind of club is this?"

"It's a strip joint," one of the guys answered.

I froze in place. I had never been to a strip club in my life and didn't plan to start going that night.

"Come on David let's go have some fun," another member of the group said.

I didn't consider watching a bunch of naked women dance fun at all. The very last thing I wanted to do, with Kim back in Austin raising my son and working for our future, was to get my groove on in a strip joint. For two years I had remained loyal to Kim, not even considering an affair while in Boston, and I considered going into a strip club a form of cheating. Furthermore, over the years, I had witnessed men who treated women as sex objects to be used and often abused as in the case of James with Mama, and it wasn't fun. "Come on David, let's go inside," another member of the group urged me on.

As much as I wanted to be a part of the group, this was something I just could not do. I excused myself and climbed back inside the cab. The driver took me over to a more legitimate club, the one where the musical star Prince's father had played years ago. I sat there alone, sipped on a drink, listened to a mixture of rhythm and blues and jazz, and thought of what a great life I had built for myself.

The following week Cargill offered me a job. I had a choice to work in East Chicago, Indiana or Dallas, Texas. That was an easy decision for me. I chose Dallas.

After the semester ended I couldn't get back to Kim and Little David fast enough. I still had two courses to complete, but they were electives, and Bentley allowed me to take them at St. Edwards University in Austin. I didn't march with my graduating class, but that was not as important to me as being home with my family. I was content with life and feeling good about our move to Dallas when all hell broke loose with Kim.

"I don't want to move to Dallas," she complained right up to the morning I pulled the U-Haul truck in front of our apartment and started to load the furniture in the back. Again, it was the same complaint. She didn't want to leave her mother and sisters. She suggested that I commute between Dallas and Austin. This time I insisted that she and David would be going with me and it was not open to discussion. I had sacrificed for two years and didn't plan to be away from my family any longer. There was no way my son would grow up not being around me. She finally agreed and we headed for Dallas. A year later, we would return to Austin and quietly get married at the Justice of the Peace.

Cargill had provided me with a good package that included moving expenses. They paid for everything to include three months rent for temporary living until we found a permanent place to live. After two months we found an apartment we liked and settled in.

It wouldn't take long for me to realize that Cargill was not a good fit for me. My initial job was as staff supervisor of the accounts payable clerks. From the very moment I took over that job I did not get along with any of the employees under my supervision. The problem was two-fold. I had become arrogant and cocky. After all I was a graduate of a very prestigious eastern university. The clerks for the most part hadn't graduated from college and I felt that they should be respectful, almost submissive to my demands. Most of them were white and there was no way they were going to take orders from what I know they considered an "uppity black man." We clashed all the time and finally they transferred me to another department.

That didn't work out much better. The company decided to lay me off with severance pay for six months. Essentially, they wanted to get rid of me in the same manner as my elementary school instructors did when they passed me on to the next grade. But this time, much of the problem was my own fault. I was like the proverbial bull in the china closet at Cargill. The clerks, for that reason, did not want to answer to me at all. Losing that job was a very humbling experience and would help me to learn humility as I moved on to my next job with Levinski, Allen and Associates.

It was during the six months I worked at Cargill that my Father's health got progressively worst until I finally lost him. Two years earlier he had been airlifted to John Sealy Hospital in Galveston suffering from colon cancer. From that point on, he was in and out of the hospital receiving chemotherapy on a regular basis.

Daddy had moved to Aransas Pass, a city where many of the older shrimpers retired. After my last visit with him, we had managed to patch up our differences and actually got very close. I was the only one of his sixteen children that spent time talking with him on the phone and I actually visited him one time. His cancer continued to worsen until finally I received a call in Dallas that he'd been admitted to a nursing home because he could no longer take care of himself.

While I was with Cargill, I made four visits to Aransas Pass to see about my Father. The first time he was in the hospital. He was still conscious and we had a heart to heart talk. He surprised me when he said that despite the fact that he had failed me, I didn't fail him or his grandson David. He had become quite frail and had to wear a catheter. The cancer had gotten so bad they finally had to cut out parts of his body. I wasn't sure how long Daddy would live, but I knew I must be there for him. I went to my supervisor and asked that they work out a schedule so that I could spend time in Aransas Pass. They allowed me to work Monday through Thursday and spend the other days with him.

By the third time I went down to Aransas Pass, Daddy was in such bad shape that he didn't recognize me. He was nearing the end, and the talk around town was that the poor man had no money and it would be necessary for friends to raise cash for his burial. There was no way I would sit around and allow my Father to be buried like a pauper.

While in Aransas Pass, I called Kim and asked her to withdraw the three thousand dollars we'd saved to purchase a home. I also had her draw four thousand dollars on our credit card. She then sent me the seven thousand dollars, and I made all arrangements for my Father's burial. Within a week after I returned to Dallas, Daddy died. Some of his friends told me that he would have died days earlier but had asked to see Mama. He held on until Mama could get to Aransas Pass and have one final visit with him. When they told that to me, I recalled the time that he was trying to make it to Mama's house after getting beat up. When he was weak and in need of love he turned to Mama, and I am so pleased that she was there for him just before he left this world.

I returned to Aransas Pass and buried my Father. I literally had to do everything for the service. He belonged to a small church, but we did not have his service there. We had it at the funeral parlor so that we could cut costs. He was buried with dignity even though he did not live a dignified life. He merely lived the kind of life that fate had dealt him. At that service I felt no animosity toward my Father, but instead pity. I realized that he was from a generation that did not have the opportunities afforded me. I know if he had been born at a different time and under different circumstances my Daddy would have soared and been one of those mythic characters in real life that I dreamt of all my childhood. Even though it set Kim and me back financially, it was worth every penny we spent to honor Daddy with a decent funeral. The one thing I regret is not taking Little David to see his Grandfather before he got too sick to recognize what a fine grandchild he had.

It was soon after Daddy died that my short tenure at Cargill came to an end. The company did, however, allow me to use their computer system to seek other employment. Prior to my last day there, I landed a consultant job with Levinsky, Allen and Associates, an accountant firm in Dallas. They assigned me to work on a contract they had with Baylor University Medical School working in the area of fixed assets.

While working there I met and worked closely with a wonderful individual, Lynn Thompson, the project manager. Besides training me in the very specialized field of fixed assets, Lynn taught me how to work in an office environment. She also taught me how to be humble, and not think the sun rose and set on me.

A year after I began work with Levinsky, Allen and Associates, I received a call from Mamma with news that rocked my world, and for which it took me a very long time to recover. I had just gotten home one evening when the phone rang. I would usually let Kim answer, but for some reason, this time I grabbed the receiver.

"David, I have some very bad news," Mamma said.

My first thoughts were of Ronnie. I knew he had been arrested again, or worst had a stroke. Instead, she caught me totally off guard.

"Last week, J.B. died from a brain aneurysm."

I was silent. I didn't know what I should say or how to respond. Two years ago I buried Daddy, and now this. Was I under some kind of curse? I finally broke the silence.

"Why didn't someone call and tell me before now?" I asked.

"Because I knew you were still suffering over the lost of your Father and that you were still trying to settle in to your new job," Mamma said.

I was angry. "Mamma, you had no right not to tell me. J.B. was my best friend. How can you not tell me something like that?"

"I thought it best to save you from the grief."

"When is the funeral? I'll get time off and be there?"

"They buried him two days ago."

"What?"

"David, you just didn't need this extra burden to carry," she said.

"Mamma, I have to go before I say something I'll regret." I hung up, ran into the bathroom and cried.

I didn't speak to Mamma or call Freeport for months after that. I just couldn't believe J.B. was dead and no one called to let me know. Why didn't Thomas call me, or Darrell, and how about Troy? Did they all know and were they present for his home going? If so, they didn't think it strange that I wasn't there? Out of the entire neighborhood group, J.B. and I were the closest. For months, my mind wandered back to the times we had spent in Houston at his grandfather's house. I thought how dangerous and irresponsible it had been for us to be in his car with no driver's licenses, and the time he lost the keys after the concert. But most of all, I thought of those many nights that we spent standing under the street light at the corner of our street, dreaming about a bright future out of Freeport. It was our dreaming together that kept us out of trouble.

J.B., who was so talented and bright, never got away, and now he was dead before forty. He would never experience the wonderful things that life had to offer him outside that empty place where he was born and died much too young.

It was during the time that I worked with Lynn that I began studying for my license as a certified public accountant. That was my next goal in life, and I approached it in the same manner as every other challenge. This was one, however, that practically destroyed me, both mentally and physically. When I wasn't working, I studied all the time, ignoring both Kim and Little David. Kim complained that I never had any time for them, and even Little David challenged me, asking why I had all "those books." My reading comprehension was that of a tenth grader, and that made it much more difficult and time consuming studying for the examination.

The first time I took it, I failed miserably. But I refused to give up. I immediately started to study to take it again. My nerves were shot and I had developed an ulcer that irritated me all the time and made my quest more difficult. I took the exam five more times before I finally passed it, but by that time, I had practically destroyed my marriage and was a nervous wreck.

I have come to love the movie *Men of Honor*. The black navy seal was willing to pay any price to achieve his goal. I share that drive and determination with him. I was going to be a certified public accountant at any cost, and after I accomplished that goal, I set my sights on a Doctorate Degree. However, I still had to work, and with the contract at Baylor over, I set out to find new employment.

My next job was with Hanson Aggregates, located in Irving, Texas, right outside Dallas. Hanson was a large manufacturer of ready-mix concrete, bricks and stone. The company employed over one thousand people and had a budget of over 130 million dollars. It was a major Texas corporation. There I worked with a man who became a surrogate father to me. Glenn Morgan is one of the greatest individuals I have ever known. He had lost his leg to cancer, but you would never know it, because he never complained or made excuses. He always had a smile and always accentuated the positive in any situation. Glenn loved to tease me about the reason he hired me. He said it was because of my haircut. He claimed any man with the kind of haircut I sported had to come from a family with good values. More so than any other individual I had met or dealt with since leaving Bentley, Glenn understood my struggle as a black man trying to adjust into an "old boy" work environment that did not want to include a Black man in a management position.

I was responsible for analyzing the profit and loss statements for 16 plants located in Arkansas, Louisiana, Oklahoma, New Mexico, and California. The managers of those plants, especially in Louisiana and Arkansas, didn't appreciate the fact that I was Black and had a Masters Degree from a prestigious college in Boston. Glenn also was not a part of their "old boy" system and showed me how to laugh off the many ridiculous situations I would find myself in with some of those old boys. For three years he helped me reign in my temper and not do anything silly that would cost me the job.

After three years, however, I did end up doing something silly that led to my leaving Hanson.

Life at home with Kim had gotten extremely unstable. Our struggles were inextricably linked to my insatiable desire to succeed at all cost. I couldn't control my need to prove wrong the string of people who had always dismissed me in life. I was still carrying severe burdens from my past. All the times I was laughed at by other students or whipped by teachers and principals built up a powerful will within me to get even with all of them. Each accomplishment simply drove me to accomplish more, and to Kim it must have seemed that the drive to achieve would never end. I never allowed her to enjoy a normal home life because that didn't exist in my world. All the time it took me to pass the certified public accountant exam was time taken from her and Little David. The chasm between the two of us had grown so large that by the time I walked into Glenn's office and announced I was quitting Hanson, it was probably too late to save my marriage. Kim and I had struggled through a great deal, the biggest being my learning to read and the support she offered. We made it through many lean years in Austin while I was a student at Huston-Tillotson, and of course we survived the two years' separation while I went to Bentley. The greatest sacrifice Kim had made was to leave Austin and re-locate to Dallas. Unfortunately I failed to realize when enough was enough. I kept pushing and asking her to be there until it got to the point that she was no longer willing to make those sacrifices.

In the spring of 2003, I walked into Glen Morgan's office and handed him my resignation. He asked me why, and I told him because Kim and I had just separated, and my health was in no condition to do my job. I needed some space from it all. I left Hanson with a little over six thousand dollars in the bank. I paid Kim nine hundred dollars a month in child support and lived off the rest. After four months, it became clear that I would soon run out of money, so I took a job at a car wash. I was at an all-time low and wasn't sure what I would do with my life. Despite my despondent condition, I never failed to see my son whenever Kim would allow me to pick him up, and that was quite often.

Kim desperately tried to create a stable environment for us, but stability had never been part of my life. Even though Mama tried to create the same semblance of order in our lives, confusion had dominated our family and especially me. I had overcome what some would view as insurmountable odds, but I still hadn't dealt with my past. In fact, I'd been so focused on my determination to achieve, I gave very little thought to the first eighteen years of my life. When I left Freeport that was all behind me. However, with Kim and my new life, all those old weaknesses and insecurities re-surfaced. We'd gotten to the point where our relationship was dictated by constant verbal fights. All my life arguments filled with abusive language had prevailed, but after the argument was over, no one remembered what had been said or what harm had been done. Kim viewed verbal fights from a different perspective. In her world, they did damage to the relationship that couldn't be overlooked the next day.

Early on we had shared a common goal, and that was for me to conquer my reading disability and graduate from college. She helped me in both those endeavors. That was the foundation of our relationship and once that battle was won the foundation crumbled. By 2003 we had very little left, with the exception of our son, so I moved out and we filed for divorce.

I don't know what came over me. I no longer sought jobs in accounting. Instead, once my funds were nearly exhausted, I went to work at a car wash. Given my psychological disposition at the time, that seemed appropriate. Besides the job at the car wash, I also worked as a waiter at Luby's cafeteria. I had reached a new low in my life. I drifted from day to day, void of ambition or any goals. But two events occurred during the summer of 2005 that brought me out of this feeling of uselessness.

One Friday afternoon I was working the back end of the cleaning detail at the car wash. My turn came to drive a new Buick from the exit point of the wash to a location where I could then dry the car and windows, as well as clean the interior. When I finished I looked up to signal to the customer that the car was ready. When I saw Tim McHugh, Chief Financial Officer at Hanson Aggregates walking toward me I panicked. I didn't want this man, who I respected and who had done so much to help my career at Hanson, see me cleaning cars. He met me with a surprised expression.

"David Floyd, what are you doing here?" he asked. He managed a smile.

I handed him the keys and said, "Just making it from day to day." Mentally, I couldn't have handled an in-depth explanation.

He took the keys and simply said, "Well take care," and then drove off.

I made it through the rest of the day feeling awfully low about myself. I can imagine what Tim must have thought. It had to be rather incomprehensible to him that a man with a Masters Degree from an outstanding university, and had a job with a multi-million dollar company was working at a car wash. Our lack of communication was a strong indicator that we were both embarrassed and uncomfortable with the brief meeting in that place.

That night I began to question why I was sinking slowly, burying myself in self-pity. Was it possible that I had been living a lie all these years? My confidence and determination to overcome any obstacle placed in my way had sustained me from the first grade when I first was labeled a slow learner and non-reader all the way through Bentley. I found myself doing something I'd never done before and that was giving up. Like Levi had quit when Uncle Lynn roughed us up on the basketball court, I was doing the same. Mrs. Hassenback was winning and I could vividly see her face when she walked out of the classroom and said, "you passed," once again. But she had also told me that I would never amount to anything and I was living up to her prediction.

I also felt bad because I let down many people who believed in me, and that included Tim. He had invested a nice sum of corporate money in my professional development only to one day see me washing cars. I vividly recalled that day I walked into Glenn's office and told him I was quitting my job with the company. His obvious disappointment was clearly discernable. I had miserably failed these two men I considered family, men who believed in me and wanted to see me develop my full potential. I had quit on them and also on life. It frightened me to think that I might be on a course that would ultimately lead to disappointing my son in the same way my Father had disappointed me all those years. Despite my ability to discern what I was doing was wrong, I just couldn't seem to break this trend. It would take one more incident for me to decide it was time to break out of my doldrums.

One Saturday afternoon Luby's had called me in to work the

early evening shift. I had just finished working at the car wash and was exhausted, but needed the money. I had been working a little over an hour when the well-known comedian Steve Harvey and his party came into the restaurant and sat at a table in my section. Waiting on him turned out to be a harrowing experience. I don't think I've ever encountered a more arrogant individual. He was extremely rude, treating me like I was less a human being than he was. I felt like gum under his shoe, being squashed every opportunity he had. He acted like a bigger jerk in real life than what he sometimes portrayed on stage.

When I returned to my apartment that evening I took a really hard look at myself in the mirror and decided I didn't like what I saw. Some changes had to be made, and it had to happen right away.

I decided that I would try one more time with Kim. She also wanted to give our marriage another try. I moved back home and then contacted my Alma Mater, Huston-Tillotson, about adjunct teaching. I talked with Dr. Steven Edmonds, Dean of the Business School. He not only offered me two classes, but also contacted Austin Community College and helped me get on part time as an adjunct there.

Kim and I decided that I would relocate to Austin and maybe later on she would join me. I packed my bags, left my Dodge Neon with her and caught the Greyhound Bus to Austin. I was determined to get back on track, turn my life around and not allow the likes of Hasenback or Steven Harvey to win.

CHAPTER 41

For the second time in my life Huston-Tillotson came to my rescue. I felt myself drowning with no hope for survival. I arrived in Austin on a bright June day and went straight to Dr. Edmonds' office. He told me that I would be able to teach an introductory accounting class at the college in the fall, but I needed to head right over to Austin Community College and meet with the dean of the business school. They had reserved a class for me to teach in the five week summer session. He asked me why I decided to teach instead of remaining in the corporate world, and I explained that I didn't find that work fulfilling. We sat and talked for a couple of hours, and then I headed straight for Austin Community College, even before I settled into a place to live.

Dr. Reed Peoples, Chair of the Business Studies Department at the community college was waiting for me when I arrived there early in the afternoon. He assigned me to teach a financial accounting class which is essentially an introductory class. After we talked for about an hour, I walked the campus, visiting the classroom where I would teach my first class. It all seemed surreal to me. The struggle was about over. A young man who used to break out in a cold sweat when it was his turn to try to read in class was now about to teach at the college level. As I left the campus, I smiled knowing that I had proven anything is possible if you only put your mind to what you want to accomplish. All those trips to the principal's office and all the in-school suspensions didn't deter me. Sheer will power had won out over a world of negatives that had threatened to destroy me in the same manner it did many young men who suffered through hell, camouflaged as school, just as I had for twelve long years. Now, in just a few days I would stand before a classroom of students and have an impact on their future.

My next stop was Mrs. Brown's house. Since Kim and I had gotten married back in 1997, and I lived up to my promise to Mrs. Brown that I would always take care of Little David and Kim, she had shown a great deal of respect for me. When Kim's sister heard that I was looking for a place to live she suggested I take over the rent where she had been living because she was moving to Dallas. I moved in that weekend. I spent my first few days back in Austin preparing for my first accounting class, this time as a teacher.

The following Monday at two in the afternoon I walked into a class of thirty students, waiting to see who would be their instructor for the next five weeks. Many of the students were from different universities and decided to take lower division accounting at the community college, because it cost less and they probably figured it would be much easier than at the university.

I never imagined that I would have a panic attack, but when I walked into that classroom and looked at the faces of the students, I froze. I actually broke out in sweat. My insecurities came racing to the surface and made it difficult for me to function. I immediately had visions of my sophomore year at Huston-Tillotson when in my speech class I also panicked. When I was called on to deliver a five minute impromptu speech I asked the instructor if I could first go to the bathroom. When she said yes, I practically ran out of the class room and went straight to Mrs. Curry's office. I told her I had to drop speech because I lacked the confidence to stand in front of my fellow students and speak. I dropped the class and never looked back.

I stood there staring at the students and they stared back at me. I wondered what they were thinking about me. Here I was a young black man, who could easily have been a student, but was the instructor. I finally worked up the nerve to speak.

"Good morning, I am David Floyd, and I will be your instructor for this five week course in financial accounting." My voice cracked as I spoke. The students turned away from me and looked at each other as if to say, "Is this guy for real? He has to be joking and when will the real professor show up?"

After about ten minutes of my explaining how I would conduct the course and what I expected from the students, they seemed to settle in and accept the fact that I was indeed their instructor. I recalled an exercise that one of my professors at Bentley had used to break the ice and get acquainted with the students.

"What I am going to do now," I said, "is write three things on the board about me, which two are true and one is false."

I wrote that I was the first college graduate from Huston-Tillotson to become a certified public accountant. The second was that I didn't learn to read until I was twenty and graduated from high school reading only at the second grade level. The third was that I had three children. I could tell I had their attention. A majority of the students picked the second one as being false. Some, however, picked that as being true because it seemed so absurd it had to be true. That exercise did more for me than it did for the students. I felt relaxed after that and had no further inhibitions as their instructor. I have used that exercise ever since.

After that first experience with teaching I knew I was anchored in what I wanted to do with my life. I loved relating to students and helping them to grow in their careers. I still, however, had one more hurdle to jump over and that was the Doctorate Degree. I had told Mrs. Hassenback that I would not only graduate from high school, but would also get a Ph.D. in the very subject she taught. Before the end of the summer I applied to Argosy University and was accepted into the Doctorate program for accounting. Fortunately it was a program that allowed me to take my courses while working at Austin Community College.

That fall I taught two accounting courses at the community college and one night course at Huston-Tillotson. I also began my study for the doctorate program. Everything was moving along smoothly in my career, but that was not the case with Kim and me.

For some reason, we just couldn't seem to get our marriage back in order. We both hoped the distance would make our hearts grow fonder. It did just the opposite as we drifted further apart. Our strained relationship became much more complicated the night she called to tell me that she was pregnant. Together, we both searched for the best way to handle our dilemma. We loved and deeply cared for each other, and we loved our son and our child to be, but we were not a good fit as husband and wife. I was convinced that over the years since we first met in the dormitory at Huston-Tillotson, we had drifted apart. Staying in a strained relationship would not be the best for either of us, or Little David, and our child on the way. We finally agreed that we would always remain close and treat each other in a civil manner also. I would definitely live up to my financial commitment to take care of my children. I would also always be a part of their life as they grew up.

We waited until Daniel was born and then divorced.

I only taught that one semester at Huston-Tillotson but eventually became full time at Austin Community College. I loved teaching and was content that I would teach for the rest of my life. I still had something to prove. Through my dedication to the craft of teaching I would disprove what I had grown up believing, that most teachers cared very little about their students. I had only one teacher throughout my first twelve years of school who really cared about me, and that was Mrs. McWilliams. In college I had a number of professors who showed a genuine concern for me and most of them were at Huston-Tillotson. If not for that school and the many wonderful people who helped me along, I would never have made it. I figured I could re-pay them by being the very best I could be when I stood in front of a class of young bright minds, and helped them in their growth.

There was peace and contentment in my life, and then that Monday morning in January happened. I received the call from James and it shocked me into a new reality. I had lost Ronnie, and that would require an entirely new adjustment.

CHAPTER 42

————◆•••◆————

It is practically impossible to explain the feelings that raced through my body trying to adjust to Ronnie's death. It took me to an altogether different level of thinking losing a brother as opposed to the deaths of Daddy and Grandma. I never had the opportunity to mourn the loss of J.B. because when I found out he had died it was after the fact. Ronnie's death was real and recent. I had missed J.B.'s funeral. I would be there for Ronnie's.

I stayed on the couch for a good three hours before I got up and called Kim. I told her I would be leaving later that afternoon and would drive to Dallas to pick up Little David so he could attend his uncle's home going celebration. Dallas was in the opposite direction to Freeport and it would take me much longer to get home, but it was worth the drive. Little David had to be there with me. As I pulled out of my driveway heading to Dallas, I thought how timely for Ronnie to die on the same day that we all celebrate the life and contributions of Dr. King. While we celebrated King, Ronnie had his own celebration and that was a release into a new world and a new beginning for him.

When Little David, who was now a young man of seventeen years, and I arrived in Freeport we went right to the funeral parlor where the wake was being held. The place was packed with family. Levi and I hugged first and then James and finally Nicole. All four of us agreed that, even though we had lost our brother, we were relieved that he was now free of any further pain and suffering. We all agreed that we didn't want the service to be one filled with tears and wailing. We wanted it to be a solemn, but rejoicing service because that's the way Ronnie would want it. We also agreed, with Mama's concurrence, that I would speak of behalf of the family. I wasn't sure how well I would hold up, but I definitely had the strength to do the job.

As the family and friends left the funeral home, I stayed behind. I asked Mama to take Little David with her because I needed that time to be alone with Ronnie. The casket was still open and I just sat and stared at my brother in his very peaceful solitude. This was the man, who as a boy I slept with in a very tiny bed for the first eighteen years of my life. This was the man, who as a child, I fought with and against for all those years. This was the brother who attacked Hayward Barnes along "nigger trail" when we were about to fight. This was the brother who would have given me the shirt off his back to help me survive during my troubled years at Huston-Tillotson. This was the brother whom I loved and would dearly miss for the rest of my life. I raised my head toward the ceiling and said, "I love you brother," hoping that he could hear me, and knowing that he would say the very same words to me.

Ronnie's service was at First Missionary Baptist Church, which was Mama's church. Reverend Jeff Williams, the pastor, officiated the service. The family was the last to enter the sanctuary. As we made it down the aisle I was struck with the size of the crowd and the many familiar faces I saw. In that brief and short march to the front of the church where the family was seated, I flashed back on different events that had occurred over the years, and could associate certain people sitting in the pews with those events. Thank God, I thought, I had escaped from that place and even though Freeport would always be home, it would be at a distance. Sitting in the pew to the right of the church were two men who had been in the Blue/White Café when the man named Don was shot to death. Right in front of them was a couple of my old friends who were with me on Fifth Street when Moppie was killed, and we actually saw him dead with his brains all over the car. I spotted Walter Pipkins, who

I had suffered many beatings from and also played basketball with, sitting at the far right side of another pew. Seeing him brought back memories of J.B. and his sisters who I often fought on the way to and from school.

I finally took my seat in the front row between Nicole and Mama. It was fitting that I sit right there because they would be the ones that needed my strength to help them make it through the ceremony. After we were seated they closed the casket and it became real to me. I would never see my brother again in this life. I had to struggle to hold on to the memories of him before they were swallowed up forever with the closing of the casket. Even though death had removed him from my presence, I would not allow it to steal him from my mind. For the first part of the service I didn't hear what Reverend Williams said because I was in a battle with the forces to steal him away from me forever and my determination to hold on. Ronnie couldn't leave because, if he did, I would also be gone. You just don't spend so many years with another individual who is a part of you and then give it up. It would be like giving up a part of me.

I turned and looked at Mama. Tears flowed from her eyes and she took a handkerchief and wiped them away. I took her hand and squeezed tightly. That brought a slight smile to her face. I had lived my entire life through her tears, and for the first time in a long while, she smiled.

Once Reverend Williams finished speaking, the choir stood and sang, "*His Eyes are on the Sparrow and I know He's watching over me.*" At that moment my eyes moistened, but I knew I must be strong. In just a few minutes I would speak on behalf of the entire family and I had to make us all look good. We had always been the family scorned by the rest of the community. A family of five with no permanent father, with a feisty and fiery mother, who never hesitated to go off on anyone that she felt looked down on us. We were burying one of its members, and it was my duty to end his service with class. My life had prepared me for this task. The many battles I fought over the years only made me a stronger person who would have to be strong for this moment. When Reverend Williams finally asked for the family representative to come forth and say words I was ready.

I stood at the podium and stared out over the packed church. I paused for a moment and stared out at Darrell, my childhood friend, who stood in the doorway along with a large number of friends. People were actually lined up along the walls on both sides of the sanctuary. That was a true testimony to Ronnie. I now had the strength to speak.

"I want to thank you all for coming out to help my family celebrate Ronnie's home going," I began. "We have always been a very close-knit family, and we will miss our brother, son, nephew and cousin. But through our collective strength we will make it through." I paused to catch my breath and fight back the tears. "Even though we will miss Ronnie, we rejoice at his moving on to the new life, free of all the problems he endured while on earth. He was the only one of Mama's five children who never left Freeport, but when he finally did, it was a grand exit. He outdid all of us. After all, our older brother, Levi, lives in San Diego, Nicole in Houston, and James had gone to New Mexico and came back home and I now live in Austin." At this point I smiled. "But Ronnie has gone all the way to Heaven on a one-way ticket with no desire to come back." I caught a glimpse of Mama smiling when I mentioned Heaven. It brought memories of the roll call back to me. I had to do it for this very last time.

"Mama used to call roll in the evenings, and I want to do it one final time for her with all our names." I took a deep breath and then in the most powerful voice I could manage, I called the roll, "Levi Douglas, David Alexander, Ronald O'Keith, James Edward, Nicole Janelle." Just as I finished the last name Levi lost it and sobbed openly. "That roll call will never be called again in this life, but if we are all blessed it will be called again by a higher source."

At that moment a poem I had come to love and had memorized flashed before me. Without any hesitation I began to recite "Invictus,"

> Out of the night that covers me.
> Black as the pit from pole to pole.
> I thank whatever gods may be
> For my unconquerable soul.
> In the fell clutch of circumstance
> I have not winced nor cried aloud
> Under the bludgeonings of chance
> My head is bloody, but unbowed.
> Beyond this place of wrath and tears
> Looms but the Horror of the shade.
> And yet the menace of the years
> Finds, and shall find, me unafraid
> It matters not how strait the gate
> How charged with punishments the scroll
> I am the master of my fate:
> I am the captain of my soul.

The church was shroud in silence when I finished. I felt that all eyes in the entire sanctuary were trying to penetrate my thoughts in order to capture the meaning of that poem, and most importantly why I had recited it at that time. But in order to understand its implications they would have had to live our lives. As kids we fought against incredible obstacles we did not ask for and did not want. But we survived in our own way. And now Ronnie had survived in his own way. I ended the testimony to my brother from his family with words from a song by the Isley Brothers.

> I'd like to say this to you,
> From the mountaintop to the valley low

We will join together again
Like hearts of gold.

We buried Ronnie in a gravesite close to Grandma, then returned to Mama's apartment and spent the rest of the night reminiscing on Ronnie and all the great memories we had stored away over the years.

That night we saw everything in a positive light because it was the only way to celebrate Ronnie. And in many ways, despite the hardships we faced all those years, our life had been filled with love for each other, and for that reason our family endured and still endures to this day.